In Search of Paradise

McGill-Queen's Studies in Ethnic History
Donald Harman Akenson, Editor

In Search of Paradise

The Odyssey of an Italian Family

SUSAN GABORI

McGill-Queen's University Press
Montreal & Kingston • London • Buffalo

© McGill-Queen's Press 1993
ISBN 0-7735-1127-X

Legal deposit fourth quarter 1993
Bibliothèque nationale du Québec

Printed in Canada on acid-free paper.

This book has been published with the help
of a grant from Multiculturalism Canada.
Funding has also been supplied by the Canada
Council through its block grant program.

Canadian Cataloguing in Publication Data

Gabori, Susan, 1947–
    In search of paradise: the odyssey of an Italian family

    (McGill-Queen's studies in ethnic history; 18)
    ISBN 0-7735-1127-X

    1. Italians – Ontario – Toronto – History – 20th century.
    2. Canada – Emigration and immigration – History.
    3. Italy – Emigration and immigration – History.
    I. Title. II. Series.

    FC106.I8G32 1993   971'.00451   C93-090231-9
    F1035.I8G32 1993

Typeset in Palatino
by Cait Beattie, Montréal

Contents

Preface

THIS BOOK WAS WRITTEN as an attempt to understand the immigrant experience, my own experience. What you are about to read is oral history put into dramatic format. Everything in this story has been drawn from interview transcripts.

I spent two years interviewing members of the Italian community in Toronto. Because I wanted to know what happens when a family from a geographically isolated area is forced to pull up roots and resettle on new soil, I began to concentrate on people from the mountain regions of Abruzzi, in the southern part of Italy. In a town like Pratola Peligna, the original home of the Pace "family," traditions have had generations to develop and become integrated into the fabric of everyday life. The jolt of leaving such security has numerous consequences and I hoped to find a family whose members had undergone a variety of experiences, both in Italy, during the war, and in their adopted country.

As I interviewed more and more people, recording and transcribing all my interviews, the type of family I wanted began to become clear.

The meetings were a process of give and take. I could only define what I was searching for through what people gave me. When someone told me their story, I was guided by what moved me personally. My questions encouraged people to reveal details about certain aspects of their lives, both private and public. I transcribed each taped interview, formulated more questions, and returned numerous times to the same subject for further interviews, each time going into greater depth.

After considerable research with people from the south of Italy, I realized I would not find a real family which embodied all the elements I hoped to convey. But I did find a family who came close and their experiences form the basis of the Pace "family." To give as varied a range as possible to the immigrant experience I rounded out the family I found with events from other people's lives. The Pace "family" you are about to meet has been woven from transcripts of different interviews. Some of the characters in the "family" are based on one individual, some are a composite of two or three.

The book may contain historical errors. I chose to leave these since this is what people remembered and what they told me.

I hope the story of the Pace family will lead to a deeper understanding and respect for the immigrant experience and will strike a note of recognition in anyone who has ever moved from one country to another.

My deep gratitude goes to members of the Toronto Italian community who have opened their homes and hearts to me to make this book possible.

"And I am come down to deliver them ... and to
bring them out of that land unto a good land
and a large land flowing with milk and honey ..."

Exodus 3.8

"Who can say how much Paradise costs?"

Vincenzo

WORLD WAR II

Vincenzo

THE MONARCHY WAS THE LAW of our fathers, the King was Italy, so I didn't want to be a fascist. That meant belonging to a political party which always changes with time. After fascism people would want something different.

Of course, all the school kids were fascists – they had to be or else they were expelled. The fascists of Pratola were always organizing parades for them, these kids were more outside the classroom than in. When did they have time to learn? They marched up and down the Corso between the Piazza Garibaldi and the Piazza of the Madonna singing fascist songs. Or there were parades to the station to pick up a guest who gave a speech about all the good things the fascists had done for the people. Sometimes a big man, like the cardinal, came from another province and everyone had to go to the Piazza Garibaldi and yell, "Bravo!" while he talked and talked in front of the *municipio*. I went a few times to hear these people but I don't remember what they said.

I often drove the big shots from Pratola to Sulmona for fascist events. The fascist officials were my best customers, I took them all over the province. Slowly they became my only customers. Pratola was a small town and people had no money to spend on taxis. Also, I don't think I was very good in the taxi business. Sometimes, in an emergency, I would drive a family to the hospital in Sulmona or Aquila and they would say, "I cannot pay you now, later." Or it was I who said, "Pay me later." I would never see the money, maybe I would get some eggs or a chicken, often not even that.

A year later after I had bought the taxi I was forced to sell it. It was a sad decision. It had taken a long time to convince my father to help me buy a Fiat 507. He had said, "Either you do what you were trained to do, be an electrician, or you come and help me on the land."

Finally, in 1937, after a lot of discussions and arguments I bought the car. So I was proud, I did not want my father to think of me as a failure and I held off selling the car for as long as I could. But there were days when there would be nothing, just waiting and waiting. Finally I had to leave the car to find a job.

Mussolini said that people could not look for jobs in another town, they had to find one in their own town. It was almost impossible to find a job in Pratola. There were people who had nothing to eat. My family was lucky, we had land and that meant there was food, even if there was no money at least we could eat. But there were people in the town with no land and no work, they had to rely on charity for survival. When the fascist representatives had nothing better to do they would prey on these poor people. If anyone was found idly walking about town they were immediately stopped, identification papers and some quick answers were demanded, like what the hell were they up to and why? Unless they had a damn good reason for not working they were beaten up or taken to the pharmacy and given castor oil. There were little dictators in the name of Mussolini in every town.

I heard that there was no shortage of work in the African colonies, plus they paid well. A good friend of mine told me that a construction company in Milan needed drivers and electricians in Tripoli, Libya. They had an office in Rome and I went there by train to take the test. I liked the idea of going to Libya, I had done my military service there in 1925.

Everything went well except I did not have a passport and I needed fascist papers to get one. But I was not a member of the fascist party. I tried to think how I could get the necessary papers. I knew that the big man, the General Consul of the party, was from my province. Every Tuesday and Friday his office in Rome received people who had problems. But this was a big program and there were a lot of offices. I wanted to go directly to the main office and talk to this man, I didn't want to be assigned to another office. I offered a packet of cigarettes to the man in charge of arranging the appointments and said, "I want to see the consul of the party, no one else."

He put the cigarettes in his pocket and asked, "Why?"

"Because I know him."

He gave me a number and I sat down to wait. I was dozing off when I heard my number called. I had to pass through a big hall full of paintings with a lot of gold. I was nervous because I had never met this man.

6

I entered his office with a big salute and greeted him loudly, "*Saluto, saluto*, I come from your province, L'Aquila."

It was a big, long office and he was sitting at the end with his back to the window, the sun was so strong I could not even see him clearly.

He took off his glasses and looked up at me, "Well, just because you come from my province do I have to give you whatever you want?"

"I have a once in a lifetime opportunity to work in Tripoli but I don't have a passport."

"Why are you not a member of the fascist party?"

"The father-in-law of my nephew is the head fascist in my town, we had a fight and he wouldn't give me the papers."

He pushed a button and in two seconds someone came in. "Give this man whatever he wants," he said and dismissed both of us.

In the hall the man asked me, trying to figure out who I was, "Do you know the Consul?"

I said very matter-of-factly, "Oh, yes, he's a good friend of mine."

This man took me to a small office and gave me the identification papers and the passport right away.

In 1938 I was off to Africa. My wife and three children stayed at home with my parents. I told them, "When I have enough money I'll send for you."

Tripoli was beautiful, no snow, only sunshine and lots of land. I was given my own apartment there. It was all white and cool inside.

As soon as I met the president of the construction company, the man from Milan, I liked him very much. He said to me, "You are the only one in my company who is a *terréno*, everyone else is a *polentóne*." Then he leaned closer to me, "Listen, Pace, I was not always a rich man like I am today. Before I was a poor man like you. Everyone I worked with helped me along step by step. I would like everyone who works with me to do as I did, step by step."

I made the best money in my life there. A lot of houses were being built for the soldiers and we were responsible for putting in the electrical wiring. The big man who was heading the operation said to me, "I don't want to make one penny on this job, all the money is for you. To me what's important is a big name with the government."

7

After twelve months I was given a good position working in the warehouse checking off all the materials coming in from Italy. Two weeks before Christmas, I decided to bring over my family. My wife came over on the boat with Roberto and Angelina. Franco, the oldest, stayed behind in the seminary. My wife wanted him to be a priest. To be a priest was a good profession, you were well taken care of physically and mentally.

It was always summer in Tripoli and we wanted to stay forever. The life was good. We organized bicycle races. On Sundays we went on bicycle outings and had picnics. The company bought a new car for me and sometimes we drove out to the farms to visit the people who had come from Italy to work the land.

Within the first year twenty thousand Italians came to work on the farms. Mussolini gave them a house, the land, and money to start. When they moved in they found everything, the furniture, the dishes, even the macaroni. The government paid these people 400 lire a month to work the land. In return, they gave a certain amount of their produce to the army. The agreement was that in five years time they were to become the owners of the property. Mussolini was good to his people. He gave us uniforms, schools, he even sent the children to the mountains and the beaches in the summertime. Everything was free.

Mussolini was a big man. He built highways, gardens, and school buildings in Africa. He said, "Our land is overpopulated, I want to create jobs for my people. I will go to Africa and the Italians will civilize the primitive natives." Abyssinia was a big victory for Italy and Mussolini kept his word, he provided his people with land.

There were rumours of war in Tripoli. We were not surprised, the Germans were always talking of war. Mussolini was for peace but we knew that Italy was ready to enter battle if the situation called for it. When Mussolini met Hitler in Munich in 1939 everyone said, good, good, Mussolini will stop the war. But later Hitler started to take Poland and Czechoslovakia and then the trouble started.

One day the director of the *sindaco* told me that they were organizing to send the kids to a fascist colony in Italy and the government would take care of them. Mussolini wanted to save the kids from a possible war. If something should happen at least the kids would be safe. They asked if my wife wanted to go on the boat to take care of the children but she was pregnant at the time, she couldn't go.

I told the children that we were going to send them back to Italy for a vacation. Lina was happy. Roberto didn't say anything. My wife was very upset, Lina was only six and Roberto was eight, they had never been away from their mother. I tried to comfort my wife, I told her that it would only be for a few months and then they would be sent back to us and Mussolini would take good care of them. He was the only man I would trust with my children.

Soon after the children left the war started. On June 10, 1940, the French bombarded Tripoli. I was in the fascist union office when the sirens announced the bombings. Even though there was always talk of war we didn't really think the war would come. The director of the *sindaco* must have known what was coming when he told us to send the kids back to Italy.

Some of my friends thought that Mussolini was making a big mistake entering the war on the side of Germany because during World War I Italy had fought against the Germans and the Austrians. We were natural enemies. We have always been fighting Germany over Austria. My opinion was that if Italy had not entered the war on the side of Germany then Germany would have occupied Italy too. Hitler was too ambitious – if he won the war without Mussolini's help he would not give one metre of land to Italy.

Notices were posted everywhere in Tripoli telling us to send back our family to Italy. All the people who were working with companies had to stop their jobs and the Italian government put every available man into the military. I was put on the pier to check off materials coming from Italy.

In September 1940 I was transferred to Tobruk. We were bombed every day and only the Germans helped us. They sent us medicine and in each bottle there was a little note, "Italia, resist! We will help you, we will help you. Italia, resist, resist!" This note was included in everything. On the thirteenth of December there was a really big bombardment. We were told to retreat because the English were close. Within days they occupied the area and a lot of people were taken prisoner.

We managed to escape from Tobruk and headed for Bengasi. We had to reorganize everything. There was chaos. This time I could not escape and I was captured by the English. But just before my capture I heard that the *Conte Rosso* was bombed on its return trip to Tripoli, carrying soldiers and doctors. At least I was sure that my wife and child were safe in Italy.

The English sent me to Kenya as a prisoner of war. There were thousands of prisoners, they sectioned us off and we were put in barracks made of jute and painted with tar on the outside to keep out the wind. It smelled terrible but by that time so did we.

Some were given shovels to dig sewers or graves for dead Italians, others were put to work on the roads, and about thirty people were assigned to work a small piece of land set aside for a vegetable patch. The produce was divided amongst everyone.

I started off working as a gardener for a big shot from England, I think he was a major. He had his own villa and I was eating there every day, the food was better than in the camp. At night I returned to the barracks. This English major had a negro to do the cooking for him. From the garden I could see into the kitchen and one day I saw the negro guy urinating into the sink where he used to wash the vegetables and the dishes. After that I didn't want to eat there, I asked them to let me take whatever I was supposed to eat back to the camp with me because I wanted to share it with my friends. Later they put me on the roads.

We set up a little community in the camp, there were a couple of tailors, a few shoemakers, a carpenter. There was someone from every profession. We also had experts who could build a shortwave radio. During the day we hid the radio in the canteen. At night we got together to listen to the news very quietly. We heard a lot of Italian and Russian news. They announced how many ships were sunk in the Mediterranean. The English said they had sunk so many enemy ships and the Italians said the English had only succeeded in sinking a few. We did not know which one was true but we believed the Italians more than the English. If they caught us listening to the news the radio was taken away and they would not give us food for a couple of days.

Sometimes we sat around and exchanged stories. Someone told us how a group of them had tried to make a coloured Abyssinian kid eat meat. He didn't know what meat was. At first he refused to taste it. So one guy held his arms behind his back while another guy opened his mouth and shoved the meat in. The kid spit it out a few times. Eventually he had to eat it. This went on about two or three days. One day he went to their camp and ate all the meat which was enough for about twenty soldiers. He learned fast.

We were all in good spirits. We were sure we were going to win the war because we knew that Hitler had the atomic bomb. We heard Mussolini say in a speech that he was going to pray to God, to ask God's permission, before using such a weapon. We knew this bomb would put an end to the war.

When we heard on the radio that the Americans had entered the war on the side of Russia and England against Hitler and Mussolini we were shocked. We never expected America to enter. Then we heard that the Americans had landed in Italy. Everyone was angry. If the Americans would have kept their noses out we would have been all set, Italy and Germany would have won.

After armistice, in 1943, the English gave us a choice – remain a fascist or collaborate with the English. They said if we collaborated with the liberation war we would get better treatment, they would give us more benefits, more clothes and more food. Most of the Italians collaborated because they could have something decent to eat. I didn't know what to do. The war had lasted for such a long time, I didn't know what had happened to my family, I had no news of them for over two years. Really, I didn't give a shit whose side I was on. What was I fighting for?

The English tried to divide us. When we were taken prisoners we were put into different categories, civilians, soldiers, and police. Each category had a different place in the camp. Before the armistice we were all friends, we shared every piece of bread. After the armistice the English mixed us up, they took one hundred people from one section and put them in another section. Then the fights started.

Big fights broke out between the people who had collaborated and those who still believed that the war was going to be won by Germany and Italy. The believers gave us a rough time. They said we were all prisoners of war and we had to remain prisoners. Those who collaborated were considered traitors.

Some of the fascists gave big speeches about how important it was to preserve your feelings of nationality. Some said, "I don't care about the family, the most important thing is the honour of my country. If we die, let us die for one reason, and if we survive, let us survive for one reason. All together, not divided. The nation is above the family. The nation is the highest ideal." But the ones who believed in this were young, they did not have families.

11

These believers gave us a hard time. At night they put blankets over us and hit us with sticks. They said, "We'll see you back home and then you'll really get it." A few people were killed.

The English officers wanted to know who had done the killings. Of course no one talked. The English punished everyone. They didn't give us bread or food for one day. They gave us water and potato peels or they gave us dry corn which we put in water and after two days boiled it and ate it.

Finally, they divided us, the people who wanted to collaborate with the English went to one camp and the people who refused to betray Italy and fascism went to another.

But there were divisions even amongst the collaborators. Two good friends got into a big fight when one applied to go to England. One asked, "Why would you want to go?" The other started to sing the Russian national anthem in Italian. He was a communist. His friend said to him, "From now on I don't want to hear about you and you can forget about me."

But no one knew what was going on outside. The news we were hearing in the camp from the Allies' radio said that they had destroyed so many Nazi tanks and so many Nazi airplanes, they had occupied this place and that place. We were hearing all the good news, good for them. Maybe it was all a lie. I didn't know what to believe. Everyone believed something different, everyone had his own idea of who and what was right.

In 1944 I was taken to England as a collaborator. We landed in Liverpool, then they sent us to Yorkshire. We heard from some of the other collaborators who had been taken to England earlier that by 1943 the British government was supplying the families with arms. Women and children had ammunitions to defend themselves because they were expecting the Nazis to beat England any day. They were in bad shape. It was said that in mid-1943 Churchill went to the States to ask Roosevelt for help, he offered to give him Canada in return for America's participation in the war.

After armistice the English had an accord with the Italian government. They gave 13 shillings a day to the Italian government for each Italian prisoner who worked but only 1 shilling to us. In the mornings a truck took us to work and at the end of the day it brought us back. Some people who worked in agriculture travelled on bicycles.

Gradually we got to know some of the English families. Sometimes we would buy an old bicycle for about 2 pounds from them and fix it up. Then we either sold it back to them or to someone else for 15 pounds. There were not many things in the stores for sale, everything was rationed. Sometimes the English sold their coupons to us in order to get money to buy something on the black market and we bought the coupons to buy something in the store.

We wore the same uniforms as the English soldiers but we had a little Italian flag sewn on both shoulders to identify us as prisoners. We finished work at five and could go out till nine. If we wanted to stay out longer we needed special permission. The government allowed us to go to the shows but some places would not let us in, they would say, "You're a prisoner, you're our enemy."

One day after work we were going for a walk and we were all very sad because we had just heard that Mussolini was killed. It was a terrible shock. We did not want to believe it. Maybe the news was lying again. Why kill him? Put him in jail but there was no need to kill him. If England had lost the war would they have killed Churchill? We passed by a pub and some American soldiers who were standing around at the entrance called after us, "Hey, *paesano*, what happened?" They saw we were not very happy. They said, "Come here, come here. Let us buy you a bottle of beer."

"No," we said. "We can't go inside." We were not allowed inside bars to drink alcohol. We could go to a small restaurant and have fish and chips with a cup of tea but no alcohol.

The Americans insisted, "No, no, come with us, come with us."

We all went inside and one of the Americans said, "Give my friends a bottle of beer."

The barman refused, "We can't give it to them, they're prisoners."

The Americans said, "Well, a man can't go without alcohol for years. Give him some alcohol." It went back and forth, yes, no, yes, no.

Some English soldiers were sitting at a table drinking beer and whiskey and they got up and said, pointing to us, "You can't drink beer here. Get out."

The Americans kept insisting, "No, no, just one bottle."

A big fight broke out between the American and English soldiers. We quietly left just as the police came in to break it up.

We couldn't leave England before 1946 because of the battle of Normandy. After it was all over they started to send us home by ship according to age, those born between 1910–1915 went first, from 1915–1920, later. We took a ship from London and in seven days we landed in Naples. Some landed in Taranto, others in Genoa – we could not all go to one place, there were five or six thousand people going back.

I returned to Italy after eight years of absence. When we landed the English gave us over to the Italian authorities and signed all the papers for us. It took a day and a half to process everyone. Then we were free to go.

We were shocked when we first saw Italy, everything was a mess. The roads were destroyed, buildings were in ruins. There were beggars everywhere asking for money, clothes, anything. I found a new population, the *mulatti*. I had never seen these kids in Italy before. I had to ask where they came from.

I bought oranges for the children in Naples. Before the war I paid 1 lira for a dozen oranges, now I had to pay 70 or 80 lire for the same thing. I thought, what's going to happen now? Before I went away we paid 4 lire for a litre of cooking oil, now I saw that it was 2,000 lire. How could we live this way? Where were we going to get all this lire?

The railroad was broken, part of the trip home was by train, another part was by truck. The train, full of released prisoners of war, pulled into Sulmona at three o'clock in the morning. It could go no further because the bridge to the next town had been blown up. We were all tired and some of the men said, "Tonight we'll sleep here and tomorrow we'll find a car or something to take us to our town." We settled down for the night. Then slowly, in the darkness, I heard a band playing in the distance and I knew right away they were from Pratola. My town always had the best band. Pratola was known as a town of musicians.

I listened and listened. Finally, I couldn't take it anymore and said to my friend, "Let's go."

He said, "You're crazy. I can hardly stand up."

I dragged him to his feet and we started to walk toward town. The music got louder and louder the closer we got. It took us an hour and a half by foot.

14

The first person we saw as we entered Pratola was Annina, the wife of a good friend of mine, she was taking her bread to the ovens. I had a beard and torn clothes, it took her a few seconds to recognize me and then she started screaming. She threw her bread down and ran to tell everyone I had returned.

When I finally reached my door I couldn't bring myself to say anything, I had lost my voice. I tried to push it open but it was locked. All I could do was bang on the door louder and louder and somehow managed to yell, "Teresa! Teresa!"

Teresa

ALL MY CHILDREN WERE BORN at home except the last one. Michele was born in the hospital in Tripoli while the building was trembling from the explosions of the bombs outside. It was hard, my family was not there, Roberto and Lina had already gone back to Italy and I couldn't be sure where my husband was. I only had the nuns to take care of me and sometimes friends would come to bring fruit.

After two weeks I walked out of the hospital with my baby. Everywhere on the street there were pieces of iron from the bombs with numbers and letters on them, littered like garbage. When I got home I found our beautiful white apartment covered with dust and more iron pieces on the balcony.

Before my husband left he told me, "No matter what happens to me, after the baby is born you must go back to Italy."

I had said, "No I am staying with you. All this will be over soon."

But I could tell he wanted me to go. "You must think of the children," he said.

I pleaded with him, "Lina and Roberto are safe in Italy. Franco is in the seminary. We at least must try to stay together."

He got angry, "No, you are not safe here. I know what's best."

I was crying, "You just want to be free of me, to do what you want."

But standing in the middle of our apartment with Michele in my arms I knew my husband was right. I had to leave. All of a sudden I felt so alone. A few months before I had a beautiful apartment, a family, everything. We were so happy. And all that was gone. My heart was torn to pieces. Without thinking I gathered up the hem of my skirt and started to collect the bits of iron on our balcony. I hardly saw them I was crying so hard. But what else could I do? Then I heard a loud shout from the street below, "You're crazy, you must come down at once into hiding, it's not safe up there. What's the matter with you, can't you hear the sirens?"

That was the last time I saw our apartment, I left everything there, furniture, pots, pans, everything.

During the trip back to Italy on the boat I constantly heard explosions hitting the water. There were explosions all around us lighting up the sky in the middle of the night. The boat was being thrown around so violently by the storm that Michele would not feed properly. I was so sure he was going to die. Two of my children had already died. With all my heart I prayed to the Madonna that she keep him alive and that she grant us safety to Pratola. If she would do this I promised to give her my beautiful gold necklace that I had received from my mother. If you really believe then the Madonna will help you. I had already given Franco to be a priest and to have a priest in the house is protection money can't buy.

I was holding the railing of the boat with one arm and Michele in the other arm and I tried to comfort him. He was crying and crying. I sang religious songs. I thought my voice would calm him. What else could I do? And then I told him stories of the Madonna della Libera, the protector of Pratola Peligna.

"A terrible plague hit Pratola in the 1500s. Families died of cholera, houses became graveyards. It was impossible to walk the streets because of the smell coming from the houses. People were going into the fields to pray. They no longer went inside the church because they were scared of each other. The contagious disease kept people apart. One day, while wandering in the fields and praying for the end of the plague, a woman who had lost almost all her family saw an eye in a big stone on the mountain. A voice called to her and she slowly approached the eye. Then the eye turned into a face and the woman got scared. But the face said to her, 'Please don't be scared. I'll help you.' The woman was still trembling. The face came out of the stone and approached the woman. Then she recognized that it was the face of the Madonna who was saying, 'Don't worry. I'll help you.'

The woman returned to the city and said, 'Believe it or not I saw the Madonna!' The people pointed at her and said, 'You're crazy. *Pazza.*' Everybody thought she was so sick from the plague that she had started to see things. Nobody believed her. But she talked and screamed so much that finally the priest and the people agreed to go and see this big stone. The face of the Madonna once again appeared. A week later the plague went away.

17

A few hundred years later there was another plague and while digging a ditch some people from Pratola found a stone with a Latin inscription, *Santa Maria Liberata.* The stone was found along the border between Sulmona and Pratola and a big fight broke out between the two towns. They both claimed this stone. Finally Sulmona won the fight and the stone was put on a big wagon pulled by two cows. The Sagittario River ran between Sulmona and Pratola, the bridge to cross this river was in Pratola so the wagon had to return to town. But once the cows reached Pratola they did not want to pull the wagon any further. The people from Sulmona tried everything to make the cows cross the bridge but nothing helped, the cows would not budge. The stone wanted to stay in Pratola.

The people of the town wanted to build a church for the Madonna exactly where the cows had stopped. But the town could not afford to have a church built, so everyone had to help. Every morning, before they went to work in the fields, the men went to the foot of the mountain to collect stones. Piece by piece they brought them back to Pratola and began to build the church. My grandfather was among the men who helped gather the stones. After a while there were no more stones left at the foot of the mountain. One of the men said, 'Now we'll have to go far for the stones and it'll take much longer to finish the church for the Madonna.' There was a big cave further up on the mountain and as soon as the man said this the cave suddenly collapsed and all the stones fell down to where the men were standing. With everyone's help the church was soon finished and they named it the Church of the Madonna della Libera because she liberated the town from the plague. This was the second time the Madonna had helped Pratola. A real artist, inspired by God, made a statue of her and put it inside the church."

Michele was quiet. He had stopped crying and he even began to feed at my breast. The storm no longer seemed to bother him anymore, the explosions did not frighten him. He was calm. I also felt comforted, I felt a certain peace but it was difficult to hold onto this peace because of the noise and danger all around. The captain came around to say that if one of those bombs hit the boat the women and children would be the first to be evacuated. This was not comforting news. I wanted to find my peace again. I had to continue talking. When I didn't talk terrible thoughts came to me. I held Michele close and told him another story.

18

"When I was fourteen years old a woman who lived far away came to Pratola with her whole family including her fourteen-year-old mute daughter. They had walked two days and a night. As soon as they saw the church of the Madonna they got down on their knees to go up the steps of the church to the altar. While they were walking on their knees the woman was crying, 'Madonna, help my daughter.' She cried this over and over again. 'Madonna, help my daughter. Let her speak. Let her speak.' As they reached the altar the girl stood up and said, 'Mamma, Mamma.' This girl had not talked for fourteen years, it was the first time she had said anything. And when the people around heard her utter those first words everybody started to scream. When the people have enough faith the Madonna helps."

After two days we arrived in Naples. I could hardly walk on solid ground after all the moving about on the boat. On the train to Pratola I felt a sense of relief at being alive and I just wanted to see my family again. A big group of people met us at the train station. My mother-in-law prepared breakfast for everyone and my sister-in-law, Lisetta, bathed Michele in wine. People say the wine makes babies strong but they also smell nice after.

When I saw Franco I was so happy, I thought the seminary had given him permission to come out to the station to meet us but then Eduardo told me what had happened, that Franco had run away from the seminary soon after I had left. When I heard that I was no longer happy to see him. If anything would have happened to Michele and me on the boat it would have been his fault because he ran away from God. That was very bad, he had put us in great danger.

The next morning I woke up at 5:30 to the ringing of the church bells. I waited for the bells to ring again at noon with that low, slow sound. It was almost a lazy sound. I had missed not hearing the bells in Tripoli. But when I heard them ringing with short high-pitched notes I was sad because I knew that the bells were announcing a funeral for a baby.

I waited for May to be able to keep my promise to the Madonna. The first Friday night in May people started to come for the Festival of the Madonna della Libera. A procession went from town to town collecting groups of people and singing religious songs. People from all over the province of Aquila walked to Pratola just to see her. Some people walked forty kilometres. As they approached Pratola we could hear the singing getting louder and louder. We waited in the streets, greeting them as they arrived. Each group carried a flag with the picture of the Madonna on it and money which had been collected from their town was pinned to the flag.

There were firecrackers Friday night. A bandstand was set up in the Piazza Garibaldi and there were two or three concerts. Different bands and opera singers performed. Sometimes important people were hired depending on how much money had been collected. The bandstand stayed on the piazza for the two weeks of the festival. The first week was for strangers. The second week was for the people of Pratola.

During the year the Madonna had a special place in the corner of the church. Before the festival began she was taken out and placed in the centre of the main altar behind the drapes. The first Sunday in May, after the one o'clock mass given by the Cardinal of Aquila, the statue of the Madonna came out of the church and was carried around town. There were so many people that we had no room to also join the procession.

Then the Madonna was returned to the church and stood on a marble stand near the altar. The first week the church was so full you could hardly kneel down and at night people were sleeping one on top of the other. Some people went from the outside steps of the church on their hands and knees licking the floor till they reached the Madonna.

The second Sunday it was the people of Pratola who went to see her. The drapes in front of the altar were opened and as soon as we saw the Madonna everyone started to sing. Then the Madonna slowly came out toward the people in the church. Six men who had paid the most money carried her. Even the poor people wanted to pay. As she came down the steps of the altar it felt as if she was coming down from heaven toward you. When the people saw her come they started to scream and said miracles were going to happen. She had a beautiful satin dress, embroidered with gold, and she had a blue satin cape. She was full of earrings, necklaces, and all sorts of jewellery that people had given her, people who have had a miracle happen to them. Year after year the jewellery accumulated, miracles never stopped happening. As the Madonna passed by me I had Michele in my arms and I hung the necklace I had promised on her hand.

The statue of the Madonna was carried around town for three or four hours with a whole procession following behind. In the first rows there were the younger children carrying candles, then there was the band and the older people singing and carrying flags. As they passed through the winding streets people pinned money to the flag in the hope of a miracle. I had given Franco some money to give to the Madonna for his father.

I had no way of knowing where my husband was. There were no letters from him, no news. I didn't know if he was dead or alive. The letters from Lina and Roberto were my only comfort, they wrote in such beautiful Italian. I knew they were safe and well taken care of but I missed them so much and there was not enough money to visit them.

Mussolini helped the family. Every two weeks the wives of the blackshirts went to the post office to collect their money from the government. Some of the women spent this money on foolish things, they wanted to show off. I was careful, I saved the money for when my husband would come back.

The war had followed us from Libya to Italy. Mussolini needed copper and gold for the war. He asked everyone to contribute whatever they had. The *podestà* came to my house and said, "Please come to the *municipio* tomorrow at ten and give whatever gold you have."

Inside the *municipio* the police wrote what everyone gave. There was a big box in the centre and people lined up to give whatever they had. I threw in my wedding ring and took a steel band from a pot next to the box as a replacement. There were people who gave watches, necklaces, everything. Another time I went to give my copper pots, the ones my mother had given me for my wedding. Mussolini said that after the war he would give back everything people had contributed, that was why the police made a note of everything.

We also had to give flour. When people went to the mill to grind one hundred kilos of grain the soldiers who were standing by took twenty-five kilos of flour. This was loaded onto a truck and taken to the city for the army.

Of course everyone gave whatever they had because we really believed that this was needed for Italy. We were sure the situation was going to get better after the war. Mussolini had said that the war would be over quickly because the enemy was not very strong and with everyone's help Italy would have an easy victory.

Later on the soldiers wanted to melt down the bells from the church because they needed lead for ammunition. But the women of the town got together and we wouldn't let them. There were three churches in our town, we let them take the small bells from one of the smaller churches, not the ones from the Church of the Madonna della Libera.

We were constantly reminded that there was a war going on. Every week we heard the church bells mourning someone's husband, or son, or brother. There were only rumours of people's whereabouts, nobody knew anything for certain. One day a friend of my husband's came to town and said to me, "I heard what happened to Antonio. The English had shot six or seven men, Antonio was one of them and their watches, clothes, everything was stolen. The English left the men as God had made them. But someone told me this so please don't say anything to your sister because I don't know if it's true."

I couldn't believe what I had heard. Antonio was my brother-in-law and he had married my sister, Maria, while we were in Tripoli. After they had been married only six months and Maria was three months pregnant the government called him into the army to fight in Yugoslavia. Just before I came back he had written to my sister asking her to send him a coat. But my sister was not feeling well with her pregnancy and when I got back I made him the coat and sent it to him. Now, when I heard this news I did not know what to think. I was afraid to say anything to my sister because something like this had happened before. Antonio had died before.

In 1935, my brother-in-law was called to fight in the war in Spain. While he was there I received a letter from him, "Teresa, I will be home in one month. Prepare my best suit." I prepared everything and the whole family was waiting for him to come home. One day, a month later, I was feeding Angelina and my mother-in-law was cooking when two policemen came in. They stood at the door looking at me. One said to the other, "What should we do?"

The other replied, "Well, if we don't say anything today we'll have to say it tomorrow."

My husband was in Africa at this time and when I heard these words I started to cry, "What happened to my husband? What happened to my husband?"

Of course, this policeman didn't know the difference between my husband and my brother-in-law. He said, "I am sorry, your husband is dead."

22

My mother-in-law was hard of hearing so she yelled from the kitchen, "Is my son coming home today?"

The policeman took out the paper and read, "Captain Pace died last month."

Then I realized that it was not my husband but my brother-in-law. Still, for me it was just the same. I got very angry. "Why are you reading that piece of paper? He wrote me a letter asking me to prepare a nice suit for him because he was coming home this week and now you tell me my brother-in-law is dead. You're crazy." I went to get the letter to show to the policeman, "Look at this! Look!"

But he just said, "I'm sorry, he died last month."

They had come to tell us this on Thursday and we started to make the funeral preparations for Tuesday. We got everything ready. We were to go to church for eleven o'clock. Seven o'clock Tuesday morning the postman, the best friend of the family, opened the door. My sister-in-law, Lisetta, called out, "Mario, what happened?"

He was holding a letter in his hand, "I bet this letter was written by Antonio. I want you to open it before the funeral. I want to know what it says."

Lisetta tore open the letter and when she read what it said she started to cry. Antonio had written, "Come and see me in the hospital in Naples and bring me some *baccalà*. I am waiting for you."

When I heard this you cannot imagine what happened to my body. I didn't know what to believe. Before saying anything I went to the police with this letter. They tried to phone Naples from the Piazza della Madonna. The whole town was in front of the phone because everyone was ready for the funeral. By the time they got through to Naples it was three o'clock in the afternoon and the doctor was operating on Antonio. The nun interrupted him, "Professor, someone is calling from Pratola Peligna. They are preparing a funeral for Captain Pace." Antonio was sick but he understood these words. The doctor stopped the operation, came to the phone and said to the police, "Who sent a letter to Pratola Peligna saying this person is dead? I am with him right now and he is very much alive."

Everyone started to cry. People came to my mother-in-law's house to bring prosciutto, cheese, fruits, and all sorts of things to celebrate. My father, Lisetta, Eduardo and myself took a taxi to

Naples. We reached the hospital at two o'clock in the morning. The guard outside said, "Nobody can go inside."

I said to him, "I'll kill you, I came all the way from Pratola Peligna after having prepared a funeral for my brother-in-law and now you tell me I have to wait till ten o'clock tomorrow morning to see him. You're crazy. Call the chief of police or the doctor. We want to go inside to see him right away."

He called another man who called another man who finally called the doctor. By the time the doctor came it was four o'clock in the morning. Antonio's face was all covered with bandages, you only saw his eyes but he was alive.

Later he told us what had happened. A bomb had exploded and ten people died. The Red Cross in Spain put all the dead men in a truck and took them to the cemetery. Antonio was one of them. As they were about to bury them someone noticed that he was opening and closing his mouth. The person screamed, "This one is not dead." Antonio stayed in a hospital in Spain for one month then the government transferred him to the hospital in Naples.

When I heard that he was dead again I didn't want to believe it. I went into the back room to cry and didn't want to say anything to Maria in case it was not true. Every morning my sister went outside to wait for the postman, "Do you have a letter from my husband?" Each time I heard this I wanted to cry because I knew he might be dead.

Six months later a friend came from another city and finally told my sister. She was breast-feeding her baby when she heard that her husband was dead. Her milk stopped right away.

Maria didn't want to believe that her husband was dead. Every day she went out to the road and waited for the postman and when he came she would say, "Oh, you never have a letter for me." I cried so much when I heard her say this because I was also thinking about my husband. I was back home but the family was still separated. One here, one there. Finally I asked Eduardo if he could go to pick up Lina and Roberto from the colony and bring them home for the summer holiday.

About the time Lina and Roberto came back the Germans also began to arrive in greater numbers. Some stayed in a villa which was just below the Piazza Garibaldi. Others stayed in the building where the wine used to be stored. The Germans took everything out and made it into barracks for the soldiers. They said very little to the people. They respected us. Sometimes you had to walk to another town and they would stop and ask you if you wanted a ride. There was no trouble, they just asked us to turn all the lights off by six o'clock. We could not go to church at night because of the bombings and blackouts.

One afternoon I took food to the people working on my mother-in-law's land and I heard a terrible noise. Everybody looked up and saw these fantastic airplanes. We had never seen such things before. There were eight coming from one direction, eight from another direction, there were thirty-two in all. We saw their white smoke and everybody was laughing and pointing, "Look! Look!" All the kids were excited. One young boy started to run toward a soldier who was crouching at one end of our land. The soldier motioned him to get back and suddenly the planes started to shoot. Six people died that day. Not one soldier. Our town was in a valley with mountains around it and there was a factory which made gunpowder near our land. The planes must have been after the factory but they missed their target and hit the people instead.

Both the English and Americans wanted to bomb this factory. But the supplies were hidden in caves, under the mountains. Even if the airplanes would have bombed the building they would not have been able to get the supplies. Still, they kept trying and trying and they continued to kill more and more people.

Just as we were starting to adapt to the Germans, I heard that they were now supposed to be our enemies and the English were our friends. And Lina and Roberto could not return to school up north. For me this was the only good news.

When the English started to come into Italy the Germans made lots of trouble. To keep the British from coming into the town they blew up bridges, mountains, and even houses.

Escaped British prisoners of war were hiding in the mountains nearby. Some had also come down by parachutes and were living in caves. They had become gaunt and almost animal-like with their long hair and beards. The first time I saw one of these men I just threw a piece of bread at him. I was scared. Some people took food to them. I did it also. I took a basket of bread and jam, covered it with manure and left it on the mountain for them. One man came out of the bushes, took the food and quickly ran away.

Sometimes the British came near the farms, hungry, begging, "Please, please, give me food." When you see someone like that you cannot refuse. I thought to myself, "My God, maybe my husband is in this condition. There is no food and no one wants to help him."

The Germans had put up posters all over town saying that whoever knew the whereabouts of prisoners of war should notify the German command. There were people in our town who were working for the Germans, sometimes you didn't know who to trust. If there was a rumour that someone was hiding prisoners the Germans would just come and tear your house down.

One night three Germans went to a man's house which was right beside the church and said, "If you see any English come and tell us." This man didn't want to go. Three nights later the Germans put a bomb inside his house. The bomb exploded in the middle of the night. The whole town shook. Everyone grabbed their pillow in fright wondering what had happened. Four people inside the house were killed.

With the English inside Italy the Germans could not get their food supplies so they had to come to us. Once when I was in the barn a German came and took four chickens and two rabbits. I could not do anything. With his hands he showed me that he was hungry. What could I say? The Germans started to steal when they were hungry. Once I hid a big salami under Franco's bed and three Germans came and turned everything upside down and took the salami and Franco off to work. Whatever they saw they took. They kept taking chickens from us till we only had one left. We were lucky to have that one. It was Franco who always found new places to hide it. It was not too hard to find a hiding place for one chicken but for ten chickens it was impossible, they made such noise. Also, the Germans kept a record of what you had left after they took animals from you. It was easy to say one chicken had died.

Once the Germans became our enemies they turned really nasty. They stole whatever they could find. People would put the dowry for their daughters or other valuables into one room and seal it up with bricks. But the Germans quickly learned about this and they would tap on the walls with the end of their rifles. If it was hollow they broke down the wall and took what they wanted. In many cases they thought we had hidden men in there.

Some women went with the Germans to get food because there was a shortage. When the Germans would be going somewhere like Pescara, a woman would ask for a lift. They would take her to their supplies and give her what she wanted after they got what they wanted. These women got oil and then they returned to town and sold it to the rest of us for a very high price. Before the war I paid 60 lire for oil. During the war I had to pay 1,000 lire to this woman for the same amount of oil.

The Germans stole men in big trucks to fix the bridges or the roads the English had bombed. The men would fix one bridge, then the English bombed it again and they would have to fix it again. Sometimes the same bridge would have to be repaired three or four times. I had two cousins who were fifteen and sixteen, one time the Germans took them away for three weeks. After their work was over they were sent back home. Lots of men were taken far away and you wondered what happened. Some of the women who knew where the captured men were made spaghetti and tomato sauce and walked for two hours with the pots on top of their heads to take food to them.

We were so scared of the Germans that when one came to our house and picked up Michele just to play with him Michele started screaming. He thought the German was going to walk away with him.

A family of actors, who had left Naples to get away from the war, came to Pratola and wanted to put on a performance in the theater to make some money for food. We had a big theater near the railroad station where they used to show films. But since the blackout there had been no films, people didn't go out at night. The people of Pratola went to the German headquarters to ask if three nights could be set aside for this family to perform in the theater. The Germans said yes.

On the first night of the performance the theater was full. But everybody in town was scared because they thought this was a trap set up by the Germans to get the men. I also thought this and was afraid to let Franco come to the performance. The play was beautiful, there was a little girl who sang like an angel. Everyone came, even the Germans enjoyed themselves. For three nights Pratola was free.

The Germans left our town two days before the Americans arrived. It was not a good place for them to stay because we were surrounded by mountains. If they would have stayed I am sure

27

there would have been a big fight. There were already a lot of dead. Four hundred people were killed when the English blew up the train station in Sulmona just as the 11:55 trains arrived from Pescara, Naples, Aquila, and Rome. They must have known that these trains were going to arrive together. A woman I knew had gone to the market in Sulmona to sell some of her produce and she never came back.

In 1944 the Americans arrived. People ran around yelling, "The war is finished! The war is finished!" The whole town went to see them. The soldiers arrived in trucks yelling, "We're Americans." Two or three big Italian representatives came with them and said, "The war is now finished. The Americans helped us against the Germans so you better welcome these soldiers." But why do I need to say good morning to people who killed my brother-in-law and might have killed my husband? I didn't want to welcome them. My husband had not written for four years, my brother-in-law was dead, I had four or five relatives still in the war. I was certainly not joyful when the Americans came. My eyes had become dry from crying so much. There was no more water inside. I didn't care who was coming.

But the war didn't end with the coming of the Americans because in April 1945 Mussolini was shot. Nobody should have killed him. Mussolini was a nice man, the best man in the whole of Italy. He was for the poor people, he didn't like the rich.

After the war there was lots of misery, poverty, no one was working. Prices multiplied daily. If you had paid 1 lira for a pair of socks, suddenly it went up to 15 lire and the next day it was 100 lire. Everything was rationed and certain things were not even available except on the black market. Some people became millionaires because of the war.

One of the first letters from my husband came in 1944. One day Mario came down the road waving a letter and yelling out my name. I was standing beside my mother-in-law and she said, "Oh, my God, it couldn't be." Mario was screaming, "It's from your husband." As he came closer with the bicycle we could see that it was his writing. I nearly fainted. When I had the letter in my hand I was kissing it and kissing it. Half the letters which arrived were either cut out or crossed out with black ink. Everything went through the censors first. If they had written something bad like, "We are not being fed," we wouldn't have been able to read it. The only words we could read were, "We're

OK, hope to see you soon." We tried to hold the letter up to the light to read the crossed-out sections but we couldn't. The censors had done a good job.

I kept getting letters which said, "Thank God I am alive, maybe I'll be home next month." But he kept writing the same thing year after year. Then I got a letter which said, "I'll be home either before or after Christmas." But I didn't believe this. The anticipation had worn off. I thought, "One of these days he'll be here and that's all there is to it."

Slowly the men started to come back. We never knew when and who would come. We went to the railroad station every day to wait. They arrived by truck, by train, some just walked into town. All were in terrible condition. Their uniforms were torn, some had no uniform at all, just old civilian clothes, some had half and half, some had no shoes.

On the sixth of January, the day of the Epiphany, a band went around the town and there were all sorts of celebrations. No one went to bed early. I usually read a story out aloud but on the sixth of January 1946 I didn't feel like reading. My mother-in-law was making socks and my sister was knitting near the fire. Everybody was doing something. I said, "I want to go to bed, I don't feel very well." But because it was the night of the Epiphany there was music and singing coming from outside and I could not sleep. When I went to bed I started to cry, thinking of my husband.

Around five o'clock in the morning I heard somebody knocking and pushing the door. I got up, opened the window and yelled down, "What do you want?" I thought someone was just making trouble. The man down below looked up at me, "You forgot me?" I closed the window. He kept pounding at the door and yelling, "Teresa. Teresa." My mother-in-law woke up and she went down to see what was going on. When I heard him crying, "Mamma, Mamma," I got scared. I didn't want to believe it was my husband and I screamed.

In five minutes there were a hundred people in my house. People came asking, "Have you seen my brother?" "My husband?" "Do you recognize me?" It was a celebration. He told them there were a lot more people at the station. Everyone took a car and went to collect the others. Soon the whole town was awake and full of activity.

I am sure God protects us.

Franco

MY MOTHER WANTED A PRIEST in the house, since I was the oldest I was her first try. As soon as I finished elementary school, at age eleven, she pushed me into a seminary. I was very unhappy there, I couldn't see this as my future. The teachers were very strict. I made a few friends but the structure of the place didn't allow anyone to make very close friends. We were under control and supervision every hour of the day. Finally, I couldn't take it anymore and about a year after my mother left for Tripoli I ran away.

The seminary was up in the mountains about fifteen or twenty kilometres from my home town, I had to walk down to the railway tracks in shorts and an undershirt. But I didn't know how to take a train or which way to go. I waited by the tracks for at least a half a day before I saw a familiar face in the window of a slowly passing train. I grabbed onto a railing near a door and quickly jumped on the train. The man I saw in the window was from my home town but he could have been travelling one way or the other, I had no way of knowing the difference, I didn't know where my town was.

I searched for this man on the train and sat down beside him but he didn't recognize me. When the controller came asking for the tickets, I had no ticket. He asked me if someone had given me a ticket and I started to cry. Then the man I sat beside recognized me and lent me some money.

It was nearly dark by the time we reached Pratola. I went straight to my grandmother's house. My Uncle Eduardo, my father's brother, was so surprised to see me. My Uncle Eduardo was a bachelor and I always spent a lot of time with him. I told him what I had done and asked him not to say anything to my mother. I was afraid she was going to kill me. My grandmother was very upset, she tried to persuade me to return but my uncle took my side.

Soon after I returned to school in Pratola war was declared. It was the tenth of June 1940, and it was pouring rain, every radio station was reporting the latest events and all the bells were ringing from every church. It was like a feast or a religious holiday, it didn't feel like war.

In school we had to stand up and swear allegiance to Mussolini. A cross hung behind the teacher's desk. To the left of the cross hung the King's picture and to the right of the cross hung Mussolini's picture. It was like a triumvirate except the fascists were the real heads, the Pope still had power but Mussolini was the boss of Italy.

All the students were put into one group or another by the fascist party, depending on age. Every week we had to attend organized activities in uniform. The state provided the uniforms for the different age groups. The black shirt was always a constant. As a teen-ager I was supposed to be part of the Fascist Youth. During school we often went out for parades, marching around with posters full of slogans, yelling, singing fascist songs. We all thought this was great fun, it was a good excuse to get out of the classroom. We were given buttons to wear which said, "God damn the English." The English were our enemies and we marched up and down the Corso and around the fountain yelling, "Damn the English." We were sure we would win because our navy was much larger than the British navy.

When my mother came home and saw me she started hitting me. From then on I think she hated me. Whenever I got home from one of our marches my mother always gave it to me, "Aren't you ashamed of yourself, your father is fighting and you are preaching war."

One morning we got up and there were about thirty-five small German tanks in and around Pratola. The Germans took over the *municipio* on the Piazza Garibaldi and they commanded. One German and two Italian policemen regularly walked around town checking up on everything and everybody.

A radio stood outside one of the cafés on the Piazza Garibaldi. This became the focal point of the town, there were always crowds of people on the streets and in the bar listening. The church bells provided us with the news of the town and the radio provided us with the news of Italy. Officially we were only allowed to listen to one station but a friend of ours who was a shoemaker had a radio in his house and I often went over there to listen to the news from England and America. A group of us huddled around this machine, the volume had to be kept very low because we were not allowed to listen to other news. If the fascists or the Germans would have caught us they would have put us all in jail.

I was too young to be drafted into the army but I was constantly arrested and released, arrested and released, the Germans never believed my age. According to them I was supposed to be in the army because there was a draft and I continually had to prove that I was not of age to enter the army. But when the Allies landed in Sicily everyone in the school went to the station and said, "We want to fight against the Americans." I went to the army colonel in Sulmona to volunteer to fight. He said, "You're only fifteen and a half, I can't take you. Go to Rome, they might overlook the consent."

I went to Rome by train. It was my first time in Rome. I took a taxi from the railroad station and went straight to the army camp. They said, "Sure we'll take you but we need the consent of your father." I said, "Of course." I waited around for two days hoping they would forget about it. They even gave me a uniform. After a few days, when they saw I still had no consent form, they sent me home. I took a taxi back to the station, got back on the train and returned home. I felt very impotent, I wanted to do something because the Americans were invading my country. The Germans couldn't help being in Italy, they were at war and they had to defend themselves. I wasn't pro-German or pro-American, I was an Italian.

Even before the landing of the Allied forces was announced there was chaos in Italy. The King had Mussolini arrested in July 1943 and Italy was left without a leader. Marshal Badoglio was appointed as the new Prime Minister but it only took a month before all of Italy saw him as the biggest traitor. At first he said, "We will continue to fight alongside the Germans, against the Allies. Nothing will change." Then on September the eighth, under his command, Italy gave up. And this same guy who told us to fight against the Allies turned around and said, "Now we will fight against the Germans, alongside the Allies." And it was he who had allowed the landing of the Allies in Sicily.

I was taught in school that the Germans were our friends, our allies, and then all of a sudden they were our enemies. I just couldn't take that. I wasn't the only one who felt that way. Some people went wild. Italians shooting Italians. It was chaos. Some

Italians said, "What the hell, yesterday I was beside the Germans, today I have to go beside the Allies. Where is my country?" Some dumped their weapons and came home as civilians. But there were black shirts who were still in favour of Germans and they were shooting Italian deserters. Someone I knew was stopped by the Germans. They asked to see his identity papers. As he pulled out his wallet two American dollar bills fell out. When the Germans saw this they said, "You have to come with us." But he got scared and ran and they shot him.

A few days after armistice German parachutists went to the mountain villa where Mussolini was being detained and rescued him by helicopter. He was then taken to Germany. From Germany he was taken to Salo where he started a fascist republic. By then the Allies were advancing and he didn't stand a chance of regaining his former power. The country was left without a leader.

When Italy signed the armistice on September 8, 1943 the concentration camp gates were opened. There were a number of camps in our valley. The English and all the other prisoners were free to go but then the Germans came and started rounding them up again, moving them into other concentration camps. Our countryside was full of escaped Allied prisoners of war who were trying to find places to hide. On the spur of the moment a group of us set up some sort of an organization to help them. We hid them in ditches, in haystacks, in caves in the mountains and the women went up the mountain to take them food.

A few English prisoners even stayed in our house. The house we lived in was actually two houses, our house and my grand-mother's house. Underneath the house, on street level, was the cantina where the wine was kept in huge wooden and concrete barrels. We hid some of the escaped prisoners in the empty barrels. At night I would go and feed these people and arrange to move them from one place to another, we couldn't keep them in one place for more than three or four days. If the Germans found out you were hiding the British they would shoot you.

We even devised a scheme to give them forged fascist docu-ments. We learned to copy the stamps. We couldn't take pictures but we had a roomful of old pictures. When we picked up a guy we looked for a picture which closely resembled him, stuck the picture onto the document, copied the stamp, and away he went.

It was fairly easy to find a photo for the dark-complexioned people, our problem was with the very blond and the Negroes.

I helped the English prisoners of war for humanitarian reasons, not because they were our friends. There were also fascists in our group because they didn't want to see their land ruled by foreigners.

My mother got used to seeing me less and less. I don't think she realized what I was involved in till later.

I had an uncle who was a priest in a convent in Abruzzi. He came to visit us once in a while to give us a little comfort. He kept saying, "God will help out." But I was very confused. God was not enough. I didn't know what to believe, there was a confusion of leaders and a confusion of God. You didn't know what to think, there was no trust, no faith. For a while you couldn't even trust your next door neighbour.

Listening to the news on the radio we all thought the advance of the Americans was so fast that the war was coming to an end. But there was no end in sight.

The Germans were getting more and more desperate. The Allies had cut off their food supply and they were being surrounded. They needed food and men to help them clear the roads. Occasionally the Germans stormed the schools and took the young men away for work so the school closed down in September of 1943, it wasn't worth continuing.

When the Germans needed people they would just take you. One morning everybody went to church and I stayed home. Suddenly I heard a banging on the door and the Germans just marched in. They pointed their guns at me and said, "*Raus! Raus!*" They put me in a truck and took me away. Someone went to the church to tell my mother what had happened. I was taken twice by the Germans. We had to help them build roads or to clean away the snow. I never knew where I was going. Once I was shovelling snow near the front lines at Casino. The first time they let me return home the same night. The second time they kept me for seven nights.

We had to hide our food from the Germans because they would come and take it for their troops. We had an eight-room house. When the war started my Uncle Eduardo hid food just under the roof. There was already a small hole in the third-floor ceiling and we put all the stock we had up there. We had to have a ladder or a chair to reach this hole. When we needed something we went up there. We had bacon, sausage, pasta, beans, even a little bit of flour.

We also had to watch out for thieves. Some Italian thieves took advantage of the war, they would dress up as Germans and come around and take everything. They even dressed up as English soldiers and said they had to feed the army. Even if you knew they were Italians, what could you do? They could shoot you.

One of the Germans was called Four Eyes because of his glasses. He was in charge of gathering food for the troops. He would just walk up to a farmer and say, "How many cows do you have?" If you had six he would say, "I am taking four, two are enough for you." Some of the soldiers would shoot the animals, cut off the head and feet and put the rest in the truck. Some of the small farmers only had two or three cows and the Germans would take them all.

In a nearby town the people decided to save as much of the livestock as they could. One evening about twenty-six young boys decided to drive the livestock of the town up into the mountains where they could be hidden in caves. They were heading up the mountain with all the animals in the middle of the night when two Germans, who were scouting the area, mistook them for a Resistance group. The Germans pointed a machine gun at them and ordered them to stop. One of the boys said, "What the hell, there are twenty-six of us and only two of them, why don't we jump them?" That's exactly what happened. They all jumped on the one with the machine gun and killed him. They only wounded the other guy. He must have made it back to town because two hours later a full battalion of Germans went up the mountain after them. They were brought down and shot one by one in the middle of the main square as an example. The youngest was fourteen and the oldest was twenty-one. Three of them had been my classmates.

The same thing almost happened to me. On the twentieth of October eighteen of us were rounded up and taken hostage by the Germans because someone in our town had shot two German soldiers. I was the youngest of the bunch. We stayed in a big barn on a farm just outside of town. We slept on the hay and each day we were given a two-inch square of black bread and a cup of coffee with no sugar or milk, that was it. At one end of the barn was a door guarded from the outside by two Germans with machine guns. The Germans were hoping that one of us would talk.

One day, while we were digging a hole, a soldier came along and said, "Either you know who did it and you don't want to say or you don't know. Either way, according to our law we kill ten civilians for every German shot."

That night Pietro, a friend of mine, and I overheard two old men about sixty or seventy talking. It turned out that they were brothers. The older brother said, "I know who did it but I'm not saying anything to the Germans."

The younger brother was surprised, "Tell me, who was it?"

"My son-in-law. He's only twenty-one, I'm an old man. I couldn't care less if I live or die."

"A life is a life. I don't care how old I am and there are others involved. You should tell the Germans what you know."

The older brother shook his head, "No, no, I don't want to say anything." The two brothers got into a fight over this.

Pietro was also twenty-one so when he heard this he was furious. He grabbed the older brother and said, "Either you talk or I won't let the Germans kill you, I'll kill you myself."

The guards heard all the noise and came in to break up the fight. Eventually, the older brother said, "All right, I know. It was my son-in-law."

The Germans wanted to know where he was living. It took some time before they got it out of him. Then they looked around at all of us and pointed to Pietro and I and said, "You two, take us there." We didn't want to go with the Germans because we were afraid of getting into trouble with the family afterwards. The guy who had shot the Germans was from a big family in town with lots of brothers and brothers-in-law. But we didn't have too much of a choice.

We arrived at the house in three tanks. Usually there were at least thirty people living there. The place looked deserted. We went inside and only found the old woman, the mother of the guy who had shot the Germans, sitting in the kitchen. They dragged her outside and opened all the windows and doors of the house. Each brother had his own section so it was a big house. We were told to pour gasoline in every room. A couple of the Germans came with us to make sure we had poured out enough. The rest of them were searching for valuables. They took all the cheese, ham, embroidered linen, jewellery. Then everyone got out. They threw hand grenades into the open windows and the house went up in flames while the old mother was yelling curses and crying for the saints.

We were already in our town and the barn where we had been kept for nearly two weeks was twenty kilometres away so we asked the Germans to just leave us off. They refused, they said we would all be let go together. Pietro and I looked at each other. Now that we had shown them the house they could still kill us. But there wasn't much we could do. We got into the tank and were taken back to the barn.

One guy among the Germans spoke perfect Italian, he was probably an Italian dressed as a German. That night he gave us a long speech about how they were fighting for us and how they were trying to save Italy and fascism. At the end he said, "Heil Hitler. Heil Mussolini. Now get lost."

We all ran as fast as we could. I lost the soles of my shoes on the way home but I didn't feel a thing, I just wanted to get away from them.

The family whose house was burnt down was mad. One of the brothers said we should have shown the Germans an old run-down house where no one was living. But the Germans were not stupid, they wouldn't have believed us.

A couple of weeks after we were released the guy who had done the shooting came back to town. It turned out that he had shot at the Germans in a moment of anger when they came to take something from his family. But he just injured them, he hadn't even killed them and then he quickly took off to the mountains. In the mountains he found an American pilot and copilot whose plane had crashed. He guided them to Naples where the Americans had already landed and set up camp. He told them how he had shot two or three Germans back home and how he had to escape before he was caught. He was hailed a hero and the Americans took up a collection for him in the camp. He came back home loaded with money. But the sisters-in-law made him pay for everything the German soldiers had taken from the house and in the end he had no money left. Secretly I was glad because he was playing the hero while we were all facing machine guns and he never said a word to us. He never even acknowledged what we had been through because of him.

The real trouble started when the Allies came to our valley. As the Germans were leaving the towns they took all the young men with them for work. My mother told me to run away to the mountains. A group of us lived in a cave for a month. The women came with donkeys to bring us food.

One man in the group wanted to go home when he heard the bombs. He was afraid for his children. He went back during the night, was spotted by the Germans and was killed.

The Americans thought they were liberating us after four years of war but they caused destruction and confusion. A lot of people died. The Americans took care of things from the air and the Germans took care of things from the ground. They were arresting everyone, burning everything and anything that moved.

The Americans first flattened out everything before they allowed a soldier or a tank in. The artillery kept pounding a nearby town for a week after the Germans had left. There were three hours of bombings in the morning. Then they stopped and the people of the town came out of hiding and went about their business, had lunch, and lived a normal life. In the afternoon the bombings started again and everyone returned to their hiding place. The Americans were about six kilometres down the road and they wouldn't advance. Finally, someone said, "We should tell those guys to stop pounding us, it's safe to come in." That's exactly what they did. Three boys went down the road during a bombing break to talk to the Americans.

When the Americans came into Pratola it was like a procession, people were leaning out the windows, standing on their balconies, cheering them as they came. I didn't cheer them. Some people even gave them flowers, but they were invaders. We went from one occupation to another. They threw around cigarettes and gum, it was humiliating. All the women ran after them.

I judged them to be more uncivilized than the Germans. I saw Americans drunk on the street, chasing and raping women. It didn't matter if they were prostitutes or nice girls. If the women tried to run away from them they shot upward to scare them. In Sulmona I saw three Italians drop a big stone on an American's head while he was raping a young girl. There was a police investigation later but nothing was done.

As a young man I felt insulted. I was boiling inside but what could I do? I talked to some of the Americans who were of Italian origin and my impression was that the war was just an adventure for them. The young men were showoffs, they tried to buy everything. They had good food, good wine, good women. The English and the Canadians had limitations, so much to drink, so much to eat, so many cigarettes, so much money. The Americans seemed to have things to throw away to the dogs. A friend's dog left the family to follow an American soldier out of town because he fed him so well.

The American army had everything. It wasn't like the Italian soldiers in Russia, without soles on their shoes. The war was easy for the Americans. You could tell the difference, the Germans were fighting a war and they let us know it, we need this and we'll take it. They were professional. The English soldiers were clean, respectful and not that friendly with anybody. The officers kept their distance from the lower classes and from their own soldiers. There was a sense of separation. There was none of that with the Americans. You saw officers drinking with plain soldiers, everybody was going around saying, "Hi, Joe." "Hi, Sam." There was no respect.

They created confusion. Someone from our town had a child from a black soldier. He looked after her by stealing from the army. He got caught and she was left with nothing. She had to go to the city to become a maid.

They encouraged the black market and prostitution. Someone paid an American soldier $1 for a blanket and resold it for $10. Cigarettes were big, you could get a carton and resell it for 1,000 lire a pack.

During the war we had some salt. Right after the war we had no salt. People went to Bari or other places along the coast to get it. They returned and sold it to us for three times the price. Five of us went on our bicycles a couple of times to San Severo di Puglia to get salt. It took us a week. We each brought back about twenty or thirty kilos.

In April 1945 we heard over the radio that Mussolini was killed while he was leaving Italy to go to Switzerland. When we were young he told us, "If I go forward follow me but if I go backwards kill me." That was exactly what happened. But to be captured in a German uniform while carrying a box full of gold wedding rings! I didn't like that. His image was shot for me. He was killed with his mistress and they were both hung, feet first, in a square in Milan. Everyone stood around spitting on them. Angelina cried so hard when she heard the news. I tried to explain to her that this man was not worth one tear but she just ran away from me when I talked like that.

There was a period of relief that finally the tragedy was over. At the same time it was a period of despair. The war had separated families, communication was difficult. The most awaited moment was for the husbands, boyfriends, sons to arrive. Sulmona had a central train station, a lot of people passed through there. Everyone had a story to tell. My cousin had been captured by the Russians. They treated him well because he played the accordion for them at night. He told us that one time someone brought back a cuckoo clock from somewhere and hung it on the wall. When the clock reached the hour the cuckoo came out and made a noise. The Russians jumped to their feet and shot at the cuckoo with machine guns. They had thought it was a bomb.

By the time my father came back I was seventeen. He was like a stranger to me. I was a little scared, I thought he would try to tell me what to do. My mother had tried to stop me from doing certain things but a woman is a woman.

There were so many people at the house when he arrived. Everyone was asking questions. People were going in and out of the house for two days. By the second evening he still had not unpacked. His suitcase was left open in one corner of the room. I saw a few cans of V8 cigarettes inside. I took a can and left, saying I would be back later. A group of us had previously arranged a little party and I wanted to show off with these imported cigarettes. By the time I got home it was 6:30 A.M. I sneaked into the house and went straight to bed. When I got up in the late afternoon my father called me over.

He said quietly, "It's about time you got up."

I said, "I got in a little late last night."

He laughed, "Last night? Or did you come back this morning?"

I didn't know what to say. Then he asked, "How many cigarettes did you take with you?"

"Just a few."

"How many?"

"A can."

He looked me up and down carefully, "So, you smoke?"

"Sometimes. I give them away most of the time."

The next evening the house was full of people again. My mother had warned me to stay home. This time my father was the one who was showing off, offering cigarettes to everyone. I didn't want to smoke in front of my parents so I went out to the side of the house and lit a cigarette. After I finished I went right back. I did this two or three times. The fourth time I went out my father followed me.

He said, "At your age I was also smoking, you don't have to sneak around."

40

Roberto

EVERY SUNDAY MORNING the Italian governor of Libya, Italo Balbo, drove to church along the main boulevard in a convertible. He was accompanied by his coloured bodyguards who were all very sharply dressed in red jackets. We lived on the main boulevard and every Sunday morning I stood on our balcony and saluted him. He always looked so proud and ready for battle with his military decorations, all those medals and stripes. There was a lot of talk of war amongst the adults. When we went on picnics my father was always arguing with the other men about what Hitler should do and what Mussolini should do. It all sounded exciting, I wanted to be part of it. I wanted to grow up quickly so I could talk with them and give my opinions. I also wanted to have an elegant uniform, participate in parades, and fight for the country.

When my father told us we would have to go back to Italy because of the war I went to the bathroom and cried. I did not want to leave. But my father said I had to go to take care of Angelina. My mother didn't want her to go back to Italy alone. I told them that Mussolini would take care of her but it was not enough for them.

Dressed in our school uniforms, we boarded a ship called Duilio. I was eight years old and my age group was called Balilla because there was a kid named Balilla who threw stones at the enemy. He became a hero and they created this group for him.

Two days later we arrived in the north of Italy and were taken by train to Cesenatico on the Adriatic Sea. Mussolini had taken all the big luxury hotels to receive the children. The hotels were renamed and they were converted to fascist colonies for us. In Cesenatico we stayed at the hotel Francesco Baracca, he was a World War I hero, an aviator.

Soon after we arrived we heard that the ship which brought us to Italy had turned around to return to Tripoli loaded with Italian soldiers and it was sunk. The English must have known that from Tripoli to Naples there was a boat full of kids and we were not dangerous to them but they sank a ship full of soldiers.

My father had thought that he was sending us away from the war to safety but here I was more conscious than ever that we were being raised to win a war, to fight for Italy. The walls of the hotel were full of Mussolini's pictures and sayings in big letters: *Vincere, vinceremo.* "To win, we will win." *Alle nostre casa ritorneremo.* "To our homes we will return." *Chi vola vale, chi non vola non vale, chi vale e non vola e un vile.* "He who flies is worthy, he who does not fly is worthless, he who is worthy and does not fly is a coward." Or, "The rooster gets up at five, the man at seven, and the pig at nine." "Better to live a single day as a lion than a hundred years as a sheep." Also, we were always talking about winning and raising wheat so we could have flour for bread.

On the beach, near our colony, a German fort was being built with thick walls. During recreation I noticed a man sketching the fort. I thought to myself, what is he doing, does he have nothing else to sketch but this place? I was suspicious so I reported him to one of my teachers. Later I saw him being arrested. I knew he was doing something he should not have been. We all felt a great responsibility toward our country and we understood that Mussolini depended on us. Every child was important, Mussolini needed us and cared for us. I knew this because he regularly sent his men, the *federali*, to visit us and look us over. Whenever they came the teacher lined us up and we proudly recited,

I believe in the genius of Il Duce and our Lord Fascism,
I believe in the communion of martyrs of Fascism,
Lord, thou who lightest every flame,
Lord, thou who rulest every heart,
Revive in me each day
My passion for Italy.

When winter came to Cesenatico we moved to a warmer place, San Remo. The hotel we stayed in was very big and beautiful. Before the war Churchill stayed there once when he came to Italy. There were flowers everywhere. At the entrance there were two big, marble, lion statues. There were long marble corridors but the teachers were very strict about running around because they were afraid we would hurt ourselves.

Everything was very organized and disciplined. Each morning there was one person who raised the flag and another who played the trumpet and we all sang,

For our Duce,
For our Blessed Duce,
We are ready,
We are ready with our guns,
And with our,
And with our flag,
Forever forward,
Forever forward we will go,
Alala.

Every time we went somewhere the whole class went together. We had to form three rows and walk in step. Talking was not allowed. There were posters all over the city telling you to keep your mouth shut because someone might be listening to you. Even on the postcards we were given to send home there was a picture of a mouth with a padlock on it. After supper we went out for recreation and played for an hour. Before we went in we lowered the flag and again said a salute.

Soldiers often went past the hotel and we stood outside waving to them. They always waved back. One day a couple of *federali* came to our school. They lined us up outside the hotel in three rows and gave us a careful inspection and a big talk. They told us we were going to be taken to the train station to welcome Hitler, a good friend of Mussolini. They said it was a great honour to have been chosen for this and proper behavior was very important. We were to cheer only when we got the signal from the *federali*.

We all marched out to the square near the train station. There were a lot of other kids and a great deal of excitement. We were all very proud to be part of this event. Our teachers had said that we might even get to see Mussolini. We waited on the square for a long time before we finally got the signal and suddenly there was wild cheering coming from everywhere. The noise was so tremendous that my ears hurt. But I could not see Mussolini.

The following Epiphany, January the sixth, German officers came to visit us with lots of presents. We went into the dining room where the teachers were putting bits of folded paper into a hat. When they were all done the hat was shaken up and one by one we were called up to pull out a slip of paper. We had to unfold the paper and read it out loud in front of everyone. Whatever was written on it was the present we were given. When

I went to pick mine I felt the teacher's hand inside the hat. She pushed a piece of paper in my hand, whispering, "Take this one." I knew the teacher liked me so I took it. I won the biggest present of all, a horse and a wagon full of books. The German officers asked if I would pose for a picture with them. I sat on the floor with the horse and cart beside me and all the officers stood behind me. I felt like a hero. When it was time to go to our rooms I wanted to take my present with me but the officers said, "It's too big to take to your room, we'll keep it for you." Everyone with a small present could take theirs with them but I couldn't keep mine. I was really mad because I ended up with nothing.

From time to time my mother sent me 10 lire. There were about a dozen of us who received money from home. The teacher kept this for us and every time she went to the city she asked us if we needed anything. Often I ordered candies or a deck of cards. One day we each asked for one hundred grams of candies. But Benito said, "No, I don't want anything." When the teacher came back she gave each of us our candies. Benito did not get anything. Later he came over to me and said, "Roberto, would you give me a candy?" So I gave him one. He did this to every one of us. At the end he had more candies than any of us. That taught me a good lesson, it does not have to cost you anything to come up on top.

At night, we often played cards. We could not play for money because the teacher had it all. We played for bread or for comic books. For supper we always got one roll but sometimes you were hungrier than other times so if you had won a game of cards against a guy you went up to him and asked for his roll. One night I went up to a guy who owed me a roll. He looked at me as if he didn't know what I was talking about and said, "It wasn't me, it was my brother."

He had an identical twin and I thought I could have made a mistake. I went over to his brother but he gave me the same look and said, "No, it wasn't me, it was my brother."

They were sleeping beside each other and that night after we were supposed to be asleep I went over to their bed and said, "OK, who is going to give me the bread?" The two of them got into a fight and the teacher ended up punishing all three of us. But the next day one of them gave me the roll.

The comic books were a big thing. The English were always the bad guys and the Germans were the good guys. My favourite was called *Bonaventure*. It was about King George of England

and his prime minister. One night King George is in bed and the bombs start falling but King George is afraid of the war and runs to hide under Churchill's bed. Also, there were lots of cartoons about Roosevelt. His middle name was Delano, Franklin Delano Roosevelt and in Italian *dell'ano* means "of the anus." We had a lot of good jokes about that.

In 1943, just before the summer holidays, everyone in my class was confirmed. Someone in San Remo picked a sponsor for each one of us because we did not know anyone. On Sunday morning everyone got dressed up, short white pants, blue and white striped sweaters, and we waited for our sponsors to pick us up. We were all debating who was going to get the most money or the best present. My sponsor gave me a bank book and he had put 50 lire into my account. After confirmation I was invited to his house for dinner. He had five children, one was a little girl who was close to my age. We played together for a while before her father took me back to the colony. Later I found out that whoever wanted to sponsor us had to give us 50 lire or the equivalent in a present.

At the beginning of the summer holidays my Uncle Eduardo arrived to pick up Angelina and I and take us back to Pratola till the end of September. We had not spoken dialect in three years. In school we were taught the standard Italian. In Pratola, when we tried to talk with the other kids on the street, they laughed at us. They knew how to speak the standard Italian because they also learned it in school but sometimes even in school when the teacher got mad she spoke in dialect. It did not take me long to pick it up again. Angelina had a harder time.

Armistice was declared on the eighth of September. Italy was split into two and we could not go back to the colony. In one way I did not mind staying at home because, of course, it was home. But all of a sudden there was no organized activity and very little supervision. I felt like I was on a prolonged holiday. I did what I wanted to and nobody asked me anything. Even school was not very strict. I often didn't bother showing up. A group of us would go and do something. We used to play soccer but we didn't have a ball. We had to make one from women's stockings. We stuffed the toe of the stocking with rags. If we could not find any rags we took the stuffing out of the pillows and used that. After filling up the toe, we twisted the stocking a little bit, then turned it inside out, twisted it again, inside out again, till it looked like a real ball. It bounced perfectly well. Sometimes we played with coins, throwing them against the wall or on a line. Five or six of us stood in a line and threw. The guy whose coin landed closest to the wall or to the line collected all the coins.

The Germans stayed in a camp just outside the town. Sometimes they drove through the town in their huge tanks. They took up the whole street and damaged some of the curbs while they were moving. I was surprised at first that the Germans were not liked in the town, most people were afraid of them. But I could see why people were afraid of them, they were tough soldiers. If someone did something they did not like, they just shot him. When you are fighting a war, what else can you do? There has to be discipline. Some of the Austrians were sick and tired of fighting and were trying to desert the army. They said the war was going to end soon anyway. They spoke Italian because they lived near the border of Italy. They often talked to me even though I was only thirteen.

The Germans did not associate with the local people. They were controlled and strict. When the Americans arrived things were different. They were the winners and they acted accordingly. They went after the women and whatever they could get their hands on. Sometimes they went up on a balcony, lit the corner of a box of cigarettes, and threw it down on the street. We would all scramble after it. We either brought them home or we sold them. We thought the Americans were great. They were throwing everything around, cigarettes, gum, chocolates.

A group of officers stayed in a nearby villa. I often went to the kitchen to help the cooks. I could eat whatever I wanted but they didn't want me to take anything away from there. I liked to eat the stem of the cauliflower, take off the leaves and eat the raw stem with salt. One day they were cooking cauliflower and I took the stem, peeled it and ate it. For me it was the most natural thing. But the Americans were really annoyed when they saw me doing this. They said, "What are you, a pig or something? You have everything you want here. Why do you want to eat that?" They took it away and threw it in the garbage.

Some people thought the war was over when the Americans entered our town. Other people thought the war was over when they left our town. For me the war was over when I heard that Mussolini had been killed with his mistress in a gas station in Milan. That was the place where he came to power and that was the place where he went down. They made such a big fuss about this actress he was living with but what difference did it make? Hitler also had someone. Are they not allowed? They are human too. They treated Mussolini like a common criminal, this man who had been the father of Italy for over twenty years. How can you trust a man for over twenty years and then suddenly he is a criminal? There must have been a better way of dealing with him. Why did they have to hang him upside down in a square after he was dead and spit on him? I was born under his regime and grew up under it. I felt extremely sad. That was one of the saddest days of my life.

Angelina

MY MOTHER WAS SERVING LUNCH and she was telling me to eat in a soft voice but I couldn't. The food would not go down. I was sobbing and sobbing. Suddenly my father slammed his fist on the table, the dishes made a terrible noise, and he yelled, "The war will start soon, do you want to die here under the bombs?"

At the age of six I didn't understand what "war" meant. But I understood what it meant "to die" because my grandfather had died back in Italy and I was sad. I didn't want to die. But I didn't want to leave my parents either. Roberto was two years older than me, he was always much calmer, he didn't cry at all.

The day we were supposed to leave my mother carefully ironed my fascist uniform, the black skirt and the white blouse. I was a *Figlia della Lupa*, the daughter of the she-wolf of Rome. My mother was sad and as she helped me to get dressed she kept kissing me. But by then I was excited to leave. At the pier everyone was crying and taking pictures. My mother bought us some ice cream which I finished on the boat. It was nice having the ice cream on the boat because it was like having my mother come with me. Three big boats full of children slowly pulled out of the harbour and I watched the little row boats of the parents following the big boats. Gradually the little boats got smaller and smaller the further out we went until they disappeared. All night long nobody slept. We were whining and crying, asking for water and for our parents. The teachers were going up and down trying to calm everyone.

It was all dark when we reached Italy. We were put on a train and by the time we arrived in Cesenatico it was day. We were taken to a beautiful hotel. There was a fence protecting the hotel and there was a big garden full of beautiful flowers. There was a long back yard with a gate that led out to the beach and the sea.

The first thing they did was to shave everyone's hair off to make sure that we were clean. Then they sectioned us off according to age. The boys and girls were separated, half the hotel was for the girls and the other half was for the boys.

Roberto and I had shared a big bed at home and I always felt close to him so I missed him very much when they separated us. We were only to be together during our two hours of play in the garden. As soon as we got outside I would look for him and wave up and down. Each time I saw him coming toward me I couldn't help myself, I started to cry. He came and sat down on the bench beside me but after two minutes he said, "Wait here, I'll be back soon." He left and I sat on the bench for two hours waiting for him while all the children played and laughed around me. Then it was time to go in and I was still waiting for him. He never came back. He did this to me so many times. I finally asked him, "Why do you always leave me?"

He said, "Because you always cry and you make me cry too."

I was very, very unhappy the first year. I missed my family. But by the second year I got used to it. There was a thirteen-year-old girl, Teresa, who reminded me of my mother. She was beautiful with long brunette braids. I told her that my mother's name was also Teresa and I wanted to love her like my mother. Each time I saw her I embraced her and she used to pat me on the head, just like my mother. Or I went into her room and just sat down on her bed and talked to her.

Whenever my mother would write the teacher would call me over while we were playing outside and read out her letter to me. Then she took out a pen and some paper and said, "Now, what would you like to say to your mother?" I told her about the beach and the sun and that I made lots of friends. I always talked too much and I loved everybody so I was popular. I also asked my mother for money for little extras. The teacher kept the money for us and if we went on a trip and wanted ice cream she wrote down, "Today I bought Angelina an ice cream, now she has 10 lire left." But we didn't really need anything, we ate four meals a day and we had cake and ice cream for big occasions like Christmas and Easter.

One day, while we were playing on the beaches of Cesenatico, a group of soldiers stopped in front of the tall iron gate and asked us what we were doing there and what part of Italy we were from. I said I was from Pratola in Aquila. I was the only one from there, most of the other children were from Sicily. There was one soldier who was also from the province of Aquila and he was so touched to hear that I was from there that he took off his necklace and passed it through the holes of the gate for me.

One day, after breakfast, our principal told us, "Today we are going to line up on the street in front of our hotel and cheer the young soldiers who will be passing by to go to war." They gave all of us baskets full of flowers to throw to the soldiers. My mother had written a few days earlier that my uncle would be coming through Cesenatico and she sent a picture of him in uniform. I was sure he was going to be one of the soldiers. I kept standing on my tiptoes trying to find him in the crowd. There were so many soldiers walking by, three and four in a row, so many young faces. Everybody was throwing their flowers toward the procession of soldiers. I kept looking for my uncle. I was searching so hard that I forgot all about my flowers. Suddenly I saw him, at least I saw someone who looked like the picture my mother had sent, and I started yelling out his name. I threw all my flowers at him but he didn't turn to look at me. He was marching in the middle and he couldn't see me.

From Cesenatico we went to another hotel in the mountains in Piazzatorre, in Lombardy. It was beautiful, peaceful. We picked strawberries and chased butterflies in the mountains. One afternoon, while I was playing in the park with my friends, my brother came running with a picture and a letter in his hands, waving them in the air. "We have a baby brother. We have a baby brother." I was too young, I didn't know what was going on but I understood that there was someone else we were supposed to love. He showed me the picture. Michele had beautiful blue eyes, curly golden hair, just like the baby Jesus. From then on Mamma always wrote Michele did this and Michele did that so we got to know him.

The teachers told us, "As the snow comes down we are going to leave." They knew that we had been used to the warm climate in Africa. The snow came and chunks of ice like stones fell from the sky. I had never seen anything like that. We put on our black capes and ankle boots and they took us to the train station. We left the ice and snow and arrived in San Remo where there was sun. I was so amazed, from the snow-covered mountains to the bright sandy beach. There were palm trees and fountains surrounding our new hotel. The teachers told us that San Remo had flower markets instead of fish or fruit markets and flowers were sent to the rest of Europe from these markets.

Boys and girls were put in separate hotels. But each Sunday those of us who had brothers could go visit the other hotel and the next Sunday those who had sisters could visit our hotel. Before we left on Sunday mornings the teachers asked us if we wanted to buy comics to take to our brothers. We were taught proper manners. The education was perfect.

We ate well, we slept well, and we had beautiful uniforms. They took care of us. As soon as there was one infection we were all given a shot. Back home I never got needles. The priest came to the hotel every Sunday.

We used to count how many fathers and how many mothers we had. For fathers we had Mussolini, the King, and our father. And I used to say the Madonna was our first mother, then the Queen, then our mother, and then the teacher, and then the principal. I counted three fathers and five mothers. We were Mussolini's children. Every morning, before breakfast, we ran into the garden to form a big M of children. We all knew our places. I was little so I was at the bottom end of the M. We pulled up the flag and said a *salute* to Italy, to Mussolini, to the King and to the soldiers. *"Viva l'Italia! Viva Mussolini!"* Someone yelled out one thing and everybody answered at once, just like the soldiers.

Whenever we were on the street going from the hotel to our school or some other place we were marching in step and in rows of threes like soldiers. Mussolini said, "The thieves walk with their heads down, people with honour walk with their heads up." The higher we kept our heads, the prouder the teacher was.

But sometimes we would talk while marching and the teacher would point and say, "You two, remember, tonight in my room." Then a couple more talked during dinner. We ended up ten at a time in her room. For punishment we had to kneel down on the floor with our hands straight up for one hour. Often we rested our hands on our heads. When the hour was up we went to her and asked for forgiveness.

When the grade two's were preparing for their first communion they had to go to study the catechism for a couple of hours after school. I didn't want to study religion. I wanted to play with the others outside. I went to my teacher and said, "My parents wrote to me that they want me to have first communion with them when I go back home." This was the biggest lie of my life.

My teacher went to talk to the principal and then came back to me. "Where is the letter that your mother wrote to you?"

I said, "Who knows? I don't save all the letters but they wrote to me."

She believed me. "All right, you can stop going to catechism classes."

I was happy. I could go and play outside with the others. Then I heard that they were going to have a party for the girls who had their first communion. Everyone was discussing the arrangements, the big party after the church. Suddenly I said to myself, "My goodness, I'm going to miss the party." And I love parties. So I went back to the teacher and said, "I don't care what my parents wrote to me, I want to do my first communion here." She believed me the second time and I returned to the catechism classes.

For our first communion we wore our uniforms, the black pleated skirt and the white blouse with our pin, the big red M. It was too bad that we did not have white dresses but we had white veils which came to the shoulder. Afterwards we had a big fancy party with a dinner and cake, just for us.

Nothing was missing except the love of the family. They took us to movies and for picnics. Some of us were interviewed for a radio program and we were allowed to send messages to our parents. One child said, "I send a kiss as big as the moon to my mother." And the *federali*, Mussolini's men, regularly came to visit us in their black boots and black hats. A few days before they would arrive a lady came to prepare us. The first time she said, "I am shocked and ashamed, these children know nothing about *la dottrina fascista*." They gave us books to study in case the *federali* asked us questions we would be ready with the answers. When these big men came we formed the big M outside and we also formed the symbol of the *fascismo*, a sheath of wheat. While standing in formation we sang songs to Mussolini. Once the *federali* came while we were eating dinner and we got French pastry for dessert.

We usually behaved when there were guests but otherwise there was always some rebellion. There were long tables for each section of thirty students and each table had a place at the head for the teacher so she could watch everybody. Every day there was some commotion because we passed food to each other under the table and sometimes we dropped things. One day, while we were eating, a fourteen-year-old had a fight with one of the teachers and she jumped out the window which was on street level. Everyone started running after her and she was brought back. If one of the children had been missing all the teachers would have been arrested and they would have had to answer to Mussolini who cared about us. Once the principal had an argument with the thirteen-year-olds and in anger she called them, "These Arabs!" One of the girls wrote about this to her father. The principal was removed a few weeks later and another one came to take her place.

Our bedrooms were upstairs. We had bunk beds, like the soldiers. There were ten girls and five beds to each room. A class president was in charge of the bedrooms at night. I was always a class president. During the summer we took naps and I had to write down who was talking, who was laughing, who was not sleeping. The teachers' rooms were next to the stairs. If we wanted to leave we had to go by their rooms. We also had a watch-lady at night, a chubby old lady who had a little room to herself. She would go around a couple of times during the night, checking the rooms. A few of us would wet our beds and she would take us to the bathroom. I loved this lady, she reminded me of my grandmother.

In the hotel there was a beautiful curving stairway leading downstairs. Once, in the middle of the night, one of the girls woke up and said to her friend, "Let's slide down the banister." They tiptoed out, past the teachers' room, and the first girl slid down the banister and she went crashing onto the marble floor. There were just a few drops of blood and she died. The friend was so afraid she went right back to bed. But later she admitted what had happened.

The Germans in San Remo were so polite, so disciplined. They regularly passed by our gate and said a few words to us in German. They knew we were children of the war. An old, old man used to sit in front of our hotel with a basket of fruit, selling it to the people passing by. We knew this old man and often spoke to him. One day a young German soldier took out a bunch of money and gave it to the old man. "Give that basket of fruit to those children." I don't know how much the soldier gave him but the old man gave us all the fruit. The Germans we saw on the street were our friends and we loved them. In the colonies we were taught that the English people had started the war and King George of England was our number one enemy.

Most nights in 1942 and 1943 we had to get up because of the bombs. The planes came so low and they made a terrible noise. Our hotel in San Remo was on the sea. They taught us that when the planes came from the sky we had to go down to the basement but when the ships came from the sea we had to go to a nice spot behind the hills. Almost every night we were down in the basement. We put our pillow down on the ground, laid down, and prayed. One teacher was so frightened, she was biting her fingernails and I could see the rosary in her hand trembling when she prayed.

Only a few people visited us during the war, beside the soldiers and the *federali*. Two parents came to live in San Remo just to be close to their children. One of the mothers died and we all went to her funeral. It was so sad, the father and the two children burying the mother. Another mother used to come on all the picnics, just to be near her daughter.

My Uncle Eduardo took us home for a vacation in the summer of 1943. By then I had become a *Piccola Italiana*. We spent the whole night on the train and arrived early in the morning. All my cousins, aunts, uncles, and grandparents were waiting. There was a procession of about twenty people around us as we were going home. It felt like such a long way under the hot sun. I was so tired of walking I just wanted to sit down in the middle of the road. My uncle kept saying, "Just a few more steps. Just a few more steps and you'll be home." Suddenly I saw my mother running toward us, crying. I had thought everybody in the family had blue eyes except my mother who had dark brown eyes. But when I saw her again I realized that it was not true, I had forgotten.

The first thing Mamma did was to prepare breakfast. She had bought milk especially for us. Michele, the little one, started crying, he felt left out. Usually you feed the little ones first and now Mamma was fussing over Roberto and I and he had not had his breakfast yet. Later on he was hiding under the kitchen table and watching us from there.

After breakfast Mamma called me into her room and showed me two beautiful pieces of material she had bought, one was blue organza for special occasions, the other was red silk with little white poodles. They were so beautiful. I was tired of wearing the uniform all the time and by then I was eight and a half. I was growing up. My mother quickly sewed the materials into dresses with little puffy sleeves and a gathered waist.

At night, when we were all in bed, Mamma said, "Tomorrow I am going to give you and your brother a nice hot bath." And Michele asked, "But Mamma, what about their mother? Will she not mind you giving them a bath?" He didn't realize we were brother and sister.

After that first breakfast we had no more milk and I was used to milk in the hotel. We only had bread and tomato in the morning. At night when I was hungry and wanted another piece of bread I couldn't get it. I got sick that summer. I almost died of typhoid. I stayed in bed with high fever for one month. I couldn't eat a thing. When the doctor came he said, "These are children of the war." The change of food and air made me sick.

All the children in Pratola spoke in dialect and we only spoke standard Italian. I couldn't understand a word and they were making fun of me. I put my hand over my ears and said, "Thank goodness I don't understand you. Thank goodness I don't understand you." My mother just laughed.

When the summer ended my uncle couldn't take us back because Italy had been split in two, half to the Germans and half to the Allies. I was happy to hear I would be staying home with my mother and I wanted to be there when my father came home. We all thought that the war was going to end soon.

There were so many bombs, the houses shook and the people screamed. My uncle, to comfort us, said, "Don't worry, these are our bombs, that's why they are so strong." He always sent us children under the bed. He said, "If you are running, you don't know where to hide." One night we didn't sleep at all because of the bombs. As soon as it was daylight we went outside to play. It was four o'clock in the morning and we saw a horse running fast, pulling a buggy with an old couple. They were both dead.

In the town there was a young and beautiful woman, Antonietta. Her husband was a prisoner of war, just like my father. They didn't have any children so she worked as a nurse in the soldiers' hospital. People talked badly about her. They said she fooled around with the soldiers. It was easy for people to talk about her, she had no family to protect her because she came from the city, from Sulmona. I heard that she had not married her husband for love. He was tall, a little handsome but not sophisticated, not a gentleman like she deserved. She was the delicate type and she had to have many operations. There was a young doctor who went every morning and afternoon to visit her.

We could hear his steps on the cement as he passed our house. The neighbours did not believe she was sick enough to need the doctor year after year, twice a day. Once she showed her stomach to my grandmother and mother to prove how many operations she had. Then she heard that her husband had died and she dressed all in black.

During the war a lot of people were in black. People were dying all the time. The church bells were regularly ringing out their funeral notes. I was told the Germans were responsible for these deaths. The Germans in Pratola did not seem to be like the ones I had met up north. They robbed people and they were rude. I could not understand that. But I still felt sorry for some of them, they were so young. Sometimes the Germans parked their trucks near our house and we gave them nuts or something to eat. Then the Germans left and the English and Americans came and everybody loved them even though they had once been our enemy. Everyone thought their coming signalled the end of the war.

Antonietta's husband was one of the first prisoners of war to return. We saw him coming with all the people around him, he had been away for five years. When he arrived Antonietta was in the hospital and the young doctor was always beside her. She was wearing a black scarf and the young doctor said to her, "Take that off, the black does not suit you."

She said, "No, leave me alone." Perhaps she wanted to pretend that she was a sad widow. He continued to urge her to take it off. She said, "No, leave me alone. Leave me in peace to my sorrow."

Then the doctor said, "I told you to take it off. Your husband is fine." I guess then she felt really sick.

Her husband went to the hospital to pick her up and take her home. Then I heard them arguing all the time and soon she was pregnant. A cute little boy was born and the doctor who was always after her married soon after that. Before the boy was one year old her husband suddenly died. She said to everyone, "He was so fine. He ate so much the night before and he suddenly felt sick in the middle of the night and died." Behind her back the people said, "She must have poisoned him."

During the day the voice of the news, always low and serious, boomed from the piazza. One day I heard, "Mussolini is dead." I felt so bad. I felt sick to my stomach. Everybody around me was happy. They called him a pig. I was so hurt. For me he was a god, an idol. I looked at Roberto and we were the only ones who were sad. How could people be that way? He was considered a god only yesterday. How could they throw him on the ground and trample him the next day? If I love someone, that's it, he has to do something very wrong before I abandon him.

I found the education of Pratola so disorganized compared to what I had been used to up north. In grade four I sat and watched the walls. By the time the teacher had finished explaining a lesson I had already written it down. Nobody cared, I was neglected. Up north the party was watching us to see if we were learning properly, but in a small town nobody cared.

In grade five the teacher asked us to write about Mussolini, what he did and what we thought of him. The next day the principal came to our class and asked to see some of the children's work. The teacher picked mine. I knew she did it on purpose because mine was different. I was the oddball. The other children had written what they had heard from their parents, that Mussolini was bad. I had written that Mussolini was a great man and he had done great things for Italy. I wrote down everything they had taught me up north. When the principal finished reading it she said, "Pace, please stand up."

Everybody was looking at me while I was given a lecture. "It's true that Mussolini built roads and buildings and he took care of some of the people but at the end he destroyed everything with the war so he did nothing."

And there I was, I couldn't change my feelings.

POSTWAR ITALY

Vincenzo

MY BROTHER AND FATHER WERE DEAD. There were Polish soldiers in my town and I was told there was freedom.

Before I left there was order. When I came back one was carrying the red flag, another waved the black flag. There were more than a dozen political parties, everybody had formed a party. They were all busy recruiting members. "Come with us, you have to be a communist!" "No, you have to be a democrat!" "No, a republican." I did not want to get mixed up with any of them. After the war how could anyone make a proper decision about a political party? Even the monarchy was in danger. The king was in Egypt and his son had taken the throne.

All signs of prewar order had been removed. The old *podestà* of our town had been replaced by a new one. But now he was no longer called a *podestà*, he was called a *sindaco*. Mussolini had used titles from the days of the Roman Empire, like *centurio* or *consul* or *podestà*. Now all these names had been changed, they returned to using the names we had before Mussolini came to power.

The lands Mussolini had won for Italy had to be returned. All the Italian people who had worked on their land in Libya for years and years were pushed out of their homes after the war. They wanted to continue working the land but the Libyan president sent them back to Italy and took their property. He said, "This is my land. Go away." What had we fought for?

In June 1946 Italy had a referendum to decide whether to have the monarchy or a republic. There were big arguments in the piazzas. The anti-monarchists blamed the King for having allowed Mussolini to take over in the first place. They said he should have called in the army to stop him. The King was also blamed for allowing Mussolini to plunge us into the Second World War. Personally, I thought that if Mussolini would have passed away in 1938 he would have had a statue on every corner of Italy. And I thought of the King as a traitor because he signed the armistice. The rest of the country must have felt the same way because the King lost out on the referendum.

There were some more elections in April 1948. This time the priests of Pratola, all six or seven of them, also got into the act. Everyone set up his own platform for his own political party and the priests sided with the Christian Democrats. They left their churches and went to the *municipio* to give speeches instead of sermons. I did not like that. A priest belongs in a church and he should stay there. I think of the priest as a person. I am an electrician and he is a priest. Everyone has his business. He was educated to preach so he should stay away from politics, that is not his business.

Myself, I don't need the priest. God is everywhere and I can pray anywhere. I believe each one of us has a destiny and if you must die you will die no matter where you are, a priest cannot do anything for you. I don't need the priest to come between God and me. St Anthony is my protector, I ask him to go to God for me. I don't need the priest to pray to God for me.

Also, priests ask too many questions. Before my wife arrived I was sick in the hospital in Libya for a couple of days. The sisters ran the hospital, I had to do what they said and they wanted me to go to church and confession. During confession the priest asked me, "How long have you not had contact with a woman?"

I said, "Well, my wife is in Italy and I am alone here."

He asked, "You have had no physical gratification since the last time you were with your wife?"

I hesitated, "Well, sometimes."

Then he asked, "With a woman or alone?"

I got mad. I said, "Listen, I came here to talk to you about something else." The priest has to listen, not ask questions. My wife and I always argue over this, the authority of the priest.

Pratola voted against the Christian Democrats because priests have nothing to do with politics. The Christian Democrats won in 1948 in Italy but not in Pratola.

No matter what the election outcome, whether the King was in or out or this party was in or out, the situation around us did not change. It was still as difficult to find jobs as when I left for Tripoli. Of course there were some exceptions, I found people in Italy who had become rich during the war dealing in the black market. Before they didn't even have land or education, now they had bought land and had people working for them.

I didn't want to work the land when I got back home. I didn't like working on the farm. Sometimes I went to help out, to pick the fruit from the trees but not really to work. I helped with little things during harvest. We grew some wheat and grain for the family and we grew grapes for a living. When it was time to pick the grapes I helped to organize the ten or fifteen people working for us. They put the grapes in big barrels which were then put on a mule or cow and taken back to the house to be put into big cement blocks. In Pratola everyone made wine. Just outside the town there was a big building which stored everyone's wine and big shots came from northern Italy, from Milan and Venice, to buy this wine.

My mother wanted me to stay and help her out on the land but I wanted to look for a job. As a prisoner of war I was given certain privileges and with some of the contacts I had it did not take me long to find a job as an electrician in a hospital in Sulmona.

After I had a job I went to the committee which was organizing the *festa* for the Madonna della Libera and offered to pay a lot of money to carry the Madonna. The people who bid the highest carried her. I had some tough competition. I was proud and grateful to be able to take her. When I saw her I felt something inside. I was moved by an emotion that I could never explain. There are no words for such things.

After the procession around town the Madonna was put back in her place and the band continued to play on the piazza outside the church. There was usually a contest for the best band in the middle of the Piazza Garibaldi. People clapped after each one and the winner got the title and some money. Pratola had the best band in Abruzzi. My cousin was a number one trumpeter. He always played during the festivals. They played opera all the time, *The Barber of Seville, Aïda, Traviata, Rigoletto*, all of them. My uncle was eighty-four years old and he had worked hard all his life, dirty work, but whenever they played *Rigoletto* or *Tosca* he got up to sing with the band. He got up there, bent over, and stood with his hands behind his back, singing.

I met my friends every night in the cafés or by the fountain on the piazza. Every night we talked about wanting to leave. People started to move, you heard that next week a guy was going to Australia. There were all sorts of stories of people leaving for places we had never heard of. Some people went to France to try to work but sometimes the police caught them and brought them back. Others went to Switzerland but it was not easy to get in. Then the way was opened for Venezuela.

A lot of men went up to the northern part of Italy hoping to find work. Sometimes they only spent a few weeks looking around, then gave up and came back home. They said it was worse up there because at least here you can always have a place to go, to sleep, and you can always grow something to eat. Up north if you had no income you had no way to obtain food.

My pay from the hospital was not bad but with four kids I still didn't have too much money, everything was so expensive. Franco was all right because my brother was taking care of him, teaching him a profession. I wanted Lina to be a school teacher, she was the type, very lively. I also wanted Roberto to become something, that was why I sent him to school. But after two months the principal, she was the sister of a good friend of mine, called and said, "Roberto is not coming to school, what happened?" I had already paid his travel for one year, I was mad. I told him he had to learn something so I sent him to learn to be an electrician with a good friend of mine in Sulmona. I had no idea what would happen with Michele. My wife was hoping he would be a priest, she had no luck with Franco.

Letters started to come back from the people who had left. They only wrote good things, about success and money. They said it was like paradise over there. I believed them because my mother's brother lived in the United States and he was a rich man. In 1946 he came back to visit us with a 1946 Pontiac. It was the only American car in town. When he had visited Pratola in 1930 he was still poor but by 1946 he must have become successful, he could afford to buy a brand new car.

In 1949 my sister went to Canada with her husband. He had a contact in Toronto who was willing to sponsor him if he gave $500 to the man's sister in Naples. Some people thought $500 was a lot of money but there were people who were asking $1,000 to put an application through. I wrote two or three guys who I knew and the cheapest one was $500. They said they had expenses, they had to go to immigration, they had to lose days of work. Then you also had to pay for the ticket to come here. But most people thought it was worth it, $500 was not much money to go to paradise. Who can say how much paradise costs?

Most people did not have such money, they had to go to a man in Sulmona – Celidonio – he was like a saint, he gave people money to come here without even getting them to sign a piece of paper. He said, "Your conscience is a good enough guarantee for me."

My sister wrote me from Toronto and said that by working for a tailor you could make $40 a week. She said her husband made $60 a week and her daughter made $40 a week. That added up to $100 a week, that was good money. Lina had studied sewing so I thought she could make at least $40. I thought in time Roberto could also make $40 and Franco and I could make $60 each. Finally, I said to my wife, "I would like to go to this paradise."

My mother did not want me to leave. She said, "We have land, you are well off here." There was enough land for the family but when my mother died the land would have to be split up into little parts amongst all the children and there wouldn't be very much left per person. But more important than that I wanted to try my luck. I quit my government job and began preparations to leave Italy.

Teresa

THERE WERE A LOT OF WEDDINGS after the war. The boys who had gone off to fight, thin and shy, came back as grown men and they wanted to get married. But there was not very much future. It seemed to me that when my husband and I had married we did not have so many problems.

My husband and I grew up together. He started to come after me when I was twelve years old. I had kept saying, "Get away from here, I don't want to talk to you. I want to be a nun." But I think my mother knew I was not going to be a nun because she had begun to prepare my trousseau as soon as I turned ten. My mother had given me four dozen sheets and she had sent me to the nuns two days a week to embroider them. A week before I married I washed and ironed everything and put it all out on five tables. Then my mother-in-law and sisters-in-law came to check everything.

I was not yet eighteen when I went to my mother-in-law's house but I understood the way you were supposed to be. My mother had taught me well. She said, "You must respect your mother-in-law because she is sick. You get up in the morning before anybody. On Mondays you have to do the washing and the pressing." I liked to go to church at eleven o'clock so I got up at seven o'clock and made breakfast, by ten o'clock I had finished the pasta. The first thing you have to do is respect your mother-in-law as you would your own mother.

For me it was easy to follow these teachings because I loved my mother-in-law. I did not have some of the problems that a lot of other girls had, the jealousies, the meanness. I was lucky. We had a house next to my mother-in-law's but we were always back and forth. It was really like one very big house.

I started to enjoy my life after I got married. Before, my father insisted that I go to bed by seven o'clock and he never allowed me to go on pilgrimages to other towns. My husband was different. We went out, had a good time, and if I really wanted to go somewhere he let me.

The grape festival in September was one of his favourites, probably because St Vincenzo was the protector of the grapes. Every spring, before the stakes were put in the ground for the vines, my husband smoked four of the stakes because St Vincenzo was burnt at the stake and then he went to his statue to get them blessed before they were put in the ground. This way the grapes were protected from frost and storms.

During the festival three or four cars, decorated with grapes, went around the whole town and the girls riding inside were all dressed up in the traditional costumes. The statue of St Vincenzo, covered with grapes, was carried around the town.

On the piazza of the Madonna della Libera there is a beautiful big fountain, four ducks are sitting back to back while the water comes pouring out of their beaks. One time someone donated a lot of wine and they hooked the fountain up to the barrels and wine instead of water flowed from the beaks of the ducks. This happened during my father's time and it was one of my husband's favourite stories.

It was good to have Vincenzo back, he completed the family. The father can always discipline the children more, especially the sons, they are more afraid of the father. Without my husband I often had difficulty with Franco. He was always very strong-minded, just like his father. I could never tell him anything. I screamed the same thing at him over and over again. But in the end I always asked myself, what does he hear?

There was a restlessness in the air. And there was very little work. During the war men had left to fight for the country. After the war they had to leave to fight for the family. My husband was lucky, prisoners of war got special attention. But I was so afraid that he would also want to leave to go up north or to one of those other countries. That was all the men of Pratola could talk about, a place to go where there was more money, where there was a future. Nobody was satisfied. Vincenzo had a good job but I could tell it was not enough for him. The stories got to him. He had to try it.

I did not want him to go away again, to have the family broken up again. When my husband said he wanted to leave to go to Canada I wanted the whole family to go together. "No," he said."There is not enough money for all of us to go. You stay and take care of the children. Franco and I will go."

Once again I was left alone. Once again he had said to me, "I will send for you." The only reason I was glad they left was because I was hoping Franco would forget about that girl and if she had a spell on him maybe with the distance it would wear off.

A few months after they left I started to get letters from my husband saying, "Soon, after I will make enough money, I will come back."

Then it was, "Maybe I will stay for three or four years. I'll make some money and then I'll come back." Three or four years? No, I didn't want to become a white widow.

Then he wrote, "Send Lina and Roberto, with their help we can make even more money and we will all come back together in a year."

I was worried about sending Lina alone but then I thought my sister-in-law would surely take care of her.

I was grateful that before Lina and Roberto left we could at least spend Easter together because after the festival for the Madonna, Easter was my favourite.

The statue of Jesus on the cross lived inside the Church of the Trinita. Easter Friday the cross was put in the sepulcher. The Madonna lived inside the Church of the Madonna della Libera. At night the Madonna was dressed all in black because she was mourning the death of Jesus. The bells of the churches were tied. There was no sound. The town was quiet. We went to pray in all three churches, one after the other. Afterwards there was a big procession of two or three thousand people. Everyone was dressed in black carrying long candles and singing religious songs. As the procession passed through the streets with their candles the people in the houses lit sparklers in the upstairs windows. My mother-in-law had ten or twelve of them. The poor people had only a few but every window had at least one sparkler.

Saturday morning at nine o'clock the bells were untied. The Madonna was taken out of her church and Jesus was taken out of the Church of the Trinita. At ten o'clock the people gathered in the Piazza Garibaldi. Lots of them had white pigeons which they had collected in cages. The Madonna, dressed in black, came toward the Piazza along the Corso. Jesus on the cross, also in black, came from a small street to the right of the *municipio*. They came toward each other from opposite directions. The men carried them, holding the statues high. As soon as the Madonna saw her son she bowed up and down, moving toward him faster and faster. One man near Jesus and another man near the Madonna quickly ran toward each other at the same time, holding a cord. The cord pulled down the black dress and veil of the Madonna and the black cape of Jesus and suddenly they were both in white. The people let go of the white pigeons and there was music and singing. The resurrection was beautiful. I felt it inside me, I felt an uplifting, a hope.

Then Lina and Roberto left and once more I found myself alone with Michele. This time I said to myself, "I don't care, I am going to follow my family to Canada." I didn't want to become like one of those white widows in town whose husbands appeared only once every four or five years, just long enough to give the wife a baby.

Before we left my father had explained, "Canada is a place of suffering. In Italy you have land, if you want to work you work, if you don't want to work you don't work, but in Canada if you are absent a couple of days they fire you." He said, "You cannot get a woman to come in and do your housework for you. You have to do everything yourself." I didn't believe him.

I sold lots of things and packed the rest in big trunks. I took pots, pans, sheets, salami, cheese, figs, prosciutto. Michele and I left in December, just before Christmas.

Franco

SUNDAY MORNINGS MY MOTHER would say, "Franco, are you going to sing today?"

"No, why?"

She would reach into her pocket and give me one lira. But sometimes I just took the lira my mother gave me to go to church or to leave in church and spent it playing cards.

I was a soloist but I was not inspired to sing for God. I was much more interested in girls, I wanted them to look at me. The church and the religious processions were the few places where you could see girls. The only other time you saw the girl of your dreams was when she came out on the balcony. You knew she went to church on Sunday mornings and she was on the balcony at certain times. But the most you could do was look at each other or exchange one word.

The church never inspired me and slowly I learned that the priests were not above mortal errors and desires. One of the priests in town got involved in a scandal. He was having an affair with a woman whose husband was living in the States. He had gone to the States before the war and now that the war was over he wanted his wife and children to join him. This woman refused to join her husband because of the priest. She refused a visa to the States three times. Most people would have given anything to be able to get their hands on such papers. She pretended to be sick. Her son, who wanted to go, was wondering why the mother kept refusing to join the father. Finally the husband wrote to Rome to find out what was going on. They informed him that she had never shown up. The husband started an investigation and the affair came to light. The bishop transferred the priest to another town. Still, he continued to function as a priest and was free to get into a new scandal.

This priest was not the only one who didn't obey his vows. I kept hearing more and more such stories and I saw things with my own eyes. It did not take me long to reject the authority of the priest to speak for me before God. My friends and I discussed this and they agreed with me. When I mentioned it to my mother she was horrified. She never accepted my questions. She told me the devil was tempting me. My mother believed and her belief was capable of transcending all rumours. I could never understand such absolute belief.

One night a friend said to me, "Franco, you know what the priest said in church tonight?"

"What?"

"That this town is full of ignorant peasants who continue to pass their ignorance onto their children."

"Why did he say that?"

"Because we don't go to church."

I said, "Well, in that case he is the one who is stupid."

Someone else said, "We have to teach him a lesson. He can't insult our fathers like that."

"What can we do?"

"Let's break his windows tonight."

His house was right behind the church. The first stone I threw hit the window.

The following morning I passed by the church and the priest called me over. He liked me because of my singing. He said, "Franco, look what they did to me."

"What?"

"They broke my windows."

"Oh, what a bunch of ignorant peasants," I said as I proudly examined the damage. There was a lady who was listening and she looked at me suspiciously.

"I was in the middle of my reading," he said. "They could have killed me."

"Oh, that's too bad. Why would they want to do such a thing to a priest?"

The following Easter I went to confession. I told the priest some of my sins, the ones I thought I could be absolved of. When I finished the priest said to me, "Franco, before you go, you have to confess one more sin."

"Which one?"

"You didn't tell me that you broke my windows."

"I didn't tell you because I thought you knew already. It's been six months."

I lost my trust in the church early and I did not yet understand politics. There was a referendum in Italy in June 1946 betwen the monarchy and the republic. But people of my age had never been exposed to political debates. Our understanding of this choice was extremely limited. In school we were never allowed to debate politics, we had to learn the fascist culture. There was no question of choice. After the war, when we were told that we now had a choice, we did not really know where to turn. We had nothing to base that choice on. After the turmoil all of us had gone through, what was left inside was a vague feeling of disillusionment. We listened to the debates of my father's generation but we only half understood what they were talking about. They kept referring to their past but it was that past that had brought us to this wasteland.

My friends were fighting to be able to work just a few days a year. There was no money. Sometimes a cigarette was passed around amongst four or five people.

I was luckier than most. I was able to finish school and then I had to go in for one year of military duty in 1948. For a while I thought of becoming a lawyer but there was no money and my father kept saying, "In my house I don't want any priests, police, or lawyers. They're all crooks." I was smart when I ran away from the seminary.

When I came back from military duty I made all kinds of applications for jobs. We were four in the family, I wanted at least to look after myself and not have to ask my father for money to go to the show or to buy a package of cigarettes. I was proud.

A lot of people started to move out of town in search of some opportunity, some possibility for the future. Fernando, a good friend of mine, went off to Venezuela. His father was in New York but he had no patience to wait till the visa went through. He just took off. Few people my age had patience to wait because what were we waiting for? Were we waiting for anything different from what my father had waited for at my age? No, we were all waiting to get jobs to survive. What had the war been all about? What was peace all about? We were left to fight over bits and pieces of rubble.

Fernando's father was sending him money from the States but he wanted to do something himself. There was nothing for him in Pratola, his only choice was to leave. He headed for Venezuela because that was the first place that offered him something, that accepted him.

We had gone to school together and I had been at his house almost every day or every second day. Now that he left, his mother and his sister, Filomena, who was a year younger than me, were left alone. They were waiting for a visa to go and join the father in New York. Since we had been such good friends I could go to the house any time I wanted. My company was welcomed by the mother because my father had a good name. Sometimes, when I would pass by, the mother and daughter would be on the balcony and they would invite me in for a coffee and show me the letters Fernando had written. He had met a South American girl in Venezuela whom he wanted to marry. The mother was very upset about this, she already had someone picked out for him in Pratola.

At that time I was going after Filomena's cousin, Giuliana, who was often at her house. Filomena knew how I felt and she helped to arrange meetings between us. No girl was allowed to go out of the house alone so the three of us would go out together and this way we would not create gossip. We went for a walk on the outskirts of the town. There was a winding road where a lot of people would meet after dark. Filomena often coordinated the time and the place where we could meet. Giuliana would pretend to go to mass at night and instead she would come and meet me. In a small town everyone wants to know what the other one is doing. You had to watch out. It was very hard to see Giuliana because the mother was tough. Often she could not show up because her mother went to mass with her. It was a very difficult courtship. Of course I was not ready to get married yet therefore I did not want to go over to her house.

My father always said to me, "You can fool around, that's your business, but watch your step. I don't want my reputation to be jeopardized. If you enter someone's house you come out married. The moment you go to a girl's house, you're stuck." Just entering the house meant a commitment.

It was much easier to see Filomena because no matter how tough the mother was, with no father or brother around she could still sneak out more than anyone else. Little by little we got closer and closer together.

Filomena's mother treated me like a king. She was good at knitting, I never had to buy socks, she made all my socks. I never bought pullovers, she made them all for me. She was a wonderful cook and cooked all my favourite things. I was there almost every day. The mother loved me like a son.

Then my mother started to scream, "Stop! What are you doing? You are not being fair to the family. That girl is not for you. You will never have my consent to marry her." According to my mother the girl was not good enough for me, not rich enough, not educated enough. But I didn't care about any of that. I got attached to them and I didn't want to hurt the mother. If I would have left she would have cried for me.

But according to custom you could not marry unless you had your parents' approval. You had to watch what family the girl belonged to. Were they rich? Did they have a good name? That was all that mattered. In certain cases, even after the marriage, the parents kept the young couple under their thumb. I wanted to be independent.

Trying to find a job had become a hopeless search. My Uncle Eduardo was a *perito agrario*, a land estimator, and he offered to take me around with him in order to learn the trade. My uncle was one of the few in that surrounding area to have court approval to make decisions on who was right or wrong when an argument broke out over a few millimetres of land. Every little corner of land counted. All the people ever did was sue each other over property or because the neighbour's fence was not straight. My uncle was constantly occupied measuring the land and going to court to say who was right or wrong. A little piece of land meant everything to the people.

A *perito agrario* also went around to the individual plots of land in the surrounding region and marked down the value of the potential production of that piece of land and the tax to be paid to the government was based on that estimate. With my uncle I learned how to estimate the fruit trees or whatever was to be grown on the property. This was a highly respected business. It was also a highly profitable one. People gave us chickens, goats, and eggs that my grandmother used to sell for Easter or Christmas.

When you went into the countryside there was no transportation of any kind, either you walked or rode a donkey, mule, or horse. Most of the time we travelled by donkey.

Three or four days before we went to a given area we usually put a notice in the piazza or in the main church or in the municipal office of the town to let the people know that we were going to be in their part of the region. People usually had bits and pieces of land scattered over the countryside and some were quite a distance from the town.

Most of the time we arrived in town in the late afternoon. The next morning, when we were ready to set out, we always found a line-up of people who wanted to help outside the house where we were staying. I never had to carry my briefcase. When it was hot and I took off my jacket there were two people ready to take it and they fought over who should carry it.

We were given extra money to pay people who carried our materials and the people whose houses we stayed in. Often the plots of land were too far from the town to return each night so we had to stay in different houses. The people gave us whatever we wanted and they refused to accept any payment. They would give us their main bedroom, even their wife, to make sure that when we reached their little parcel of land we would not tax them very high.

In a little town of four or five thousand people the three big bosses, the *sindaco*, the *podestà*, and the *commissario*, usually owned half of the countryside and the rest of the population owned the other half. These three gave the orders. Whenever we went to determine the tax on their land we were treated like kings to make sure we would not classify their holdings on a first-class basis. We had big dinners every evening. But I would always tax them to the nose.

In my town I was the son of my father and the nephew of my uncle. Because of my uncle I succeeded in having a job which I knew nothing about. But no matter what I did, I would have to follow the footsteps of those two. I could not make decisions on my own. Whatever I did was a reflection on the family as a whole. I had a responsibility not to dishonour the family name, not to taint it in any way.

When my father started talking about coming to Canada I saw that as a possibility for freedom. As soon as the plans for leaving became definite I began to take English lessons from a priest in town.

Filomena and her mother were preparing to go to the States to join the father who had been there for the past twenty years. Since my father and I were going to Canada, the plan was that I would go over to the States later to join Filomena and marry her. But she did not get the visa because she had just turned twenty-one. Her mother went to Brooklyn, New York, while the daughter remained in Italy on the quota list. She was sent to stay with her uncle who was living in another town, fifty kilometres away.

Her mother left four months before my father and I. During that four month period I went to visit Filomena every day and I always took something with me. I even bought her nylon stockings when they first came out. I had quite a distance to travel to see her. And each time I returned I had to endure my mother's screaming.

I had to go to Rome for the visa and I was so afraid. I thought, "What if I don't pass my physical? What will I do if I cannot get the visa?" Till the visa was actually in my hand every moment of my time was consumed with anxiety.

The consulate in Rome was sitting in his big chair when I entered his office and he said, "Young man, show me your hands." I did not understand at first what he was asking. He repeated his request. I put out my hands. He examined them, shaking his head all the time. Then he asked, "What do you think you are going to do in Canada?"

I said, "Don't worry, I'll do something. I know people there."

"Well," he said finally. "Good luck to you." He gave me my visa.

Then I started to count the days before departure. I felt a strange sadness. I was going into an unknown. In the Middle Ages they used to punish people by sending them to another land. It was one of the worst punishments you could have, to be sent away from your place of origin.

On the other hand there was also a sense of adventure. I was going into the unknown, to a strange land where I might be able to dictate my own rules.

Roberto

AFTER THE AMERICANS LEFT, the possibility of easy money also left. I had no money at all. I had to ask for whatever I wanted. It wasn't just me, everybody was the same. Of course, we all had our ways to get money. A friend of mine whose father was an artist for the cemetery had a good system. At the entrance to the cemetery there was an altar with a human skull on top. Beside the skull there was a little box with a slot where people put their donations. This friend of mine used to take all the money out of the box with the help of his mother's bobby pins. Whenever he needed money he just helped himself. He was loaded. He often paid for me when I did not have any money. He was very generous to his friends.

When my grandfather died he left fifty silver coins to my mother. She kept them in a drawer in the bedroom and every time I needed some money I just helped myself to a coin and sold it for 30 lire. It was like a gold mine. I sold about twenty of these coins to a watchmaker in our town. I knew there was going to be trouble once my father found out but by the time I had already taken half the coins, I thought, "Should I leave the others there?" Then I figured I might as well take them all since I would probably get the same punishment. I went to Sulmona and sold the rest there.

The watchmaker I sold the first twenty coins to was probably afraid that someone might find out he had taken advantage of a kid. He told my father that I had sold him the coins and asked him if he wanted them back. My father told him to keep them since he had already paid for them. But when he came home the roof almost fell on me.

My father is a very emotional man. He could not say, calmly, "OK, you did this." Then bang. It was not a dispassionate kind of punishment. He would be screaming almost in a state of madness and trying to hit me all over the place and I was running around trying to find a place to hide. When my father finally caught up to me he hit me with an aluminum pan till it was all out of shape.

Many kids quit school to work on the land. When they asked their parents for money at least they felt they had worked for it, they had a right to ask. But they also had ways of making extra money. Sometimes they took oil and cheese from their family and sold them to someone else.

I remained friends with the ones who did not continue school after grade five and my mother would always criticize them. They were not good enough for me or not educated enough. The professionals were the real elite, the doctors, the lawyers, the chief of police. My family was well enough off so there was a closeness with them. Frequently I was forced to take some of these kids with me when I went somewhere because my mother would say, "This is the doctor's son, you have to talk to him, he is a nice boy." I guess she thought your friends can make you or break you, depending on the crowd you hung around with.

We skipped school often and of course we needed notes. We just wrote them out ourselves because the parents could not write. Most of the parents had not gone beyond grade two. Sometimes we went out to the farms and just picked fruit. One day we were almost caught. There were about six of us in the group walking along the road. There was a fruit tree up ahead and as we passed it one by one everyone picked off some fruit. The other guys went ahead of me and by the time I got there the tall ones had already picked all the fruit from the bottom. I was not very tall so there was nothing for me to pick. Another guy and myself had to climb up on the tree. He climbed up on one and I took the one next to it. While we were up there picking off the fruit one of the boys below yelled, "The owner is coming. The owner is coming. " And they all broke into a run. I thought to myself, "Aha, those guys have picked off all the fruit and now they don't want me to pick any." But as I looked down, sure enough the owner was standing about twelve feet away from the tree. The guy on the next tree was also still on top and we just looked across at each other. The owner saw a bunch of kids running away but he did not bother looking up. All of a sudden we just dropped straight down. We hardly touched the ground and we were off. The owner just stood there totally bewildered. The other guy had lost a shoe as he dropped down so he had to go back to get it when it was safe again. He practically tiptoed back, he was so careful.

One day I needed money to buy some cigarettes. I took the bank-book my sponsor had given me in San Remo and went to the bank in my home to cash in the 50 lire. The guy at the bank looked at me and said, "I'll give you the 50 lire but you have to pay me 150 lire for the transaction." I took my book back and said, "Forget it."

On Palm Sunday in 1948 I had no money and neither did any of my friends. My mother had just bought about six or seven litres of olive oil for the house. I decided to take one litre bottle and sell it. I rented a motorbike and took the oil with a friend, Alberto, to the next town. I could not sell it in our town because people knew me. We sold the bottle for 400 lire. On the way back Alberto wanted to drive the bike. He had had an accident and all his fingers were missing on his left hand. I knew he would have trouble driving it but I didn't want to say anything. I thought, "Why not?" It wasn't my bike anyway. I let him drive it back and I sat behind him. He took a sharp curve on the dirt road lined with trees but he took it too wide and crashed head on into one of the trees. At the point of impact I was thrown from my seat and was sent flying over him into the tree, head first. The tree was about six inches in diameter and as I smashed into it the tree broke into two, just like that. The top half of the tree with all its branches just fell across the road. We were covered with dust. I was lying on the ground, half conscious. Alberto was still on the bike. He had just cut his pants but the bike was all smashed up. We were lucky this had not happened while we still had the bottle of olive oil. I would have had trouble explaining to my mother what I was doing with olive oil on my clothes. An old man who was living close by came out and examined the tree with great care. All he said was, "This is good wood for burning." And he went back into the house. He was only concerned about wood, nothing else, as if we were not even there.

Every year Cocullo, a small town four or five miles from Pratola, had a festival of serpents for San Domenico who protects against snake bites and toothaches. A friend who was a few years older asked me to help him catch snakes to put around the statue of San Domenico. I had never done that before. I thought it would be a good way to spend the day. It could also be useful to know how to catch a snake. He approached the snake from the back and grabbed it close to the head. As the snake opened his mouth I had to quickly put a piece of cloth inside. The snake bit down on the cloth and the poison was absorbed by the cloth. Then I had to quickly pull the cloth out so that the teeth came with it. It must be a painful way of pulling teeth. I had to practice a couple of times before I got the hang of it. You had to give a strong yank to the cloth before the teeth came out. The snakes which had this operation were put into a sack. Some people said that this was the way the witches extracted the poison of the snakes to use in their potions. They would take the cloth and just boil out the poison in water or some other liquid.

We went to Cocullo for the procession with our sack full of serpents and as San Domenico was brought out of the church I helped my friend throw the snakes around the statue. The first one I threw fell back into the crowd. It took practice to get the right aim. San Domenico was full of snakes, hundreds of snakes, all of them coiling around his body and hanging onto his hands.

Everybody was waiting to be eighteen to go to a House of Tolerance. We could not talk to the girls in Pratola, all we could do was look at them. If you talked to someone everyone considered the two of you to be engaged or at least almost engaged. I knew that if at that age I started to really like someone I would end up marrying her. I was not ready for marriage so the safest solution was going to a House of Tolerance. Older kids would tell us about their experiences and they explained to us how these places worked. To get in you had to pay an admission fee and they all had different rates. In some places you had to pay 50 lire. In the cheapest places there was no admission, you could get in free. These had a big room and all the people were sitting around waiting. The women came in and tried to lead you to the rooms upstairs. You went with whoever you picked. If two people wanted the same girl the one who came first got her. Ten or fifteen minutes later the next person could have her. You could also buy time. The big problem with the cheap places was that you could easily meet people you knew, a father could accidentally bump into the son.

Then there were the expensive places. Before you went in you had to knock and a woman would open a small opening in the door to check you out. She first asked for your identification to make sure you were eighteen. If everything was in order she signalled a woman upstairs to make sure the passage was clear. This way there was no danger of meeting anyone, there was only one person at a time in the passageway. Inside you were led up to a small waiting room where you were the only one. You were seated on a couch and the lady would parade all the girls, one by one, in front of you. Each one stopped for a minute or so and said her name. After they all left you told the woman the name of the girl you wanted.

The day I turned eighteen I went to one of the expensive places in Sulmona. But all I had was 50 lire. In the expensive places besides the 50 lire admission you also had to pay 500 lire for the girl. I knocked on the door and the lady who answered asked for my identification. She looked at the papers and said, "You just turned eighteen today. I can't let you in." There was another lady beside her who said, "What do you mean! He's eighteen. Let him in."

I didn't want to let them know that I did not have any money so I had dressed well. I acted as if I was loaded with money. One of the women took me upstairs to a nicely furnished room. The girls paraded in front of me, each saying her name. After they left I was supposed to tell the woman which one I wanted. Instead I said, "Today I just came to see the girls, to have an idea what you have. I'll come back another day to see if they are as good as they look." She just said, "Come any time." I paid the 50 lire admission fee and left.

That same week I went to a cheaper place. I told the woman I had picked that it was my first time. She was very good and I went to see her a few more times. One day she asked me if I wanted to be her steady, then I could pay the regular ticket but get the extras. Besides their customers these girls also had boyfriends. One of the girls asked me to be her lover and then I could have come back during her spare time and have her for free because while they were working they were on commission. I was bragging about this to all my friends.

I found my cousin over there once. He had been married for only a year. He said to me, "Roberto, please, don't say anything." He told me that the reason he had come was because his wife was expecting any time and he didn't want to touch her. That was reasonable.

My father had two brothers in L.A. and in 1948 they made an application for him to join them. Then my aunt Lisetta went to Canada and wrote back how good it was there. All my father could talk about was leaving. None of us were very happy about this but when my father made up his mind to do something no one could convince him otherwise.

Several months after he left with Franco he wanted Lina and me to join him. All I knew about North America was that everyone was working there and they had Hershey's chocolate bars because my uncles from the States used to send us packages with these chocolate bars inside. The movies we saw, the westerns, also gave me a good impression of North America. The Tyrone Power and Gary Cooper films were popular.

As soon as I knew we were going to leave, my interest in learning to be an electrician, which my father had arranged, was gone. I quit and was doing nothing. I just wasted my time in pool halls before coming to Canada. Alberto really wanted me to help him come out but I knew he would never have a chance, he would never pass his medical because his fingers were missing.

Angelina

DURING THE WAR WE NEVER heard a song. Afterwards, we started listening to music on the radio and my uncle from the States sent a record player to my grandmother with opera records. Slowly we began to buy records for dancing. I was growing up. When my father came back he taught me to dance the waltz and the tango and it was the time of the samba and rhumba. My cousin, Vittorio, taught me all the latest steps. Vittorio had gone to Milan as a policeman but he was also studying at the same time. He often came back to Pratola with new records and the two of us would dance together in front of my parents. Everyone watched as he taught me the fancy steps and they laughed. The kids! But the kids were in love. He was eighteen and I was twelve but we knew how we felt about each other, we had never talked or touched but we knew. Roberto was also there but he was too shy to dance with the girls. He danced alone by hanging onto the door handle. He learned to jitterbug with the door.

I had one friend, Rosa, who I loved very much. We went to school together. I never looked my age but she at thirteen looked older. She was tall and beautiful and boys were always after her. She walked up and down the Corso between the two piazzas and the boys would chase her. Her father had died during the war and her mother had to work so she was freer, she didn't have to be that afraid. I didn't dare to go. She would often call on me to go with her to the piazza to buy thread or something else. My mother sent me once, just to be polite because her father was my father's best friend before he died. But after that one time she said, "From now on when she calls for you say no. You cannot go with her." They said she was *sfacciata*, easy.

My mother told me when she was young she would just watch the boys from the window and they would watch her. She never had boyfriends. When she went out to buy something her father would say, "Never stop. Come right home!" Her father sometimes followed her as she was coming home from an errand to make sure she did not loiter.

I finished grade eight in my town and I told my mother I wanted to go to Sulmona for high school. She said, "Oh, yes, so you can go up and down in the train and meet boys." She didn't send me to school for that reason. My brother was allowed to go and instead of going to school he went to the beach. I would not have done that. None of my friends went on to high school, some because they could not afford it but others because the mothers worried about what they would do the whole day. They thought it was better for daughters to learn sewing and housekeeping.

My mother sent me to the nuns to learn embroidery. They had a house behind the Piazza Garibaldi where they looked after the children and they also taught sewing. I enjoyed my time there. We sang and embroidered. But we had to follow the rules. Every time we went in we had to kneel down and say a prayer and then we could start to work. At lunch time the big bell rang and we had to go down on our knees again and pray. I used to go at nine o'clock in the morning, have lunch over there, and finish by five or six. We were not allowed to eat meat on Fridays and the nuns checked our sandwiches to see what was in the middle. If we had something we were not supposed to we would sneak downstairs to eat it.

Rosa was also studying sewing. The two of us always sat together in the same place and no one dared to sit there. While we were sewing she told me all sorts of things about her boyfriend. She told me they kissed on the mouth. She told me about the Houses of Tolerance. I had never heard about them before. She learned about them from her boyfriend. She told me that the boys said to the girls, "If you don't want me to go there then give me what they give me." The boys would trick the young innocent girls because the girls thought this was a dirty place, they didn't want their boyfriends to go there. Rosa told me that they would not go to bed but they would touch. When she told me this I started screaming and laughing. I was so embarrassed and shocked. She pinched me and said, "Stop it! Stop it! Be quiet." I was red and everyone was looking.

In the evenings, after sewing, all the girls, against their parents' permission, would go to the park and the boys would follow them. I ran straight home every night. I was afraid of my father.

The only time I ever had any kind of contact with boys was during the religious festivals. Religious festivals and weddings were my favourite events. We always waited for the festivals because we got new dresses and new shoes and there were plays and dances. During the *festa* for the Madonna the main streets were so lit up it always looked like noon. People sold peanuts and lupini beans. Others roasted pigs in the bakeries and sold pieces of *porchetta* with bread while people were listening to the bands. The bars on the piazza sold ice cream and espresso coffee. Outside there were round tables with metal chairs. If the grown-ups did not have enough chairs they brought their own from home. There were all sorts of rides, the merry-go-round, the flying chairs, and my favourite, the bumper cars. Kids were running around yelling. Clowns joked with the people. The girls and boys who were already engaged hid in the dark streets. But I was too scared to do anything. Boys just looked at me and said, "Hi, doll."

Vittorio was always there but we were six years apart so he was walking up and down with the big boys. Once we met at the bumper cars. I was with Marcella, my cousin, who was three years older than me and we loved each other like sisters. I confided all my little thoughts to her. Vittorio and Marcella's brother bought tickets for all of us to go on the cars. The ride hadn't started yet and I was beside her brother and she was with Vittorio. She leaned over to me and quickly said, "Lina, you come her and I'll run there." I loved her for that. She knew how I felt about Vittorio. I ran so fast that I ended up with the wheel of the car in front of me but Vittorio leaned over and was doing the driving. It was a little uncomfortable but fun.

Before a wedding the talk of the town was how many trousseau chests a girl would bring or how much dowry she had. When a boy went to a girl's house his parents always wanted to know what she would bring into a marriage. When I was twelve a cousin of mine got married and the week before the wedding they emptied out my aunt's bedroom, put all the furniture somewhere else, and filled the room up with sheets, clothes, everything. It looked like a store. This was supposed to be the exhibition for the in-laws. They counted everything to make sure that what had been agreed upon was all there. The mother of the bride was proud to show off what she could give.

People would ask, how much is she getting? Twelve? That usually meant twelve of everything, twelve sheets, twelve nightgowns, twelve underwear, twelve brassières, twelve pairs of shoes. Some people went up to forty-eight. The couple would not have to buy anything for years. There were also dresses and coats, perhaps not twelve but four or five. All the neighbours went to look. Liquors and cookies were served and there were green candies, with almonds inside, everywhere.

Another relative was to be married to a girl from another town. We all walked over to the bride's house to look at her trousseau. We were supposed to have lunch there, pick up everything she had, and take it over to the groom's house. While the in-laws were evaluating all her things the sister of the groom discovered that the sheet for the first night was not a full sheet. There was only the top part of the sheet, nicely embroidered, which was to be folded over the bedspread but there was nothing to go underneath. The parents must have thought that they were not going to sleep on that anyway. It was for the first night and just for show so why waste the rest of the material? But an argument started over the missing part of the sheet and everyone got so upset that we didn't even eat. We just picked up what was to be moved and left.

In one case the father said, "I will give this piece of land to my daughter."

The other father said, "I will give this piece of land to my son."

Later the father of the girl decided that he would be better off if he could sell all the wood on the land first. He went to the father of the boy and said, "Before I give this land to my daughter I want to cut down the trees."

But the father of the boy said, "No, you should give her the land the way it is. That was the agreement." The father of the girl refused and he cut down the trees. Because of that the couple never married.

A sad story happened to a friend of mine who lived close by. She had been to the priest and to the *municipio*. They were due to have their wedding in a week. The father of the bride had promised to give his daughter a piece of land with fifty trees on it. A week before the wedding the groom's family went to count the trees. One tree was missing and the wedding was cancelled. My friend was crying for a month and she blamed her father.

Some couples eloped if the parents would not allow them to
get married. The young couple would come back after spending
a week together and the mother would call them names.

But sometimes the parents had to sell their souls to marry off
the daughter. The boy's parents could say, "He will leave her if
you don't give them an apartment." They wanted an apartment
and a dowry.

The boy had to listen to the parents. Sometimes if the parents
of the boy heard that the girl did not have very much they told
their son not to go with her. This happened to my Aunt Maria.
Her boyfriend was a policeman. That was a very good position
so the parents expected the girl to be a lady. It was a big thing to
have a policeman in the family. He could speak nicely and was a
little educated and my aunt was the fine type who always wanted
to study. But she was the oldest of nine children, her family was
not wealthy and she had to sew for other people. When she was
young the people didn't pay with money, they paid with flour,
eggs, and oil and this was used by the whole family. Still, she
managed to make herself some sheets and she got engaged to
this boy. The bride's parents usually gave the mattress, the
pillows, everything for the bed. Rich people gave a mattress filled
with wool. My grandmother had five daughters so she could not
give a wool mattress to all of them. She could only give a mattress
filled with fine straw. Because my aunt could not have a woolen
mattress the parents of the boy would not allow him to marry her.
My aunt suffered a great deal.

In some cases the girl's reputation was devalued and the next
boy who came to her was poorer. But in some cases they might
do better the second time around. Antonietta, the one whose
husband had suddenly died, was extremely lucky in the end.
She married another doctor who was single. In Italy the men
always chose the best, they wanted the single ones. The widows
were the ones to have a good time with, to take advantage of.
Only if she had money would they consider marrying her. But
here was Antonietta, a widow with one child, and she married a
handsome doctor. When she got married she wore a pale blue
dress with a beautiful hat. The groom's family came to Pratola
from Sulmona for the wedding. They were all high-class people
with university degrees.

When I was small I heard that there were witches and if you
hated someone you could go to an old witch and say, "Put a

malocchio on this person." I also heard people say, "Don't accept anything from anyone, especially when you go to a girl's place. Don't eat or drink anything because they are going to try to attract you. They will put a spell on you and then you will never be free." My Aunt Carmina, Vittorio's mother, believed these things. Marco, her other son, liked all the girls he saw and his mother was always telling him to be careful, not to go to a girl's house unless he was really sure he wanted her. But a lot of times he took his mother to the girl's house and then he didn't want to marry her and my aunt felt very bad. She was also afraid that the mother of one of these girls would try to do something to her son. She kept warning Marco not to eat or drink anything at their houses. One day he fell in love with a girl from another town and he said to his mother, "Her parents want to meet you." If the mother of the boy went to visit the girl's family then they were sure the boy was serious. If the mother did not go that usually meant the boy was fooling around.

His mother said, "I am not coming unless you are really sure you want her."

He went back to the girl's parents with two of his friends and said, "I am sorry but my mother is sick, she cannot come."

The parents said, "We are very sorry about your mother. Why don't you take this to her from us and tell her we hope she will feel better soon." They had made cookies for the occasion and they gave him a tray of cookies and a bottle of liquor. Marco was afraid to take this to his mother. Instead, on the way back, the three of them sat down by the road and his two friends ate all the sweets and drank the liquor. Marco would not dare touch them. When the two friends finished everything they started to tease him, "I must return to her house. Help me. Something is pulling me toward her town. I feel a terrible attraction. Help!"

There was a story of a boy from Pratola who went to the next town with a group of friends for a festival. In the group was a girl who was in love with him and she wanted him to notice her. When they arrived at the town she reached into her pocket and gave him a cookie. As soon as this boy finished the cookie he started to shiver and they had to come back right away. The boy was sick for one year. The family went to all the specialists and nobody found anything, except one man in Chieti who had the biggest knowledge of witchcraft in the province. He said, "Your boy has really been fixed. Nothing can be done." The girl must have put something in the cookie to get his love but she put too much in there and she poisoned him. He was twenty-one when he died. She went to Lyon in France to become a nun. The whole town said he died because of that girl.

One day, while an uncle was planting vegetables, he found a lemon full of needles in the dirt. He said it must have been placed there in order to put a spell on someone. They wanted the person to rot as the lemon rots with pins. The lemon was still fresh. It must have been placed there recently. He took all the pins out so nothing bad would happen.

One part of me always believed in such things. Dreams were something else I always believed in. When I was fourteen I dreamed that I woke up in my bridal bed beside a man whose face I could not see clearly. And I felt such sadness.

Suddenly I heard that my father wanted to go to Canada. I was sixteen then and I cried to my mother, "Please, leave me with Aunt Carmina." My mother just smiled when I said that and shook her head. My Aunt Carmina was my favourite aunt. She was a little bit like me, very affectionate, talked a lot, and she was very scrupulous. Once she said to my mother while I was dancing with Vittorio, "They really do make a good pair. They are both so fine, so delicate. They are different from the others."

Whenever Vittorio came for a visit we would kiss like a brother and sister but we knew. The last time we danced together before I left he said to me, "Some day, I am going to take you to Milan."

We were always among people. All I could do was joke around and say, "Oh, yes, you will take me on a broom."

"No," he said, "by car." Only the rich had cars. Then he said, "I will take you to a nice place and we will go dancing. You will have an evening gown and I will wear a tuxedo."

And I could not say anything.

PARADISE

Vincenzo

BEFORE WE CAME WE HAD brand new coats and suits made. When we arrived in Halifax, in August 1950, we looked good. We were well-dressed, everything was tailored. But by the end of our three-day train trip from Halifax to Toronto all our clothes were rumpled. Those three days were a bad introduction to Canada. We were packed into the trains like cattle. The only food available was corned beef in cans and a strange looking white bread that resembled an accordion, the whole loaf could be squeezed into a small ball. That's all we ate.

We arrived at my sister's house starving. The first thing she did was make us a breakfast of bacon and eggs. We had eggs in Italy but for supper. For breakfast we had milk with coffee and a piece of whole wheat bread. She said they ate meat every night for supper, that was why they could afford to have eggs for breakfast.

Lisetta and her family were living in a poor, small house with four boarders. Franco and I had to share a room with two strangers. It did not take me long to discover that my sister had lied to me. She was being paid one penny to sew on one button, a penny a button. She was making $18 a week, not $40. I wanted to kill her. Why didn't she tell me the truth? She said it was her husband who told her to say these things. If she would have told me the truth and just said, "Come for awhile and see if you like it," then I could have taken a leave of absence from my job. I would not have gotten paid for a few months but at least I would still have had a job. But why hold on to a job if you are going to paradise?

For fifteen days I couldn't talk to her I was so mad. I didn't want to see her. Franco and I met some people from Sulmona. They were living in a three-storey house full of men and we moved in with them. Often we had to share our room with four or five men because as the people arrived from Italy this was one of the first houses they came to. At one time there were twenty-one people living together. We had to do our own washing and cooking. I washed my own clothes and Franco ironed them, he had a talent for that. I didn't like to iron but I was the best cook. I made one big pot of spaghetti sauce on Sunday and it lasted the whole week. One of the men bought a TV and after work we either watched bowling or wrestling or we played cards and talked about the family. When a letter arrived from home it was read by everyone, no matter who it was written to. It was a little like being back in England as a prisoner of war where every letter or little note was passed around and anxiously read by all.

One time we went to visit some friends who had recently arrived. Five of them had found a basement apartment to rent. When we got there they had just finished cooking pasta and beans and were about to sit down to eat. Then they realized they had no spoons. They didn't know what to do. One of them went to the cupboard and took out a sack of onions. He peeled them and used the sections as a spoon. They went through five onions before the meal was over.

Whenever we heard that people from Pratola were coming we all went to the train station to greet them. We went even if we did not know them very well. Sometimes we even went down there when no one we knew was coming because you could be sure to find some Italian people at the station. The church and the train station were the two main places to meet people. Finding a job here was harder than finding a job in Italy before the war. I looked for work every day and came back with nothing. The money I had brought with me did not last long. I was so poor that I had to stop smoking. But even when I did have some money and wanted to buy a packet of cigarettes I didn't know how to ask for it. It was hard to find Italian-speaking people. Those who had come here before the war did not want to speak Italian – they were ashamed.

The Italian people who had come out here before the war had no education and they disliked us. They were jealous because we were better educated. Under Mussolini everyone had to go to school till the age of fourteen.

The second week I was here the nephew of my brother-in-law, who had been here for forty years, took me to find a job. He said to me, "You can't expect to find a good job in two weeks. First you have to go and work in construction."

I was so mad at him. "How can you, as an Italian, say such a thing?"

But I could not find a job. It was always, "You speak English?"

"No, I am sorry."

My first job was as a dishwasher in a restaurant on Yonge Street for $25 a week, six days a week. The boss was from my home town. We had coffee together and a nice talk, we got along. But I did not like the job, inside I was angry. Besides having to take care of the dirty dishes I had to mop up the floors twice a day. I did not want to do the floors. I asked the boss if he could find something else for me. We had big arguments over this every day. He said, "When you come to this country you leave the big San Paulo."

One day a fuse went in the ice box and he called an electrician to come out and fix it. Just to have this man come out to look at the ice box cost $5, whether he could fix it or not he still had to be paid his $5.

"Why do you call this man? I'll fix it for you," I said.

He just waved me aside. "You people who come here now think you can do everything."

"I can do this job. This was my job in Italy," I told him. He did not believe me.

Then one day he came over to me. "All right, we'll see what you can do. Take a look at the dishwasher."

"OK, I'll fix it." And I fixed it. It was as good as new.

"Good, good." He was pleased.

"Look," I said, "I won't ask you to pay me for this but I don't want to mop up the floors anymore because I can't stand doing that."

He agreed. Two days later he came over and said, "Pace, you have to do the floors again."

"Why?"

"Because another man complained that he has one week seniority over you."

"Listen, what kind of a boss are you?"

"What do you mean?"

"Yes, because he can't do the same things I can. He can't fix the icebox, the dishwasher, he can't do any of these things. You're not a good boss. Not for me." I just walked out and started looking for something else.

I found a job doing silver plating. But there was too much acid and it made me sick. It took me two or three months to find another job.

95

I wrote letters home saying everything was fine. I said to myself, "Why should someone else suffer? When I will go back home I will tell them what really happened here." But first I wanted to make some money. I couldn't go back without a cent. I did not tell my wife what I was doing here. I was ashamed. And I was not the only one to feel this way.

My cousin, Domenico, was a shoemaker by trade. In Italy he had his own little shop and he was a well-respected man in the town. He was called Maestro Domenico, he was a master of his trade. The carpenters and tailors were also called *maestro*, so were the house builders because in Italy they designed the houses and were responsible for putting in the mosaics and the marble. But they had to be tops, not everybody was called *maestro*. When my cousin got here he had to work on an assembly line in a shoe factory. He was yelled at by a stupid boss because he didn't understand English. He could make a whole shoe by himself and a much better quality shoe than what the factory was producing. Here people had no taste, no sense of what was fine and important. Domenico would never have made such garbage in Italy, he would have gone out of business, nobody would have bought anything from him. He felt humiliated having to work on an assembly line where he was responsible for only one part of one part of a shoe. He felt he had lowered himself, he had fallen in disgrace. How could a man be expected to hold onto his self-respect? When Domenico's son arrived he was embarrassed to show him his place of work. He didn't want his son to see that here he was no longer a *maestro*, he was just another worker being pushed around by a crazy boss.

I put in a job application to DeHavilland Aircraft as an electrician. The inspector was Italian so I went to see him. He was a very nice man and he tried to help me. He said, "I know you made the application in February but I am sorry, we will not have anything before October."

I said, "October is a long way off. I can die before then. I have no money and I have my family and kids."

I could tell he was thinking of a way to help me. Finally he said, "You really want to work?"

"Yes."

He took me down to a construction company close by and spoke to the boss. They were paying $1.20 an hour. To me that sounded like big money. The boss asked me if I had done construction work before. I said, yes, otherwise he would not have hired me. The next morning I started my new job doing pick and shovel work. There were some old Italians who spoke a little bit of English and a little bit of Italian, they had been here for about twenty or thirty years. The foreman was Irish. He told me to dig twelve feet down. I didn't know what he said. I understood you had to go down but how deep was twelve feet? I asked one of the Italians working next to me. He said, "It's two metres and so much." After I finished the foreman came over. He said, "Very good, very good. Not everyone can go straight down, some go crooked."

At the end of the day I had calluses on my hands. I could not straighten out, I was bent over. I said, "God, please help me." I prayed to St Anthony, my favourite saint. He is good for miracles and all sorts of things. Then I felt better but still a little mad because I had never had to do such a job before. There was a man with big boots and a big hat working nearby. He called over to me, "Mister, are you Italian?"

"Yes."

"I speak Italian. I speak five languages, Hungarian, German, French, Spanish, and Italian."

I said, "Hey, what are you doing in this kind of a job?"

"I just left Hungary with a wife and two kids. I have to live. Someday I will return to my real job. I am a lawyer," he said. "What were you doing in Italy?"

"I was an engineer."

"Don't worry. With every passing hour I say to myself, I have just made $1.20."

Most of the men I knew were working in construction. A lot of them told me that unless you had a bottle of whiskey and $20 or $30 for the foreman at the end of the week you found yourself out of work. They didn't always expect money, sometimes a bottle of whiskey or an invitation home for a meal was enough. But the Irish liked to have both the money and the whiskey or scotch.

When the airport on Dufferin was being built a lot of people gave a bottle or two of whiskey to the foreman to start. They were allowed to work one or two days and were fired. Then the foreman hired more people and got more bottles of whiskey.

Some of the contractors took your blood. You worked ten to twelve hours and they only paid you for nine. There was no union. If you complained, the boss said, "You don't have to come tomorrow morning." On the record it showed the company paid me $3.45 an hour as a skilled labourer but in reality I was getting $1.20.

Sometimes, instead of pouring in three tons of cement they poured in two tons. The job looked just as good and the inspector was paid off and the company saved money. No attention was paid to safety. A friend's son died in a construction accident when he was only twenty-four. A wall just collapsed on him. The Workman's Compensation Board paid $1,000 to the family and the contractor paid for the funeral.

We knew people who had been injured for life or unable to continue their work and the Board gave them maybe $42 a month. One guy broke his spine and was paralysed from the waist down and had to stay in a wheelchair for the rest of his life. He managed to get $330 a month from them. That was the maximum pension. He went back to live with his family in Italy and with that money he was able to live comfortably. Amongst ourselves we often said, "Maybe he was one of the lucky ones."

Sometimes we would sit around and exchange construction stories the way we sat around in Kenya and exchanged war stories. In Kenya everyone had dreamed of returning to Italy. I was the only one who had wanted to go back to Libya and live in the sunshine forever. Here, in Canada, my dreams were of Pratola.

When I arrived I thought I would just make enough money to go back. By the time I made $1,000 I said, "I'll stay a little longer and make another $1,000." Then I thought, if Lina and Roberto came out, together we could make even more money and in 1951 I called them out.

With Lina coming here I did not want to stay in a house full of men, I wanted to find another place just for us. I went to look around, talked to some people but if the owner knew you had a family he did not want to rent you the house. I could not find anything. Then a person who was living with us bought a house, partly because he was expecting his own family to come out from Italy and because he knew I was looking for a place. He bought this house two months before the children were due to come and he told me I had to start paying rent right away. I lost $200 for nothing. But at least when Roberto and Lina arrived there was a house for us to live in.

We had the top part of the house which had three bedrooms and we had to share the kitchen downstairs with the owner.

He screamed at us every night because we flushed the toilet too often or we kept too many lights on. Every room had wooden windows with three little holes at the bottom of the frame and a wooden latch to cover them. In the winter we lifted up the little latch to get some fresh air. During the day, when we were not there, he went upstairs to check if the latch was down. At the end of each month, when the bills came in, he ran upstairs and complained for an hour.

One night we got tired of this guy always screaming, "Don't flush the toilet! You are wasting water! Do you know how many gallons of water you use each time you flush the toilet?" We decided not to flush the toilet at all for one whole night. When it was his turn to go in we all listened carefully. The first thing he did was flush it, he couldn't stand the smell. From then on he didn't scream anymore.

I took Roberto with me to work on construction, I had no choice, he spoke no English. I felt bad because I wanted him to go to school. I sent him to learn English at night. He went a couple of times and then said he was going to learn it by himself. And he did it. He bought all the books and learned by himself, just like Franco.

With all four of us working I soon had enough money to go back to Italy. Plus I had more money in Italy because I had been sending money to my wife all this time. But I didn't want to go back to work on the farm. I was proud. I thought with the money we saved I could go back and start a little store. I wrote about this idea to some relatives but they said, "You don't have enough money to do what you want here. You'll only have to start over again." So I had to forget that idea.

DeHavilland Aircraft notified me that I had a job with them if I was still interested. I decided it might be better to stay a couple of more years. When I wrote this to my wife she insisted on coming out to join us. She was right, it was better to have the family together.

One day my sister, Lisetta, sent a picture of Lina to my older sister, Maria, in Italy. Maria showed this picture to the doctor who lived close by. He said, "What a beauty! She would be good for my nephew, Alfredo." I laughed when Maria wrote us about this because I knew Alfredo, he had been a good friend of Roberto, they had gone to school together. A couple of weeks later Dr Di Nino wrote a letter to me suggesting that Lina might be a good match for Alfredo. I replied that I had nothing against it but Alfredo had to send a letter to my daughter, she was the one who had to decide.

I went to work for DeHavilland Aircraft a year and a half after I had arrived here. We had to pay $2 to the union but I didn't like the unions. When people work from five o'clock in the morning to ten o'clock at night then you need a union but just to race for one more dollar, I don't see the point.

I always voted against strikes. People don't realize, strikes are only good for the businessman. If you pay $10 for something which the factory is manufacturing and the workers in that factory go out on strike for a pay increase of $1 then tomorrow the public will pay, instead of $10, $20 for the same item. So, who pays for that increase in salary? We do.

We had to go out on strike for five months. I had to join the picket line and walk up and down with a sign for two hours every day just to get $18. Every day for two hours! I felt ridiculous.

I liked the union Mussolini created, the *sindaco* and the *confindustria*, protection for the worker on one side and the businessman on the other. He did not have strikes. He had debates before the judge who decided in favour of whoever was right.

More and more Italians were coming out every year and with my wife and Michele here slowly we began to return to a normal way of life. We started to have a good time. My wife complained that I was spending too much money because we always had people over to the house. But we had nowhere else to go. We couldn't walk up and down the streets like in Italy, not in this weather. So people either came to my house or we went to their place.

In the summer we could not go to the park to drink. When we went for picnics we had to put our wine in empty Coca-Cola bottles or ginger ale bottles because the police came around to search the parks. One day the police caught a friend of mine drinking beer and he had to go to court. Another Italian we knew stopped beside the 401 highway for a picnic. He spread out everything on the grass and took out a bottle of wine. The Ontario police came and put him in jail. The poor guy didn't know the law, he was just having a picnic and he was arrested. The liquor laws were made for the Canadian people because they could not drink. When they drank they turned into animals. They lost control. We were used to drinking wine with our meal. We had a bottle of wine on the table and we might have one or two glasses or however much we wanted. We didn't finish the bottle just because it was in front of us. But these Canadian people had to finish everything they had in front of them. They didn't know how to stop. They died under the bar and the next morning they told their friends what a good time they had.

I invited a young man I was working with to Lina's wedding. I saw that he was drinking too much so I went over to him and said, "Tom, why must you drink so much? Why can't you control yourself?"

He said, "Mr. Pace, I want to forget everything."

How can you say that? Me, I want to remember everything. I want to remember the times I am enjoying myself, not forget. Why would you want to forget the beautiful day of my daughter's wedding?

It was very hard for us to understand the customs here. If you met non-Italians the first thing they wanted to know was what you did for a living. In Italy people put their arms around you and said, "Let's go for a walk or have a drink." People in Italy didn't care so much about tomorrow, they cared about today. But people in Canada only seemed to care about tomorrow, nothing else. We Italians stayed together because we understood each other. We were more comfortable with people from our own country. If you heard that an Italian girl was marrying a non-Italian, a *mangia-cake*, it was a scandal. It was a dishonour for the father. If the son in an Italian family moved out of the house before he was married, the father would disown him, he would never allow him back in and the whole community would side with the father. The relatives would gather together to mourn the death of the son. Here it was a custom to have the son move out of the house before he was married.

A lot of people were coming over from Pratola and we wanted to stay together for a social life. The young people started a home town soccer team. The Canadians didn't know what soccer was. The soccer team went to Buffalo regularly to play against a club from another town. All of us went to watch. We would have a picnic and exchange news. A big community of Pratolani was growing in Hartford, Connecticut, and in Brantford, Ontario.

The young people wanted to have a sports club where we could all meet. They tried to get organized but they could not put it together. Everyone had different ideas. Then they called some of the older people with more experience and we drew up a charter and had a lawyer fill out the right papers to become a corporation.

The people in Brantford organized a yearly festival for the Madonna della Libera. They even ordered a statue from Italy which was the exact replica of the Madonna della Libera in Pratola and they asked the Pope to bless it. We had to hold the festival in June because in May it was still too cold. But it was different, we were in another country. The people were not accustomed to see such a procession and they laughed at it. There we were, walking behind this statue. They seemed to think we had stepped out of the Middle Ages. When we got back to the church the priest said, "I admire you people, you are really devoted. But there is only one Madonna della Libera. Not one here and one there."

The people in Hartford had also ordered a statue of the Madonna and the Pope had blessed it. When it arrived in 1962 the people at the New York customs thought there were drugs hidden inside her and they took her apart. They took off the head, the arms, everything. They did not even bother to put her back together again, they just sent her to Hartford in pieces.

I got to know some important people at the Italian Consulate because of my involvement with the community and we attended fancy Italian functions. I met with my friends, played cards, organized activities. When big shots came over from Italy we went to the airport to pick them up. A number of important people stayed at our house. Sometimes priests came here from Pratola to ask for contributions for a new nursery. Those of us who donated over $100 had our names printed on a plaque and this was hung up inside the new building in Pratola. I always gave. Sometimes my wife would complain that I was out too much, doing too many things, but then I told her she went to church too often.

Franco was doing very well for himself and he tried to get me involved in his business but I was happy at DeHavilland. I had my job, the pay was fine, I had no worries. After work I was free to do whatever I wanted. In 1955 we bought a house with a big basement and I made wine there every year. Franco had no time to make his own wine, he was too busy. In the beginning he came over to help me but later he just came over to collect his bottle of wine.

The first time we went back to Italy was in the mid-sixties. Four thousand people had left Pratola to find their future elsewhere. There were only about nine thousand people left in the town. We went back again in the seventies and everything was different. People thought differently, they had a better education, there were lots of doctors, lawyers, teachers. In my days only the rich people's sons could have such an education. All of a sudden this was available to everyone. People were working in industry, there was a FIAT plant between Sulmona and Pratola. On the land I had inherited from my parents people were growing grain instead of grapes. The town was almost brand new, there was a new *municipio*, new schools.

We took the train to visit some relatives who had moved to Milan and on the train my wife's purse disappeared. On the streets of Milan you had to be careful, some of the young people sitting around the parks looked dangerous. Every day in the news you heard about murders. I didn't feel safe. During the time of Mussolini everything was safe because there was a guard on every corner and you would not dare to do anything against the law.

Under fascism nobody bothered me on the streets. The fascists were the national party. Now there were all sorts of parties and you had to try to satisfy everyone. People did not really believe in this or that. They had become opportunistic, today you give me this, I'll believe in this or that. You couldn't trust people. You should believe in one thing and follow that. When there was only one party people were more friendly. Now you don't know what the other person thinks. You go out and you don't know what you might find. You have to watch yourself in this democracy.

Canada has the best people, one day they will realize this. We are solid and honest. We lived under Mussolini and we learned how to work hard. Today the young generation does not want do do anything. If a bunch of Italian men would come over here today they would be shipped right back to Italy.

Teresa

THE TRIP TO CANADA was almost as bad as the one from Libya to Italy during the war. Every time I moved on the ship my stomach was in my throat. Michele was the same. We held onto the railing, with my hands on top of his, and we were sick. In nine days I lost twelve pounds.

In Halifax hundreds of trunks were unloaded. The ones that had been inspected were marked with a big white X. Some people had known this was going to happen and they brought their own chalk with them. After landing they marked their trunks with the white X. The customs people just passed these by thinking they had already been checked. A lady from Calabria, who I had met on the boat, explained this to me and gave me a piece of her chalk. I sent Michele to find our trunks and told him what to do.

People's trunks and suitcases were opened and all the food was taken away, sausages, salamis, cheese. The people working on the docks must have eaten well.

Inside the customs building there were translators who spoke a broken Italian. They were hard to understand and I don't think they understood us. They asked us so many stupid questions like how we were going to like Canada. How could we tell, we had seen nothing.

While waiting for the train a man said, "People here don't understand us and we don't understand them but maybe the language of animals is the same." He threw a stick to a passing dog and spoke to him in Italian. The dog jumped for the stick and barked. The man smiled, "You see, the dogs are the same as the ones in Italy."

When the train was ready everyone was pressed in. Some people had to sit on the floor. Not one window could be opened, they were all frozen. Two hours after they had told us to get in, the train finally started to move. We were given cotton bread with marmalade, mayonnaise, and jello. I had never seen such things. I tasted them and got sick again.

At night I could not sleep and tried to look outside but it was all dark, all I could see were a few lights. I felt as if we were going through a long dark tunnel. Not until the next morning could we see where we were. Everything was covered with snow, I had never seen so much snow. The homes looked like shacks. I thought, "My goodness, is this Canada?" In Pratola my home was better, it was bigger.

When we got to Montreal they started to unhook the cars. We were hauled around from one track to another. No one knew if we were going to make it to Toronto. No one could speak the language to ask what was going on.

Early in the morning, on the ninth of December, we arrived in Toronto. It was still dark outside and there was grey snow on the ground. When I got to my sister-in-law's house the first thing I noticed were the wooden steps leading up. We didn't have that in Italy. In my house I had a fireplace, here there was no fireplace. Everything was different. I saw cockroaches inside the house and I was scared. I wanted to go back.

Lisetta lived down the street from where Vincenzo had rented a house for us. The second day I was here she took me to a small store near our home and introduced me to the owner. She told him that he should allow me to take whatever I wanted and she would pay for everything when she came in. She said to me, "Teresa, I am going to work. The fresh bread arrives at nine o'clock, you can go and buy some whenever you like."

Now in Canada, all of a sudden, I was poor. In Italy only poor people went to buy bread, the rich ones made their own twice a week. I didn't want to go and buy bread. I cried, I wanted to go back. I cried for six months. I didn't like the bread or the meat, I didn't like anything. I didn't eat. I decided that I had to start eating if I wanted to go back because I had lost so much weight that I even looked poor.

One morning it was raining and before Vince left for work he said to me, "Why don't you make some gnocchi for tonight?" I made a nice sauce and then I noticed that I did not have enough potatoes. I went down to the store but I didn't know the word for potato. The man motioned for me to look around. It was a little store and I didn't see any potatoes. I thought he might have some in the back. I tried to tell him with my hands to wait a minute, I would come back. I went home to get one potato and returned to the store. I went up to him, pointing to the potato, and said,

"Mmmm." There were two ladies beside the counter and one of them started laughing at me. I just took the potato, threw it at her with all my might and ran out of the store. When Vincenzo came home he found me sitting on the bed, crying.

Every morning my daughter left for work and I was scared. I didn't speak English, if something happened, I wouldn't know what to do or where to find her. In Italy I always knew where she was. Here she showed me where she was working but perhaps I would not be able to find it alone. Once I went for a walk and got lost. I wandered around for a couple of hours and couldn't find our home.

I had difficulty buying clothes because I didn't know the names of things. I didn't even understand the value of the money. I paid for everything with paper money and returned home with my pockets heavy with change.

There were a lot of things I didn't understand about this country. One of the first big surprises came at Christmas. Lisetta set up a big decorated Christmas tree in her house. There were presents under the tree which everyone opened after a big meal on the twenty-fifth of December. And that was it. That was Christmas. I had never heard of such a thing. In Italy we didn't have a Christmas tree with presents underneath. We had the nativity and gave gifts on the sixth of January. We bought little figurines made of clay and a week before Christmas the nativity scene was set up in one corner of the house. Every family had this. The poor people had small ones with paper figurines and two candles. Families with money built a bigger nativity scene where the figurines had robes, there was a real house with a light inside and outside there was grass, trees, water, and even a bridge. Each day more and more figurines were added as the nativity was enacted. At first the three kings, the Magi, were put up on the mountain behind the rising moon which was made out of silver paper or it was just a light behind the scenery, behind the hills of Jerusalem. Every day the Magi moved closer and closer. It was the duty of the oldest child to move the figurines but in our house it was usually Michele who moved them. Finally, the Magi arrived at the manger with presents on the sixth of January, the Epiphany. Here the Epiphany, the most important part of the occasion, was completely ignored.

But my worst impression occurred in the church while I was trying to pray on Friday or Saturday nights. I heard dance music coming from the basement. In Italy this was unheard of. To start with, our churches did not even have basements and there was certainly never any dancing inside the church.

My father had been right. I wrote to him, "I don't like this country. I want to come back."

My father answered, "If your husband asks me to send you the money for a plane ticket, I will do so. If you alone ask me, I won't." But my husband wanted to stay and try it.

I thought if I also went to work and earned some money we could go back sooner. But Franco would not allow me to work. He told me if I went out of the house to work he would stay at home. When the whole family came back after work they wanted to find food on the table.

After a few months we found an eight-room house to rent for $100. A lot of people were coming out from Pratola and they often came to stay with us until they found something else. Soon I was cooking and washing for eleven people. I also cleaned all the rooms. I was always working. The men came in the winter and there were no jobs. They paid $10 a week for room and board but when they had no jobs they could not pay.

One boy could not find work for two or three months. He felt bad because he could not give me any money. I told him not to worry. I knew the mother in Italy needed the money so I told him to send money to his mother first, then he could pay me. He kept telling me, "You're just like my mother."

The Canadian people didn't like Italians. One time I saw an empty seat on the bus and went to sit down. The person sitting beside me stood up and moved to another seat. Another time a man came on the bus and stood in front of me. I could smell he was drunk. He said something to me but I didn't understand so I just nodded. He sat down on my lap. As soon as he did that I jumped up and started yelling at him and shaking him. Everybody on the bus laughed. Nobody understood what I was saying. That night I begged my husband to go back.

A Canadian boy from our street always stole the money I put in the milk box. His parents didn't understand me when I tried to tell them about this. I thought, "I'll fix him." The next morning I stood behind the milk box waiting for him. When the boy came and stuck his hand inside I pricked him with a needle. I had a good laugh to myself. It was the first time I really laughed since I had arrived in Canada. I told the story to everyone.

One night I was sitting by the window looking out and saw a sixteen-year-old boy coming back from work and four or five Canadian boys surrounded him and beat him up. I knew the boy was Italian because sometimes he yelled, "Oh, mamma." There was blood on the street, in his mouth, everywhere. Lots of people were looking from their door or window and nobody helped him. They just left him on the ground. I didn't know what to do. I couldn't go there alone, what could I do against five boys?

I was scared of everything in Canada. I told Michele to come right home after school. In a small town there wasn't too much to worry about, everyone knew you. If a child did something wrong, before they got home the parents knew about it. But you don't know what can happen in a strange country. You did not know who they would meet.

One day it was already four o'clock and Michele wasn't home. Five o'clock and still not home. Six o'clock! I thought, "My God, something has happened to him." I went next door and said, "Anna, please come with me. Maybe someone beat him up." She was a friend from Italy and had a thirteen-year-old son who was a friend of Michele's. We went to the school and found the boys in the yard, playing. They had forgotten the time. My son saw me and ran away but I managed to grab him and both Anna and I gave our sons a good spanking right in the middle of the school yard. A policeman on a horse passed by and saw us. He got off his horse, came over to us, and tried to drag us away. I didn't understand what was happening. What did this policeman want from us? Another Italian lady was passing by and asked us what was wrong. She had been here for a few years and spoke a little English. She explained to the policeman that we had been worried about our sons, the school had finished at four o'clock and at six o'clock they were still not home, so we were giving them a good spanking to punish them.

But he said, "You can't spank your son, it's against the law. If you spank him you go to jail."

I said to this lady, "Why doesn't he take care of his son and leave Anna's son and my son alone?"

The policeman wanted to know what I had said so she told him, "Why don't you mind your own son's business." Then she quickly had to explain that we had only been here for a few months.

Finally he said, "This time it's OK, but next time I'll put you all in jail. In this country you can't spank your son."

I thought to myself, what kind of a country is this? If the mother cannot bring up a son to be well educated then who can? The government? No. They don't feed him, I do.

During the day, when I had some time, I listened to the Italian radio shows. Sometimes they read out romantic stories. Other times it would be just the news. I heard that there was an Italian lady who was so poor she could not feed her children and she was forced to steal some meat from the store. She was caught and put in jail where she hung herself with the sheet. For a little thing like a piece of meat, she hung herself. Another time I heard that an Italian man who spoke no English was working outside and he needed to go the bathroom, so he urinated near a tree in the park. The police saw him and took him to jail for one month.

While I was shopping in a store on College Street I saw a woman and I went up to her and asked, "*Italiana?*"

"*Si, Italiana.*"

We started talking and I liked her. I asked her where she lived and it turned out that she lived one street away from us. She came to my house, saw Michele and said, "You have a nice boy, God bless you. Tell him to be careful because last year my brother was badly beaten up." She explained what happened and where. I could not believe my ears. I said, "I saw him from my window. Everyone was looking and no one helped." The boy's nose was broken and he was in hospital for three weeks.

Sometimes I got together with friends in the afternoon for a coffee. All we could talk about was our fear. All of a sudden we were afraid to ask our children to run down to the store after dark. One friend sent down her fourteen-year-old son to get some milk and he came back with torn clothes and all the change was stolen. You could not trust anyone who was not Italian.

Roberto knew Canadian boys who were living with their friends. They had moved away from their parents' home and they were not even married. One time we heard that an Italian boy moved out of his father's home. Everyone was talking about it. The father changed the lock on the door and wrote home to his relatives that his son was dead. It was such a disgrace. I did not want my children to have non-Italian friends. I kept telling them that these Canadian people were not well educated, they had no manners, they should not get mixed up with them.

Slowly I got to know the city, the bus routes, the names of streets, the stores for the best bargains. Even after we moved away from the Italian section I could keep in touch with friends. I could pick up the phone at any time and call whoever I wanted. In Pratola there were only two or three phones in the whole town. The only way you could talk to someone was if you went over to their house or if you met them on the piazza.

We could even call Italy when we wanted to and, in emergencies, they could also call us. I could not see my relatives but I could at least talk to them.

The first phone call we received from Italy was in 1957 from my sister to say that my mother and brother were in the hospital. I wanted to go to Italy to see them but I had to ask my mother to help me pay for my ticket, we did not have enough money. Roberto wanted to come with me and we took out a bank loan to pay for him.

I returned to Pratola to find a lot of old people and women with young children. I was shocked to realize how many people had left. I looked around and saw things had not improved very much. Still, being in Pratola with my relatives was like going home to a mother, I was welcomed and accepted. Everything was so comfortingly familiar.

When I was ready to leave I cried. I was still torn inside. In one way I wanted to stay with my relatives and in another way I missed my family and wanted to be with them. At the airport, in Rome, I had to pay a lot of money for my luggage. I was so overweight, everyone had given me presents to take back to Canada for their uncle or father or cousin. One suitcase was filled with gifts, nothing else.

On the plane I felt a sadness. But by the time we landed in Toronto all I could think about was seeing my family. A dozen people from Pratola welcomed me at the airport. When we got back to the house there were over fifty more people from my home town all wanting to know how the trip was, how their relatives were. Everyone was laughing as I handed out their gifts. For hours and hours they surrounded me with questions. There was a lot of drinking, good food, and fun. For the first time I felt comfortable in Canada, I was amongst my people.

Franco

AFTER WE HAD PASSED THROUGH customs in Halifax a few of us decided to try some Canadian beer before the train was due to leave. We saw a sign for a restaurant which is very close to *ristorante,* in Italian. We went in. I had a little knowledge of the English language plus I had brought an Italian-English dictionary with me. I tried to ask for a beer in English. I thought the waiter did not understand me because he was not giving us any beer. I looked for the word in the dictionary and pointed it out to him. He still did not give us any beer, instead he gave us a big speech. We decided we must have had the wrong restaurant and left to look for another one. The next one was a café, but again there was no beer.

We found a guy inside who gave us another little speech and then he motioned with his hand for us to follow him. He led us to a restaurant next door. Inside, it was dark and full of people, noise, and smoke. The smoke was so thick you could not see the other end of the room, you could barely see the next table. Everybody was talking loudly and yelling, some people were drunk. And it was only one o'clock in the afternoon. The guy who had taken us there spoke a few words to the waiter and finally the beers arrived. I was thirsty and grabbed the bottle right away. The guy touched my hand to stop me. He talked to the waiter for a couple of seconds and pulled out some money to pay. Then I understood that you had to pay before you drank. As soon as we had finished our first bottle of beer the waiter was there, "Do you want some more?" It was drink or get out. At home we were never rushed, we played cards for a while, then had another drink, or played pool, talked to friends or to the guy at the bar. But then in Italy you could have alcohol in any restaurant and most places had patios where people could sit and drink in the sunshine.

As we were going out I looked up to make sure that we would have the right place in the future. The sign said, Tavern. We had something called a *taverna* back in Italy but for horses.

High-class people had luxury buggies with a horse and when they went to a restaurant or a hotel they left their horse and buggy in the *taverna* where an attendant would take care of them while they went about their business. In Canada this was the place to go for a drink.

On the way to Toronto I looked out the window of the train for a whole day and only saw a few towns where the houses looked like little churches with their peaks. But there were long stretches of time when there was nothing. In Italy the landscape always changed. There were lakes, valleys, mountains, the roads curved, every few minutes you passed a town. There was variety.

By the time we arrived in Toronto the white shirt I had put on before leaving the boat had become all black. I felt dirty and cheap.

Overnight, I went from one status to another. Whatever you knew in Italy was not worth a penny here. When I tried to speak English nobody could understand my accent and I had difficulty understanding theirs.

I could not get a decent job. The first thing I found was washing dishes. I did not come to Canada to spend the rest of my life washing dishes. I was determined to learn the language properly. I went to night school twice a week and I spent the few extra hours I had reading the newspaper. I read one line and understood five words, it was like doing the crossword puzzle, if there was a word I did not understand I found it further down in another context. But I picked up the language quickly. The greatest satisfaction was going to a movie and knowing what the hell was going on. After two or three months I was able to communicate with people to a certain extent. Then I started to learn slang and other words you could not find in the dictionary.

One thing I detested here was not being able to really talk to anyone. The Italians who were here were my father's age, I had nothing in common with them. I could only carry on a certain amount of conversation with my father. "How are you?" or "What have you done today?" But nothing that really interested me.

One day I saw a man close to my age in front of a store window. I thought I knew the guy or at least I was sure he was Italian. I went up to him, "Italiano?"

"Si. E Italiano?"

We started to talk and it turned out that he was from my province, Abruzzi, and he was living with a bunch of young guys who had also recently come out. I asked him to take me home with him and I finally met a few people I could go around with.

We tried to find coffee houses or restaurants where we could meet but all we found were places where you had to sit in booths with the small jukebox in the middle. You were separated from everyone else. There were no round tables with chairs.

We could not understand why everything closed down on Sundays, the restaurants, the cinemas, the stores, everything. The only place left open was the church. On Sundays everyone went to church. Afterwards we gathered outside to exchange news and letters. Italians liked to take walks, to stroll outside in the sun, to meet people. Here there were no avenues or piazzas. There was just College Street. We used to walk along College Street after church or at night and maybe three or four of us would stop to talk. Right away the police came to push us out of the way, "Move, move, you're blocking traffic." Which was not true. They were big policemen and they were rough, pushing with their elbows. It was very bad. Some of them were stabbed and kicked by the Italians because they treated us like animals. The police were an authority, fine. But they did not understand our way of life. We were not harming anyone by stopping to talk.

I soon began to notice that Europeans, whether Italians or another nationality, did not get the same treatment as a Canadian or an English person. If a radar stopped your car and your name was Italian then they treated you according to the name. If your name was MacNamara or MacDonald or Mac something then it was, "OK, my friend, just watch it next time."

I could be in a store or on a streetcar and I could feel that people did not like me because I was Italian. Some even said to me, "DP, go home, this is not your land." There was no way I could answer back to defend myself. And I was furious, I wanted to kill someone. All I could do was say to myself, "You don't know who I am or could be, you know nothing about me. Give me a chance and I'll prove what I am capable of." Or often I thought, "The Italians discovered this land, Giovanni Caboto was Italian. We have more right to be here than you."

I understood some of the discrimination, a lot of Anglo-Saxons had lost relatives during the war. But the understanding did not make the situation easier to live with. Even the older Italians were our enemies, they held us responsible for the war. When Italy entered the war in 1940, all the Italians living in Canada who had become Canadian citizens after October 1922, the date fascism came to power in Italy, had to check in at the police station every month. Whoever was married to an Italian was also required to register. During the war people could not write home to their relatives. Someone told me he wrote a letter to his sister in Argentina and inside the envelope he put another letter for his wife in Italy. The letter either never made it to Argentina or was returned from Argentina. One day the police called him in and said, "We have a letter in our possession which proves that you are giving information to our enemy."

The guy said, "No, that's a letter I sent to my sister and my wife."

There was a certain envy and resentment on the part of the older Italian immigrants who had come here around 1910 or 1915. They saw the way we were dressed when we arrived, we were more elegant than the others, we had better manners with the girls. Some of the new immigrants had enough money to buy a house after two years of hard work. That for the older immigrants was like a slap in the face because some of them still did not own a house although they had been working here all their lives. They said, "You were lucky, it was harder when we came here." But it wasn't that, most of the people who came here before the war were illiterate. Some of them had come here to run away from the police. But when we came we were really scrutinized by immigration. Also, the earlier immigrants came from an Italy that had rejected them, they came out of desperation and their memories of Italy were bitter. Those who came after the war spoke of Italy as a nation with problems but we had a lot of affection for it. The older Italians could not understand that affection.

Everybody kept talking about going back. Everyone was saving their money to first pay back their debts for the trip over here and then to have enough money for the return ticket. But I kept thinking that there must be a way to live well here, it was just a matter of discovering the right approach. I did not really want to go back because no matter how difficult it was here I still felt a greater degree of independence than I would have in Italy.

My father finally found a job in construction. When I heard how much he was making I asked him if he could get me in there. I thought I could do construction for a short time before I got my bearings.

I had never done such manual work before in my life. We were working on big apartment houses. I used to mix the *malta* and put it into the *arco*, a wooden box on a stand. Then I had to carry the box on my shoulders up a wooden plank. The first day my back was full of blisters from the pressure. I was slow and the people from the windows upstairs were yelling and swearing at me.

In the winter we left our overalls on the site and the next day we had to make a little fire to warm them up because they were frozen stiff. It was terrible. The other Italians tried to make fun of me. A lot of people I was working with had been farmers or had worked in construction in Italy, they were used to physical work and they thought I had had an easy life back home as a student. They thought I was soft. Of course I had to prove to them that I was man enough to do exactly what they were doing. But I was going home at night crying. I was depressed. My hands were always full of cuts and blisters and sometimes they were so stiff that I couldn't even tie my shoelaces. Sometimes I was so tired I couldn't sleep at night. I didn't know how much longer I could last. I hated it but I needed the money.

One day I saw some bricklayers singing and whistling while they were breaking their backs. I said to myself, "What the hell, what do they have that I don't have? I am twenty-three and healthy. Why should I be suffering while they are singing?" From then on my attitude changed. I decided that I was going to enjoy this life.

I worked hard and, of course, I went out with other girls but in the back of my mind there was Filomena in Italy and the mother in Brooklyn. The mother came to visit me a couple of times to see how I was doing.

One day I saw an ad in the paper asking for an insurance salesman with an Italian background. I had never sold insurance in my life. I went for an interview. It was a Jewish insurance agency on Bay Street. A man behind a big desk asked me all sorts of questions. I had to lie. I said, "I know a little bit about life insurance, not because I have been involved in it, but my uncle in Italy is a travel agent and he sells insurance too."

Finally he asked, "How is your Italian?"

I said, "I don't have to worry about my Italian. It's my English I have to worry about."

He said, "You're fine. You are the man I want, don't run away." He gave me a thick briefcase full of papers. I didn't know what

I was supposed to do with this, eat it or burn it. He gave me his home number and said, "If you have any problems just call me. I am here to help you."

I went home that night to read all these pieces of paper. Even with a dictionary I only understood 25 per cent. But by that weekend I had sold fifteen policies. In the evenings I knocked on the doors of the people I had met around. I had helped some of them with the language and had helped them to fill out papers.

In a month's time I noticed that everyone was complaining. They said, "Why do I need a life insurance? Why should I buy something now for when I will die? After I am dead I don't care." I quickly realized that there was no sense in going to an Italian and asking him for money now so that he could have money after his death. There was no logic in that for him. I had to find a different pitch.

I said, "Look, you get the family allowance for the children and instead of putting it in the bank you can put it into a life insurance policy." I knew that 99 per cent of the Italians opened a little bank book in the name of the child and put the family allowance in there.

Then I said, "You will only use this money to buy a TV or a radio or a new fridge and then you will have no money. But, if you have no money in there in the first place, I am sure you will still find a way to pay for what you want. Then you will have the money and the fridge. And, as you continue paying into the policy, you will actually begin to make money. But be prepared, the first year you will not make anything, the second year you will get a little bit, and from then on you will keep getting more and more. Of course, if you stop paying, you will lose part of your money."

I was telling the truth but I was telling the truth my way. I told them to fill in the application because they had nothing to lose, they would just be saving money, in fact this would force them to save. But that was not really the truth. The second year they would get a few cents, from the third year on they would start to get some money, but they could never get their money back. If they cancelled the policy after ten years then they came close to collecting the amount they had paid in, but if they cancelled the policy before the end of three years they got almost nothing. Most salesmen never mentioned this.

I slowly brought the conversation to the point where I succeeded in convincing the family that this was the best way to protect their child. I would write up the policy in the child's name and point out that this was an even better protection than putting the family allowance into the bank. Nothing about death, this was for the child.

Later I would convince the husband to buy a policy in his name and another one in his wife's name so they would protect each other. One Sunday morning I sold six policies to one family.

The discussions almost always took place in the kitchen because that was the only place where I could stop the man or the woman. The kitchen was the centre of the family. I don't know how many kitchen tables I cleaned with my elbows and then I used to come out of the house smelling of sauce and fried oil.

The families often got into arguments in front of me. Especially the women. They argued over nonsense, that was the way of life. Sometimes the man was playing cards when the wife wanted him home or the woman was not paying proper attention to the man or the supper was late. If the wife bought a new dress and she looked good the husband might be jealous. He was afraid someone might look at his wife and the next day phone her and make offers. Sometimes the husband thought the wife was no good or she thought she was too good. Some women complained that their husbands were beating them. But if the man's father had beaten his mother then it was like a tradition to him, he saw no reason not to beat his wife, it was a way to control her, to keep her down. If the wife answered back to her husband she got a good beating. In many cases the man said, "I am a man. I can do whatever I want."

Then the woman turned to me and said, "You see what I mean, you see how stupid he is."

It was easy for me when the woman was fighting because most of the time it was the women who were against buying the insurance. They would say, "Let me use the children's allowance for what I want." After an argument I would always sell a policy. One of the styles of selling that I developed was to get involved in the arguments. I would encourage them to argue and then say, "All right, let's stop this and forget about it." By then they were both tired of arguing and they listened to me. Or the wife got sick and tired of sitting there and went to another room with the kids or did her washing downstairs. I could convince the man easier when he was alone than when he was with his wife.

I saw people worrying continuously and saying, "I am going to go back, I am going to go back." But few people did because, no matter how rich they might be in Italy, they would never be able to have the same house and the same luxuries as they had here. Over there you could be as rich as you want but if there is no electricity, there is no electricity and you have to live without light. If there is no water, there is no water.

People were always complaining that here there was no respect, people did not care about other people, and this and that. I said to them, "What did you expect? If you walk into a stranger's home you have to first accommodate yourself to their way of life. Only after you have proven yourself to be better can you make the rules." While I was trying to sell people a policy I would find my own way to make them understand reality. In Italy they didn't even have half of what they found over here and without knowing the environment and the language they were starting to become complainers, they wanted to be the boss.

I looked around the houses and saw a fridge, a TV set, a radio, and both the TV and the radio were on full blast because they did not know what to do with these things. They never had such things before. I was there trying to sell them a policy and these machines were never lowered or turned off, I had to yell above their noise.

At the same time as selling insurance I was also helping people to file their income tax and I explained how to pay the mortgage. Often I made the payments for them because they didn't even know how to write a check. I filled out thousands of forms and never asked for payment. I gave out my home number and told them to call me if they had any problems. They used to call me as soon as a piece of advertisement was thrown inside their door. They thought it might be an important document. They wanted me to go over and take a look. I went there only to find that it was nothing, just junk mail. They would call me for every stupid thing. I had no peace. They used to call me at seven o'clock in the morning, "It's very important, it's very important." They could not read and they were scared of any little piece of paper.

Of course, it was easy for me to sell insurance to everyone related to the family I had helped. They recommended me to all their relatives, "He's fine, you can buy anything from that man.

He will help you." There was a period when I didn't have to buy any liquor or wine, people used to bring them home to me or put them into my car.

Filomena was writing to me every day because she had nothing else to do. But she was always writing the same thing, remembering when we were together in Italy. Or she told me what she did during the day. But little by little I would get annoyed with the letters because it was always the same story. In the beginning I answered her once a week. Later on I answered only once every two weeks and she was mad. In the next letter she would scold me for not writing and that would be the whole letter.

Her parents wanted me to go over to New York. But I had already established myself here in the first three years. I even took a correspondence course in bookkeeping. I was confident that I would have no problems.

As soon as my mother arrived she started trying to talk me out of marrying Filomena. I think she even threw away some of her letters when they arrived. I told her that in Canada there were no class differences, she could no longer tell me Filomena was not good enough for me. Here I didn't have to be under anyone's power or direction. But my mother was always on the lookout for other girls. She was full of suggestions which I regularly ignored. I didn't want her to think that she could tell me what to do.

In 1954 Filomena and I got married by proxy. She came over and moved in with my family. She had been used to not working at her uncle's house in Italy, plus I sometimes sent her money so she had whatever she could want. Also, I think she was under the impression that her father was very rich and this gave her an air of arrogance. She had never seen her father because he had gone to the States when her mother was still pregnant and he never returned. The father had left without one lira in his pocket but from the States he was able to send enough money to his family so they could live comfortably. When we went to New York and Filomena saw her father for the first time she was shocked. He had a shoe repair shop in Brooklyn. It was a little shop, smelling of boots and dust. The man did not know any of the streets in Brooklyn or Manhattan other than the ones along the streetcar line which took him to the shop and back home. Each time I asked him how to get somewhere he just shrugged his tired shoulders and said, "I don't know. I don't know." After that visit Filomena never mentioned her father. I think she almost hated him.

Filomena made no comment about what I had achieved. I had been here, studying and growing and growing. And she said nothing. All she could do was complain. Something was always wrong. Of course, my mother and her never got along and my wife kept pushing me to get out of the house. The first year was terrible for her, she could not cope with anything yet she had everything.

I tried to take her to shows and she would fall asleep. I would wake her up, I knew how hard it was. I was trying to encourage her. I wanted her to learn English, I thought it would be easier for her if she knew the language. Then the children started coming and I hoped that they would solve some problems.

By now the insurance company was giving me 75 per cent commission. My production alone was more than eleven salesmen put together. Besides life insurance, I also started to sell health and accident insurance.

The men would buy a policy worth $100 a week in September or October. All of a sudden, in November or December, they had an accident, a back or a neck injury. It was very difficult to prove anything in a back or a neck injury. The guy started to walk funny and he was sent for therapy to the hospital and they sent him here and there while he was collecting money from both Workman's Compensation and from his insurance policy. He managed to collect $2,000 or $3,000 in the wintertime and then he went back to work in the spring. The word got around, a person told his brother, who told his brother-in-law, who told his son, who told his cousin. They told each other what to do and what not to do in order to get the money. The health and accident insurance became so popular that I had to stop selling it. I used to bring $10,000 a month into the company in sold policies and they were paying out $15,000 a month. The company refused to take the risk anymore.

The Workman's Compensation Board also caught on to what was happening. They opened their own medical department and started to play tough. Some guys were really sick but the doctor could not prove anything and automatically they were discharged and sent back to work. There were endless arguments. People had to go to court trying to prove that they were really sick. On the other hand others were collecting money without having anything wrong with them. That taught me a lot. You cannot get that kind of experience by going to school.

I was very much aware that no matter how hard I worked or how successful I might be, the Italians were still viewed with a great deal of suspicion. In 1954 a guy from Calabria killed somebody with a knife in the east end of Toronto. That same day a Canadian attacked a nine-year-old girl in Scarborough. Both events were reported in the *Telegram*. That day I happened to go to the Insurance Agency on Bay Street and one of the guys said jokingly, "Watch him, he might have a knife." This was a very bad joke for me.

I said, "What are you talking about? Did you read the papers?"

"Yeah, one Italian killed another Italian."

"I also read something else. A Canadian raped a nine-year-old girl." They were both bad. But which one is worse? The one about the Italian was on the front page, the one about the Canadian was a small item inside the paper.

A little later I read an article in the *Globe and Mail* which said that the world inherited fascism and the Mafia from the Italians, therefore they should all be put on a small island and drop an atomic bomb on them. These things made me feel angry inside. But such stupidity and ignorance cannot get in your way. You have to continue to live your life according to your own plans. If you allow people's ignorance to interfere with your life, you are finished. You become like them.

At the beginning of 1955 I opened up my own agency. I was doing bookkeeping for Italian contractors and selling insurance. I started on Queen and Bathurst but the area was full of Polish and Ukrainian bums. As soon as I could I moved to College Street, in Little Italy. When my parents bought their house, we went to live above the office, in the second-floor apartment. It was very satisfying to be independent.

I saw that I didn't have to worry about the future. I started to consciously assess what I could do with my ability and the contacts I had available to me. I knew that I could sell people a policy. Selling life insurance was easy for me, I had learned the psychological game. But it was taking too much time. You had to set up an appointment, then you had to discuss the policy for an hour. I was on the lookout for other possibilities.

While I was selling insurance people began to ask me where they could buy a house. Every second week I had half a dozen people wanting to buy a house. A friend of mine was the biggest real estate broker in the city of Toronto and I referred my clients to him. In return he was paying me $50 or $100 per sale while he was making about $500 per sale. I paid close attention to how he did things. I was getting an education in real estate without having to take a course.

It did not take me long to realize that if I got my real estate license I could pick up $500 or $600 on every sale. I had to sell twenty policies in order to make that kind of money. I already had the clients to be able to sell five homes a month. There were nearly a thousand names in my files, each one had to buy a house. They had been here a few years, they had saved a few thousand dollars, and their first investment was a house. This was the first investment for any European.

I knew I could not have a double license, I could not be an insurance salesman and a real estate broker. I convinced Roberto and my cousin to learn the real estate business. I did not want to lose all those renewals for the insurance contracts and neither did I want to lose all those clients for houses.

Selling real estate was easier, I was selling something tangible. When I sold insurance I sold a piece of paper and, no matter how much explaining I would do, when I went back the next day they didn't remember anything, they would not know which form was for what. They relied on me completely.

So many people wanted to buy houses. There were not enough to go around. I had to find a house and convince the people to sell. Then the person who sold his house had to buy another house and automatically I had two sales.

I had to give people a motivation to sell their house. Maybe they never dreamed of selling it. But as soon as I went there and asked if they wanted to sell it I already planted the idea in their mind, it was a psychological move. Sometimes they would say, "Who told you I want to sell the house?" And they shut the door in my face. But some people listened.

I developed a good pitch. I would knock on the door and say, "A client bought a house down the street and now he would like his brother to buy a house close to his. Have you by any chance thought of selling your house?"

Many times if the husband was not home the lady would say, "I don't know, you have to speak with my husband." I would ask for their phone number and I would never leave them in peace.

I would phone them every second day, "Have you changed your mind? Would you consider selling the house?" Finally, one of them would say, "Yes, I do want to sell the house. How much do you think I can get?"

I would say, "First I have to look at the house." I didn't want to sell the house to my client without being able to explain what the house looked like inside. When I got there I would never say, I think I can get you this much. I would say, "Tell me how much you want and I will see what I can get for you." I wanted them to give me a price first, even if it was a crazy price, to get an idea what I was dealing with. Sometimes the price they gave me was too low, then I would bring them up halfway. I would not accept a very low price. Some real estate agents took advantage of this. I never cheated anyone.

Later I made money by speculating. A speculator bought a house, repainted it, put a new chandelier up and resold it. As a speculator you could make money in an intelligent way. You bought the house and made the first commission. Then you resold the house and made the second commission because most of the people were selling their old house. Then the speculator had to refinance the house because the newcomer did not have $10,000 or $15,000. The speculator did have the money and he sold it to the people for a $2,000 down payment and he kept the $10,000 mortgage. He then sold the mortgage for $1,000 and he made money without doing anything. We were making $500 commission the first time, then $500 commission the second time, and sometimes the third time. Now that was business. It was very simple, you didn't need to go to university for such things. Some people who went into this business did not even know how to read or write.

We gave business to carpenters and builders. Then the politicians stepped in. They introduced the Speculators' Act and the Land Transfer Act and they ruined the whole business for us.

I really enjoyed what I was doing and I worked very hard. Other people would sit down to watch a soccer game and I would go out to sell. There were times when I got together with friends and played cards. A group of people started a home-town club and they organized picnics twice a year. But I would not participate very much because the children were too young, my wife got no pleasure out of it, and I was also working too hard. I did not have much time.

One of my salesmen who was from my home town was planning a trip back to Italy in 1960. I decided to join him. My wife could not come because by then she had two children to look after. I had bought a big American car, a Pontiac. The salesman took it back with him on the boat. I flew over and joined him in Naples. The plan was to drive from Naples to Pratola.

I never drove a car when I was in Italy, I was not used to the way people were driving there. They were crazy. People went through red lights, they paid no attention to signs, they drove like maniacs. Also, the streets were very narrow, the American cars were not made for Italian roads. The Pontiac was huge with horns at the end, it was a luxury car and it could barely get down some streets it was so big. If another car came from another direction then I was in trouble. The other car would start honking loudly. Everyone would come out on their balcony yelling, *"Cazzone Americano!"* – Dumb American. Or *"Uzurame!"* – Uncle Tom. When I drove down some of the streets, there was hardly any room for another car. As soon as I saw another car coming I went close to the curb and they just zoomed by at high speeds, honking at me. I felt like an idiot in that car and my salesman was terrified.

Once I ended up in a one-way street, driving the wrong way. Suddenly I saw a car coming toward me. On a one-way street, especially if there was a parked car, it was impossible for two cars to pass. The other car kept coming toward me, honking his horn wildly. But what could this guy do to me, his car was half the size of mine. I tried to make him understand that he should leave me enough room to go by. Finally, I succeeded in making him understand but at that time I didn't realize that I was going the wrong way on a one-way street. When I finally came out at the other end I found myself in the middle of an intersection, at least six streets emptied into this circle. A policeman with white gloves was in the middle directing traffic and as I came out of the street I went through a red light. There I was, in a big American car in the middle of an intersection with a red light. My eardrums almost burst from all the honking. The policeman came over to me and started yelling.

I said in English, "I beg your pardon?"

He was talking with a Neapolitan accent which I didn't understand very well so I just played dumb. He finally got tired of yelling and gave up. Angrily he banged on the hood of my car with his fist, called me a *cazzone Americano*, and returned to the middle of the intersection. He stopped the traffic coming from one direction, then stopped the traffic coming from the other direction. It took about five to ten minutes before all the cars came to a standstill. Then he motioned for me to go.

My next problem was along the narrow mountain roads. The Italians never slowed down for the curves and they left only a few inches between themselves and the next car. The American cars were made for the straight and wide highway, they were not made for curves. Each time I approached a curve I had to slow down to ten miles an hour or else the car would just swing out and we would be down the side of a mountain. I thought I would never make it.

It was the style to go back with a big American car. It was the thing to do, to show that you had made it. As I drove into Pratola I drove right past my house, I had thought it was much further. Everything looked smaller, closer, narrower. But my heart was pounding, I was so nervous. Right away when my friends saw the car they examined it inside out. They had never seen a convertible with the top going up and down. They had never seen the water squirting onto the windshield. They loved the car but if they spotted anything that I wore that was typically American they would laugh at me. But I was smart, I had heard about this before I went and they told me I was the only one who went back not looking like a typical American with the coloured polyester jacket. I tried to look Italian, to dress like them. Once they saw me wearing a pair of shorts and they laughed, "Aha, *Americano.*"

I heard stories of people who went back and they couldn't speak Italian anymore, or they tried to impress the people with their broken English, or they mixed their Italian up with English words. When people live in another country and get together with Italians from other regions who speak different dialects then inevitably they pick up bits and pieces of other dialects. In Canada there were so many Italians and so many dialects and accents. Certain Italian words had become Anglicized. People had gone back and they were using words like *jobba* instead of *lavoro.* I had to be really careful.

Some of the Italians in Canada had picked up terms from Johnny Lombardi who was the first Italian to have a radio program in Toronto. But he did not really speak Italian. He was called *la bonna jobba.*

Shortly after I got back from Italy I began to try to get my own radio program together. I went to the director of one of the stations and told him that there was a whole new area building up with a lot of Italian people and there was nothing for them. I managed to convince him. He gave me one hour every Saturday morning. I wanted to have an educational show. I tried to teach people how to pay the mortgage and I advised them to go to a lawyer before they signed anything. There were salesmen who sold sewing machines at the door and told people they did not have to pay the full amount, just small monthly payments. People ended up paying twice or three times as much as they would have in a store for the same thing. I knew how easy it was to take advantage of these people, I was trying to help them.

The radio show was easy for me, it was a way of publicizing my name and my business. By law I was only allowed twelve minutes per hour for commercials. There were people who listened to the program, counting the minutes of advertising. If you went over the limit they cancelled the show. But I soon learned that it was possible to advertise while talking about education. There were so many sneaky ways to add more commercials which did not look like commercials. Just mentioning names meant money. In time I hired a radio announcer to work for me and I only showed up for special occasions.

I still helped people. In fact I could help them even more because now I was becoming more knowledgeable. These people's children were growing up, going to school and they were also becoming more knowledgeable. But people still kept calling me with the same problems. After a while they could no longer get through to me. I was too busy to be able to help them the way I used to a number of years earlier. Then I stopped giving out my home phone number. I had new business cards printed up giving only my business number. A lot of people could not understand why I was not giving them the same service as I did ten years ago. It was impossible, at that time I had five hundred clients and now I had six times that many. Even if I would go around with a helicopter I would still not be able to serve them as before.

You treat people with a certain style and they expect that for the rest of your life. A salesman who discussed the sale of a house with one of my older clients was told, "Your boss does not care about us anymore. When he was going with a briefcase under his arm he was always here when we called him, now he is never available." In other words, I would have to be with a briefcase under my arm all my life to please the public. If I progress and have employees who can give the same service as I had done earlier that is not good enough, they need to speak to me. If I don't talk to them, I am no good.

All the time that I was working, growing, developing, I tried to keep my wife informed of what was going on, where I wanted to go. I tried very hard to make her understand that we had a good future here, that I could accomplish things but I needed her help. I wanted her to stand by me, to invite certain people for dinner, to accompany me to certain social functions. I sometimes tried to talk to her for hours and hours. She did not understand what I was saying. There were nights when I would get home, very tired, and I would want to talk. She would not answer me or not pay attention to what I was saying. Suddenly she had to check on the baby, or the baby had to be changed, or the dishes had to be washed. Whenever I started to talk I never received any attention. The only response I got was that I was crazy, that I was too ambitious, that I only cared about myself, and that I was ignoring her and the family. She made me feel very small. Gradually, she put me in a position where I would not tell her anything anymore. I got sick and tired of talking. And she never asked any questions.

Roberto

LINA AND I LEFT NAPLES by boat in April 1951. I met a beautiful Mexican girl on board. She kept smiling at me in a very encouraging way so I went over and talked to her. But I had to watch my actions because my sister was there, I didn't want to set a bad example. So nothing happened between us, we just talked and danced.

When I came to Canada I was eighteen and a half and had never worked in my life. I arrived on a Friday and on Monday my father took me with him to do construction work, pick and shovel. There was no other place I could go, I didn't know a word of English. Before I could accomplish anything I had to master the language. I enrolled in night school to study English. But it was very tiring working on construction during the day. At night, I did not have very much patience left. One night I was really mad, the teacher spent the whole lesson trying to explain what an orange was to an oriental guy. After that I said, "That's it, good-bye, no more." I had only been there for a couple of nights and I never went back.

I did not mind working on construction. I kept my eyes open and learned a couple of things. Right from the start I felt that all the avenues were open for me here. Whatever I wanted to do I could do. It was up to me. Therefore, the construction work did not depress me, I knew I was not going to do it for the rest of my life.

When I came here I went to church much more than I ever did in Pratola. Here church was a good place to look at the girls. After mass a group of us just stood around outside at the entrance watching the girls leave with their mothers. Also, going to church was one of the few things you were able to do on Sundays in Toronto. Everything else was closed. A store had to pay a $50 fine if it stayed open. There was only one store which did not close on Sunday, Honest Ed's, he was doing tremendous business. All he had to do was pay the $50 and he made a fortune on Sunday. He was smart.

A bunch of us from the same town stuck together and regularly went dancing. In the early days I was dancing seven nights a week. The Seabreeze, down by the Lakeshore, was open in the summertime and you could dance under the stars. I was there every night in the summer. The biggest dance hall was the Palais Royal, or the Pali Royal, also on the Lakeshore. There was the Masonic Temple at Yonge and Davenport, and the Columbus Hall at Sherbourne and Bloor. I knew all the places in Toronto, dancing was the only sport I ever did. My father wanted to form a soccer team made up of people from my home town and he wanted me to be on it, but I never really enjoyed playing soccer. I liked dancing so much that when my mother arrived Saturday afternoon I spent a couple of hours with her and then went out dancing.

One of my regular spots during the winter was the Pali Royal and when you go there almost every night you form your own crowd. The dance floor was big but we always hung around in one corner. One night there was a girl in our corner who was a stranger. I went over to her and asked her to dance. She said, "No." I think she was sorry that she had refused me. Two or three nights later she asked me to dance. I didn't dance with her right away. I said, "Normally I make a point of not dancing with someone who has said no to me once."

She smiled sweetly, "Sorry, I didn't feel like dancing that night."

One Saturday night I took a friend of mine, who had just arrived from Italy, to the Masonic Temple which was a strictly English place. We were standing around looking at the girls and talking in Italian. One of the bouncers came over to us and asked us to talk in English. I just ignored him. He continued to insist and would not leave us alone. We ended up in a fight and were thrown out. That certainly gave my friend a bad impression of Toronto. What on earth were we doing wrong? Did we only come to Canada to work? What about enjoyment?

A year after I arrived here I quit the construction work and wanted to join the Canadian Forces. I went to the recruiting office. They gave me a test and I passed. I don't know how, my English was very poor. I was supposed to go for my medical the next day. That night I showed all the papers to my mother and told her I would probably get accepted. She was not happy to hear this. She said, "What are you doing? Why would you want to go to the army? In Italy people pay to avoid a compulsory draft and here you are volunteering." I listened to her and didn't sign up.

From then on I did everything. I worked in a bakery, Christie Bread, for almost a year. Then I went to work for a candy factory where they made mints. After a few months my stomach started bothering me because it was too sweet. I sold stocks for a while and I also worked with Franco as a real estate agent. I did not know what I wanted to do but slowly I was forming my own ideas and gaining experience by watching other people.

My father got me a job with DeHavilland Aircraft. Soon after I started we went out on strike for about five months. During that time I taught dancing at Arthur Murray's Dance Studio. But I knew that I would never make a living out of dancing, it was strictly for pleasure. I knew that as soon as the strike was over I was going to go back to work. Teaching dancing was not a profession unless you wanted to be a gigolo. Some of the young girls who were teaching there went out with the rich old men. I also met some guys there who made a living out of being a gigolo. I had my chances too. I used to teach a widow, who was the owner of a big company, and her daughter. I could have been a gigolo for the mother and married the daughter. I would have had no worries. But I didn't want to. I had my pride. Another time I was teaching an old lady. She was wealthy and asked for private instructions. Fine. The lessons were held in a private room, lined with mirrors. Every time I started to dance with her she made a grab for me. She said, "Come with me. I'm going to make all my friends jealous." I went to my supervisor and said, "That's it, give her to someone else." Again it was a question of pride.

I went out with one Canadian girl for six or seven months. She was the only one I ever dated for so long. She was blond and very attractive. She wanted to get married but I was not sure what the consequences might be. What would happen later on with the kids? If you don't have any kids, fine, but if you are going to have children then it's different. Also, she was not Catholic. We had different points of view, different customs. I kept postponing the question of marriage because I was always thinking of the children. One day she said to me, "Someone from the office proposed to me. What should I tell him?" I told her to say yes. For a couple of months I was mad, but it was my fault, I cannot blame anybody else. I know she married that guy and I never saw her again.

I met an attractive woman one night at the Pali Royal. She told me she was divorced, we talked and got to know each other. I liked her and I knew she was interested in me. I knew it was just a question of time. But before I even touched her, she said, "I want a child from you."

I was so shocked. I said, "What? Forget it." I just left.

If she would not have said anything, if it would have happened accidentally, then I could have accepted it. But to come right out and say it! It sounded as if she did not want me for sex, she just wanted a child.

Some girls said, "I want to get married. I want to have lots of children but I want to do what I like. My husband should not run my life." What kind of family is that? This was one of the reasons I always hesitated about marrying a non-Italian. The mentality of the Canadians was different. A family is supposed to be together, not the mother in one place and the father in another place because they have different interests. Both your interests should be the family.

I never took a girl home and I never gave out my home phone number. I didn't want my parents to know what was going on. When girls asked for my number I told them I didn't have a phone. I used to call them.

I met very few Italian girls when I was single. I didn't want to get involved with an Italian girl because I knew that once I was involved, I had to get married, and I wanted to be free.

My mother was always asking me if I was seeing anyone and both my parents were making suggestions about which Italian girls they thought would be good for me. I think my mother was really worried that I might end up with a Canadian. My parents wanted me to go to all the Italian social functions with them but I just went to a few weddings. Sometimes my father would point out a girl to me at a wedding and say, "She would be a good match for you." He usually said this about girls whose parents were rich. There was one very wealthy girl I could have married. She was always asking my best friend about me. But she did not attract me. There was nothing wrong with her, she wasn't the best looking girl in the world but she was all right. The only reason I felt no attraction was because I once danced with her at a wedding and she had bad breath, maybe it was temporary, but in my mind I didn't care about her millions, I just could not see myself with someone who had bad breath.

I heard that when she did get married her father gave her half a million dollars as a wedding gift. Maybe if I would have married this girl with all that money I might have felt like a slave or a failure. I might not have tried anything on my own. I like to feel that I have paid for everything I own, I don't want anyone coming to me and asking what I did with the money.

When I first started to work I gave my father my whole paycheque and kept just $2 or $3 for myself. The whole cheque went to them and I was making good money, $1.20 an hour. We were all giving money to my parents and I could see that there was no progress, they were using the money for entertainment. So I thought, am I crazy, I could be using that money myself. I said to my father, "I'll give you $20 a week and I'll keep the rest." My father was spending a lot of money, people were coming over all the time, there were parties. They did buy a house but my father liked to live big.

I had a very simple job at DeHavilland Aircraft. I was part of the assembly line making airplane parts. I had to stamp a number on each part to identify it. The job I was doing was nothing special but I was doing a good job. It is all very well to do a good job but it also has its drawbacks. If you are thinking of a promotion and your boss knows that you are good at a given job then he does not want to lose you on that job, so you will have a tough time trying to get ahead. I wanted to be a panel inspector. I put in several applications and each one was turned down. Once I was really mad because they hired a person from the outside without even considering me. I went to speak to the union about it. Finally, I was given another job but not the one I wanted. I became a sheet metal dresser. A sheet of aluminium, wrapped around a big block, was put under a big rubber press. The press tried to form a dress around this block with the sheet of aluminium. When the block came off the press it had wrinkles in some places because of the way the aluminium bent. It was my job to dress that block. I had to take all the wrinkles out with a hammer. That would distort the metal again and I had to give it back for another pressing until the sheet fitted the block smoothly. It wasn't a bad job, it paid more than what I was doing before, but it wasn't much more exciting.

I took a month leave of absence from the job in 1957 to accompany my mother to Italy because my grandmother and uncle were ill. We did not have enough money for the whole family to go and she wanted one of us to go with her. But it was such a sudden decision to return, I had no time to prepare myself. It happened too fast. I had no time to dream of what it would be like. All of a sudden I was just there. And it was like a dream. I could not believe I was really there. I got together with my friends but I found that whatever we were discussing we were arguing all the time. My mentality had changed, it was no longer the same as theirs. They noticed the difference as well and even commented on it.

I said, "Yes, of course I have changed. I have been away and I can see things with new eyes. I can see what is right and wrong better than you because you have not seen a different way of life. You have not changed. I cannot blame you. But if you could have gone to another place and then come back you also would have compared."

We disagreed on everything. I was thinking big and they were thinking small. One guy was talking about opening up a small store. I would tell him to open up something bigger. You can start small and then become big, but sometimes if you start small you remain small.

I noticed that their way of life was different, their attitudes were different. Even when it came to little things like waiting for the bus. People did not form a line like they did in Toronto. People just stood around and when the bus came it was chaos, everyone tried to get on at once, they were all pushing and no one got in. Why was that necessary? If I arrived before you did, why would you want to push in front of me?

I went to visit the House of Tolerance in Sulmona. This time I had money. I could afford to go to the most expensive one. But it wasn't the same. I was already twenty-five years old and I had much more experience.

My mother returned to Canada after one month. I decided to stay for another two months. I thought that since I was in Italy I might as well stay for awhile and enjoy myself. I went to San Remo, to the hotel where we had stayed during the war. I talked to one of the waiters and when I told him who I was he said, "Oh, you were one of those guys who scribbled *vincere, vinceremo* on the walls." They had wallpapered over all of Mussolini's sayings. I wanted to stay at that hotel but there were no rooms available. I asked about the other kids but no one could tell me anything.

I still had the bank book for those 50 lire. I had taken it with me thinking I might get a chance to visit San Remo. I went to the bank where the deposit was made. This time I did not want to take the money out, I wanted to deposit 2,000 lire on top of the 50. The guy at the bank looked at the book very curiously, he turned it around and examined it. Finally he said, "I am sorry. We have no record of this deposit."

I said, "What do you mean? Someone must have used that money." I took the book back and left. I also tried to locate the person who had confirmed me but I could not find him. I remembered his small daughter, I was particularly interested in seeing her again. By then she must have been about twenty-two or twenty-three.

I decided to return by boat. This time I was all by myself, I could do whatever I wanted, I did not have anyone to look after. I met a twenty-one-year-old girl from Trieste who had married an American in Italy. After the wedding he had stayed with her for seven days and then went back to the States. Now she was following him over. We stayed together on the boat for ten days. I had a better honeymoon than he did. Three times a day, every day, she received a telegram from her husband, "Good morning, dear." "Good afternoon, dear." "Good night, dear." She showed them to me.

When we landed in New York she had a hotel room which had been booked by her husband. She was supposed to fly to Memphis to meet him the next day. She asked me to spend the last night with her in the hotel. But I said no. As long as we were on the boat everything was fine. I was safe. What if the husband decided to surprise her and arrived in the middle of the night?

I discovered that I no longer had a job when I returned. They had given me a month and I took three months, they did not like that. Suddenly, I found myself with no trade and no real future. Franco helped me to start a travel agency. Since I was living at home I could take a chance on some things, I did not have to support a family. Still, my mother was always telling me to save more money, that I spent it too easily. I never worried about it.

I was not doing very well with the travel agency but I was having a good time. Right across from me there was a wholesale clothing store and I used to arrange flights for the owner. One day a girl came into the office and asked for two tickets to New York. I just sat in my chair and stared at her for a couple of minutes.

She was beautiful, gorgeous. She told me she was the daughter of the owner of the wholesale clothing store and she was going for the weekend to New York with a girlfriend. I knew her father's name was Anderson but she gave me a different name. She was married. I thought to myself, "Aha, you're married and you're going to New York with your girlfriend. What's wrong with your husband?" Naturally I tried to make a pass at her. When she came back from New York I tried to take her out. She would never say yes, but she would never say no either.

She was helping out her father and since my office was across the street from her father's business I could see when she went out to the corner coffee shop. Every time she went for coffee I went in after her. We always exchanged a few words and I would flirt with her. One day there were a couple of kids in the store and as I was looking at them it occurred to me that I didn't know anything about her. I said, "By the way, do you have any kids?"

She said, "Yes, three."

When I realized that I had made a pass at a woman with three children I felt really bad and I apologized to her. Once I found out that she was married with kids I lost interest in her, not because I no longer found her attractive but I didn't want to break up a family. From then on she was the one who was chasing me. She said, "What difference does it make whether I have kids or not, am I different from other people?"

This time whenever I went to the corner for coffee she also came in for coffee. Since she was coming after me so persistently I thought to myself, "Why not?" We started to have an affair. She had a car and she would pick me up after work and we would go to a hotel or a motel. She was wealthy and she paid for everything, the hotel, meals, everything.

One day she called me in the office, "Are you alone?"

"Yes."

"Can I talk to you?"

"Go ahead."

She said, "I told my husband everything about us."

"Yeah?"

"Now he wants to talk to you."

I was swearing. It is one thing if the husband hears from someone else that his wife is having an affair but to be told by your own wife! I could not understand it. Now I had to agree to meet her husband. What could I do? If I refused he could come after me and kill me without me ever having met the man. I thought if he was going to shoot me, I want to at least see his face. We arranged to meet in front of the museum. She told me he would be waiting in a car at five o'clock. He was going to be alone, it was to be a meeting just between the two of us.

Before I went to meet him I told my father what was going on. This was the first time I had said anything to him about my personal affairs. But in case anything might happen to me I wanted them to know who to look for and where.

I saw a car waiting in front of the museum. I went up to it and looked in. The driver asked, "Robert?"

I nodded.

He opened the door, "Come in."

The first thing he said to me when I sat down was, "Why don't you take off your jacket."

"No, no, I'm OK."

I knew that by telling me to take off my jacket he wanted to see if I was armed. It was the summertime, it was hot, and I was very uncomfortable. As he started to drive he said, "Why don't we go to the lake. It's cooler there."

I was scared, I thought this guy must have ideas if he is suggesting the lake. We drove along in silence for a couple of minutes. Finally he said, "You must have a lot of guts to come and meet me."

I said, "I have nothing to hide."

We started talking about his wife.

"Do you love Debbie?" He asked this without any emotion. It was a straight question, as if he was asking me about the weather. How do you answer a husband, in person, when he asks you if you love his wife or not? If I would say yes, I could put myself in a bad predicament. If I would say no, he would have all the reason to kill me because what am I doing with her if I don't love her? I didn't know what to answer. Finally he asked, "Would you marry her?"

Again, what could I say? Why should I want to marry someone else's wife? On the other hand, if I would say I would not marry her, he would have every reason to say, what are you doing fooling around with my wife if you don't intend to marry her?

I played it safe. I said, "Yes and no."

"What do you mean yes and no?"

"Yes, I would marry her because I like her. And no, because I can't. I can't afford her."

"What if I fixed you up financially?"

"No, thanks." I knew I had the whip in my hand now. "I want to do it on my own. Right now I am not in that position."

We had been driving around for a couple of hours and I was beginning to get the impression that he wanted to get rid of her even though they had three children. I also had the impression that this was not the first time she had done something like this.

Finally he said, "Now we have to meet Debbie."

She was waiting for us seated in a booth in a restaurant. I wanted to sit on one side of the booth and allow them to sit together on the other side. But the husband came and sat down beside me, leaving his wife to sit alone, facing the two of us. The three of us did not have much to say to each other. The husband got up and said to me, "I'll leave the two of you alone to talk but don't stay too long because I want to talk to Debbie after." He left and fifteen minutes later she followed.

She tried to contact me but how can you trust someone after something like that? I wanted to be left alone. One day she called me at the office and said, "Bob, I have $10,000. Let's leave the country."

I said, "Are you crazy?"

I suppose someone else might have taken her up on the offer and when the money was finished just come back home. I could not do that.

That same night I was playing cards at the sports club. Someone came over to me to say that a girl was waiting at the door. She knew where she could find me and she just drove over. When I finished the game I went outside, Debbie was waiting in the car.

She said, "I want to talk to you. Come with me." I got in the car and she drove to the University of Toronto campus. She parked and as she was about to get out she said to me, "Bob, remember that whatever happens to you I will always love you." I didn't know what she was talking about. I opened the door of the car and as soon as I stepped out she took off, leaving me alone.

Right away I knew that something was going to happen. It was late, the campus was dark and there was no one around. I quickly looked behind me and saw four big coloured guys coming toward me. I didn't stand a chance. I knew I was going to get it. I curled up because I didn't want them to hit my lower part, and I covered my face. They really worked me over. I was covered in blood. I could barely walk out to the street to get a cab home.

I realized that her husband must have offered her the $10,000 to go away. He obviously wanted to get rid of her. The next day I visited her husband's office with a friend who was really big. I asked him to wait just outside his door while I went inside.

I said to the husband, "This time I'll forget what happened. But the next time if you so much as touch a hair on my head you can kiss your family goodbye."

He said, "I had nothing to do with it."

"I'm just warning you."

After that she was afraid to get close to me.

The travel agency did not work out and at the end of 1959 I decided to join the Canadian Air Force. I thought I was old enough to do what I wanted. If you did not have a trade the Air Force would teach you. If you did have one you could get $30 more a month. Since I had worked at DeHavilland Aircraft for a number of years I told them that I had experience in sheet metal.

I went to a training camp in St John's. Every night Debbie tried to call me. I refused to talk to her. One night the Air Force police grabbed me from my bed and forced me to answer the phone. She had insulted the Air Force and they were mad. I told her to leave me alone.

After the training camp I was sent to Nova Scotia. I had to go into the hospital for a circumcision because every time I had sex I had problems. Debbie came to visit me in the hospital. She arrived in this small town, elegantly dressed, and all the men looked at her with an open mouth. From that day on I was famous, everyone knew my name.

She wanted to get a room in town and stay with me. I told her it was over, finished. I told her to go back to her family. She went back to Toronto. Every time I visited Toronto she came to see me. She refused to leave me alone. I couldn't understand how she knew I was in town. Then my friends told me that they had all taken advantage of her. They knew she was madly in love with me and they were the ones who told her when I was due to come home, in return for a little favour. She would pay them for the information by having sex with them. But they knew I didn't care. Let's face it, she wasn't someone I was going to marry.

In 1961 I asked the Air Force to take me to Italy with the service aircraft. The trip didn't cost me anything, the only agreement was that I had to wear my uniform, which I didn't mind. I spent my first thirty-day leave of absence in Italy.

There were no more Houses of Tolerance. After they closed, thousands and thousands of women were plying their trade on the streets with no medication. In those houses they had a place to sleep and eat. A doctor visited them regularly for a check-up. If there was anything wrong, they had their licence taken away. They had a pension after a certain amount of years, like everyone else who works in a company. They could retire, move from one town to another, and nobody would know about them.

While I was in Pratola I went to a party where I met two sisters. I danced a few times with the younger one, Luigina. Later she told a friend of mine that she liked me. But what was I going to do with her, buy her ice cream? She was only sixteen and I was twenty-nine. I remembered seeing her older sister at that same party and told my friend that if it was the sister I could be interested but not her.

They must have told the older sister that I was interested in her and they set up a meeting between the two of us. We were introduced to each other in front of the fountain and we talked. I liked Maria, she was extremely shy and very pretty. I vaguely remembered her as a kid because she used to be our neighbour but I never really paid any attention to her in those days, she was seven years younger than me. She had developed very nicely since those days. I decided to prolong my stay by another week.

During that week I could have seen Maria alone if I had wanted to. But the town was small, people were always eager to talk, and why ruin something you want? If I had other intentions, then it would have been a different story. By the end of that week we were engaged. At first her parents didn't like the idea of their daughter leaving Italy. After two or three days I brought them around to my way of thinking.

I returned to Canada and we wrote to each other for a year. The next year I made arrangements for another thirty-day leave of absence. Before going to Italy I bought a tuxedo and my mother bought Maria a wedding dress. That summer I went back and we got married. For our honeymoon we took a three-week cruise and returned to Italy by boat.

My friends had a stag party for me while I was away. When I came back they gave me $300 they had raised from the selling of tickets for the party. They said I had missed a great time, lots of food and gambling.

Since my sister and parents were here, Maria was not that lonely. Even though she did not say anything, I knew that after a year here she was homesick. I sent her back to visit her parents. That's the only way to cure a person. When she returned, she was fine.

I had reached a stage in my life where I was ready to settle down. I married because I wanted a family, I wanted a mother for my kids. I didn't marry because I wanted a woman. I could have married a glamorous girl who was good for dancing but perhaps not for raising a family. I didn't want a Sophia Loren, I wanted a mother.

My lifestyle changed completely from one day to the next. That was it, all of a sudden I said to myself, "Now I am a family man." When a person gets married too early he does not have time to really get to know life, to really enjoy himself, and he will always feel that he has missed something and he will go with someone else the first chance he gets because he did not allow himself time when he was young to get that out of his system. Of course, sometimes it's the woman who causes the problems. In my case I became a family man and my wife had no reason to go outside of the home to meet someone else because I was there whenever she wanted me.

After I got out of the Air Force a couple of investigators came to my house. They asked me to step outside and get into the car with them. They started to ask me questions about Debbie. I knew they had a tape recorder with them in the car so I was careful what I said. They kept asking me if I had sex with her. I just laughed and said, "You must be nuts, you don't ask such things." They threatened to tell my wife. I said, "Go ahead, she knows everything."

They were investigating Debbie's death. I knew that she had died because a friend of mine had heard about it and told me. She was electrocuted in the bathtub while taking a bath. It was supposed to have been an accident, something fell into the water. But perhaps her husband killed her. Maybe I was a suspect in her death. But I was miles away when it happened. A few days later I told my wife about it.

I came out of the Air Force with five years of experience as a sheet metal technician. Previous to that I had four years of experience in one profession. If I would have turned to another area of work I would have had to start from the bottom up. I realized that I was stuck with a trade. Why waste those nine years? I ended up being a sheet metal man, not because I wanted to but it was there. That was the area of work where I could make the most money if I had to work for someone else. I said to myself, "OK, Roberto, this is it. Do the best you can and really learn it."

To every trade there is an easy part and a hard part. It didn't take me long to find the hardest part of the sheet metal trade. It was trigonometry. As soon as I realized this I concentrated on that aspect of the work and ignored the rest.

Angelina

EIGHT MONTHS AFTER MY FATHER came to Canada Roberto and I followed him. Once more the two of us were travelling alone on the boat. We were making jokes about it, telling my mother not to worry because we were just going on a holiday.

This time there were no teachers to watch us. I was always hanging around on deck with a group of young girls and all the boys were coming after us. Roberto was there, watching me, making sure I did not do anything bad. I would not have known what to do anyway, I was so naive. There was a tall, handsome Greek guy who winked at me each time he saw me. I just looked back at him, I didn't know what that meant, I didn't know what he wanted from me.

The train we took from Halifax was cheap. The seats were made of wood and there was no padding. When we arrived in Montreal we had to transfer. We had to go up the stairs and down the stairs to get to the other train. We didn't know where we were. The suitcases were so heavy and there was no one to carry them. Finally we reached the train. A certain amount of trains had been set aside for the immigrants and the rest were for the regular passengers. We found ourselves among the regular passengers. I was glad because the seats were much more comfortable.

When we arrived in Toronto it was the same story, up the stairs and down the stairs. I could see all the people waiting for us but it seemed to take forever before we could reach them.

My cousin got married a week after we arrived. I knew I would have to go to this wedding and I came prepared for it. I brought nice new clothes, blue shoes, a blue purse, and a beautiful suit with a pure silk blouse. I was amazed when we arrived at the church. There were so many people, at least four or five hundred of them. In Italy I was used to small family weddings with a few intimate friends.

As we walked into the church everybody looked at me and whispered, "She just came from Italy. Look at the way she is dressed." I could not believe what some of these people were wearing, cork shoes with no stockings, a simple cotton dress that we would only wear inside the house. In Italy we didn't have so many weddings and when we went to one we would dress up from top to bottom, everything was new and fancy. That's what I was prepared for.

Then I heard things like, "People say you're starving in Italy and look at the way you're dressed." Who told you we were starving? The people who had come out just before or after World War I had told their children that in Italy people worked and worked all day long on the farms and they never got anywhere. I think they told their children only the negative things. They never said that Italy could be special, that there were also the beautiful times.

I knew that I would have to work when I got here but I still found it a little humiliating because girls from good families never worked in Italy. Some of my cousins were complaining all the time, they found life here very degrading. Two weeks after I arrived I went to work in a cookie factory, my second cousin who was also there recommended me.

Early in the morning, when I went to work on the bus, no one looked at me, nobody paid any attention to me, no compliments, nothing. In Italy, when you are sixteen, boys start looking at you, they pay you compliments and you feel good. But here in Canada I felt buried.

People here were not at all fashion conscious. They did not seem to care what they had on. When I left Italy the pointed toe shoes were in style, here they were wearing wide shoes. In the winter the people wore heavy boots, the kind you had to put over your shoes, they looked very awkward and unfashionable. And the clothes were not very well tailored.

In the cookie factory my supervisor, Margaret, was Scottish and she liked me. She put me on the assembly line for packaging cookies. The cookies came along on a conveyor belt and I had to put them in a bag with a scoop, then I let them go and someone else continued. As the cookies came down on the belt they were very hot, the fig bars were the worst. We all had red spots on our finger tips because of the heat. My best friends were two French-Canadian girls and an Estonian girl, Eva, who was five years older than me. We were a team in the factory. The Canadians from Toronto were always bothering the French-Canadian girls, telling them to go back to Quebec. Verna was the leader of the group and everyone followed her. She made loud jokes and called out names. She would say, "Hey, Lina, is it true that Italians sleep naked?" And they all laughed. I was so young, I didn't know people hated each other.

But our small group was happy. We were laughing and singing while we worked and that bothered Verna. She had it in for us. One day she yelled, "Still laughing?" She started to push more and more cookies toward us so we had to work faster and faster to pack them. Her face became all red, she was screaming and swearing and pushing bunches of cookies down. Nobody had treated me like that before. At noon we all went down to the lunch room. I was so shook up that I started to cry really hard. Joyce, a friend of Verna's, saw me and ran to the cafeteria to call her.

Verna rushed over and tried to calm me, "Come on, Lina, it was nothing. Don't let Margaret see you like this." She was afraid Margaret would fire her. But what had I done against her? I was just doing my work, I didn't bother her. I was so nervous that I had lost my appetite. I threw my lunch into the garbage. Verna grabbed the brown bag, opened it, and placed my sandwich on my lap, apologizing. I looked at her and just asked, "Why?" She didn't say anything.

From that day on it was always, "Hey, Lina, how are you doing?" She was never mean again.

But there were people who had a much worse time than I did. One of my relatives was working in a factory, sewing sleeves for children's pyjamas. She was paid 25 cents an hour. In one hour she managed to sew twelve sleeves. The girl beside her was only making six sleeves in one hour for the same amount of money. After one month the trouble started because the boss saw that one person was making twelve while the other was only making six. He wanted everyone to make twelve.

She came over to our house and was crying, "I am scared. If I don't work hard enough they will put me out. If someone makes two I will try to make three. But the Canadian people don't like that. They get up and smoke, drink coffee. But I am scared. I don't go to the bathroom, I don't go to have a drink, nothing. And I feel that the Canadians hate me for it. But we immigrants need the money. Maybe the Canadians don't need it that much, that's why they don't work so hard. But you don't know the language, you can't explain anything, you can't talk."

She suffered a lot. The other women in the factory told her to go back to Italy.

I was here with my father, Roberto, and Franco. When I came home from work I had to do the cooking and cleaning for all of them. My father taught me a few things. He used to say that he taught my mother how to make a good sauce. Whenever she got a compliment for her sauce he would say, "I taught her how to make it."

In the fall I started going to school to learn English. I had to eat fast, leave the dishes, and go to school for two hours. Then my father or one of my brothers picked me up to take me home because by 9:30 it was dark. The dishes were there waiting for me. Then I had to wash my hair, put it in bobby pins, and when I finally went to bed it was eleven o'clock. Sometimes, before I went to sleep, I wanted to write letters or to read but the owner would come upstairs and say, "Please turn out the light, the bill is very high." I didn't know how he knew that the light was on. He must have been watching for it. At 5:30 the next morning I had to get up. I was so tired, I fainted twice at work.

When my mother arrived it was easier. I didn't have to worry about the washing, the ironing, the cooking. She took care of everything. I just had to do the dishes.

One summer night we had a little party to welcome a relative who had just arrived from Italy. A cousin with a banjo and another cousin with a guitar came over. We all sat out on the veranda, there was music and singing. We were having such a good time, we felt as if we were back in Italy. Suddenly we see a police car stop in front of our house.

Two young policemen got out, "We are very sorry, the neighbours are complaining, there is too much noise. We don't want you to stop having a good time, finish your party, but please go inside." They were very kind. They could see we were not the wild types. Still, we felt bad. In Pratola, when it was hot, everyone went outside.

There were a lot of Italian boys coming to Canada alone. My parents often took me to the dances at the Italian Hall. Sometimes there were ten Italian girls to thirty or forty boys. I danced with thousands of them every Saturday but I didn't find anyone I really liked. I always looked for the well-educated boys, the fine types. Even though I didn't have very much education, I felt noble inside. I felt high class.

At the factory there was a handsome Canadian boy with dark wavy hair and big brown eyes, he looked Italian. He had just graduated from grade thirteen and he came to work in the office. They told me he was very rich and he had a beautiful car. Bill walked up and down, whistling, and there I was blushing and the cookies went upside down when he passed by. He also blushed. I knew he liked me but I was so shy, I was afraid to smile at him.

One afternoon we stopped work early and had a party. Bill and I danced together the whole afternoon. But after each dance I ran back to my place to sit down, I didn't know I could stay. In Italy the boy has to invite the girl for each dance. Later I realized that the Canadian girls stayed there and talked to the boy so he would dance with her again.

They had a Scottish dance where we had to form two circles, the girls were on the inside facing the boys. When the music stopped you had to dance with whoever you were facing. I stopped in front of Bill's best friend and Bill was beside him. They quickly switched places so Bill ended up facing me. That was when I knew for sure how he felt.

One day, Bill said to one of the French-Canadian girls, "I like Lina very much." She turned to him and said, "But, Bill, do you know she is Roman Catholic?" Bill was a Protestant. I didn't know there were differences in religion. All I knew was that Italians were Catholic.

I gave everything I earned to my parents. The Canadian girls laughed at us. At the beginning I got $27.50 and kept 75 cents. I spent 50 cents for tickets a week, I kept the rest for drinks. Sometimes during a break Margaret, my supervisor, would come over to me and say, "Lina, why don't you take typing lessons? You should go to school." She always encouraged me to try to do something else, something better than just working in the factory. I told this to my parents but they didn't say anything.

After two and a half years the factory closed down. We had a party on the last day. By then there were ten Italians and we were all sitting together laughing. Suddenly Bill came over to the group of us and he invited my best friend for a dance. He had gotten married a couple of months earlier to a girl in the office. I heard that he had to marry her. But his wife was not at the party. My best friend came back to me after the dance. She was all excited, "Lina, he asked about you."

Then he came to ask me to dance. After two years I had learned a couple of things, plus I knew he was married so I was not that shy, I was calm. After one or two dances he had to go and pick up his wife. When she arrived she sat with Bill's best friend the whole evening while we danced. He kept calling me, "Honey." I thought, "My God, if I would have married this Canadian and he would have treated me this way I would have killed him. I wouldn't let him dance with someone else the whole night." Then I started to think that maybe all Canadians did this.

He said, "Now that the factory is closing down why don't you find yourself a nice place in an office?"

I said, "I don't speak English very well."

"I'll teach you English and you'll teach me how to dance." That was the time of the jitterbug. He was such a good dancer, he certainly didn't need any lessons.

Then he looked at me seriously and said, "In an office you'll meet lots of boys."

I said, "I don't want lots of boys. I would like to find one." I knew how the Canadians were, they went one night with one and another night with another. Not me, that was not the way I was brought up.

He said, "Would he have to be Italian?"

Since I liked him so much I said, "No, as long as he was a fine boy."

When he was not talking to me he would sing, "You, you, you, I'm in love with you ..." Finally, his poor wife couldn't take it anymore and when the night was almost over she came and tapped me on the shoulder. "May I?"

"Of course." I was so confused that I ran away from the dance floor.

After the factory closed down my cousin and I ended up at Loblaw's warehouse, packing tea. It was better than burning our fingers on the cookies.

My Aunt Maria in Italy showed a passport picture of me to the di Ninos who lived next door to her. I was nineteen by then and I had bloomed. My father proudly showed me a letter she had written which said that Alfredo di Nino had seen the picture and was interested in me. He asked me what I thought. I said, "Well, I don't know if I am interested. I want to see a picture of him first."

When his picture arrived I realized that I knew him. Alfredo's family was one of the wealthiest and best-known in town. All his uncles had university diplomas. His father worked in the head office in town and the mother was wealthier than the father. I had seen Alfredo on the street but had never danced with him or spoken to him.

But I was still thinking of my cousin so I didn't say anything. By chance I read a letter my father had just finished writing to Alfredo's father, "I asked Lina and she said yes. We are all happy." My parents had not even bothered to sit down and ask me. If they would have talked to me and encouraged me to tell them what I thought or how I felt I would have told them my secret. Now I was afraid to say anything.

Alfredo and I started writing letters to each other. "I love you." "I love you." But we didn't even know each other. A few months later my cousin, Vittorio, came to Canada with his sister, Elisa.

While we were dancing one night I told him that I wanted him to be the best man for my wedding when Alfredo arrived. He shook his head and said, "I don't want to be the best man."

"What do you want to be?"

"The groom." I laughed. I couldn't do or say anything.

Alfredo's family wrote to the Italian Consulate asking for information about me, about my father's economic situation, our social life. My father knew the Italian Consulate, we were always at their dances, so of course they said good things about us. It was a custom in Italy for families to do such things. If a foreign boy would want to marry someone from my town the first thing the girl's family would do is ask him where he was born. Then they would write to his home town asking for information about him. The first time Alfredo's family asked about us everybody was happy. By the third time I was fed up. I knew he came from a good family, but still, what did they want from me? Although I was only twenty years old and inexperienced this bothered me very much. I complained to Vittorio about it. "Well," he said, "stop writing." I did and my father supported me in the decision.

One night everybody was over at our house, including Vittorio and Elisa. My father was upset with me. He said, "You have so many nice boys here who ask about you. They already have their future here, they don't have to come and start all over. They have put money aside. Why aren't they good enough for you?" I did not answer. I could feel Vittorio looking at me.

After my father left, he said, "Did you hear your father, how many boys he has for you? But I am going to marry you." I turned pale. I felt weak.

From then on I called him at work. I didn't want him to call me because I was afraid. I called him every day at lunch for two months. He worked in a factory. I knew he wasn't going to stay in a factory all his life, he was ambitious, like me. Every day after work we met at the streetcar stop and rode home together. We had a twenty-minute ride, but we were not alone, my other cousin was always there.

He often invited me to go to the movies. "Say you are sick one day. I will come to pick you up by taxi." But if I would have told the head of my department that I was sick she would have believed me. Then I would have been so nervous knowing that I had lied. I never had the guts to do it. We only saw each other on the streetcar and he would say, "I wish the red light would last an hour."

He said that when he heard Alfredo was writing to me he thought to himself, "I am not going to do anything now. I will be there before him anyway."

We made plans to get married. Vittorio had one worry, "What if your father doesn't give his consent?"

I said, "No." I thought to myself, how could my father refuse? He loved him like a son, Vittorio was the best of all his nephews.

After five weeks I told my parents and they said, "No." My mother was always the kind who listened to my father. I tried to talk to my father. He said, "First cousins cannot marry." But he went and talked to his friends about it, he wanted to hear their opinion. Everyone was so negative, "No, no, you shouldn't let them do this." Another said, "No, no, just like animals." If you are going to say no, at least keep quiet about it. This was a family matter.

My father wanted me to marry Alfredo. I was not writing to him but there was still an understanding between us.

One night I could not sleep and I heard my mother and father arguing. He said, "Don't worry."

My mother said, "We should give her time to think. Drop everything."

"No, don't worry. Love will come later."

Both Roberto and Franco sided with my father. They wanted Alfredo as a brother-in-law. Roberto said to me, "Remember, if you dare to run away or elope with Vittorio, the first time you see me I am going to kill you both." I was afraid. If it was only me, I didn't care. Fine, kill me. But he said both of us would die.

Franco said to me, "Remember, if you don't marry Alfredo you're not going to marry anybody."

Our priest was Irish but he spoke Italian very well. The priests in Italy were always so severe, people were afraid to talk to them. In Canada they were more gentle, they were there to serve people. This Irish priest was a handsome man, with the face of an angel. I felt I could go and talk to him. My mother was a religious woman and I told her I wanted to ask the priest's opinion about this. My mother agreed.

I was only interested in one thing, was it a sin to marry a first cousin? If it was a sin, I would not dare to do it. In my heart I have faith. I might not go to church every Sunday, but I have faith. The priest said, "No." My mother said nothing. He also said the usual thing, sometimes the children are born deformed. But how many children are really born deformed?

When my mother and I got home and we told my father what happened he was so mad. He said, "How can you embarrass me like that, going to talk to the priest?" My father knew the priest because we did everything there.

I had an uncle in the States who had married his cousin and I wanted to write to him to ask for help. I didn't do it. I was shy to ask about things. I also wanted to write to the Pope because they said the Pope was the only person who could give permission for first cousins to marry. But I never did anything. I was too inexperienced and naive. I was twenty years old and nobody had kissed me, I had never been alone with a boy. I was even afraid to dance with them. I would tell them, "Please, don't talk, my parents are looking." I was afraid that my parents would scream at me.

After my father had said no we met a couple of more times but Vittorio was so sad. My father wrote a letter to his sister, my Aunt Carmina, saying that her son was a traitor because he had come between Alfredo and I. My father said, "I don't want any nephews in this house till my daughter is married." My aunt was hurt, she wrote back, "We always knew that Lina liked him too."

The news that I was practically engaged to my first cousin flew back to Pratola. Alfredo's father wrote to mine to ask what was going on. My father answered, "No, it's not true. She's free."

Alfredo's best friend came to Toronto and visited me. He said, "Alfredo doesn't talk to anyone and he is always sad. Please, write him a note. They say you're engaged to your cousin."

I said, "No. It's not true."

He said, "Why don't you give your father a note for Alfredo and he can put it in his letter the next time he writes home."

I wrote this note and my father showed it to my cousin as a way of saying, forget it, she is not really interested. But my cousin advised my father not to send it because Alfredo might use the note to show it around and say, "See, she still wanted me and I never answered her note." Vittorio told my father I should hold onto my pride and let Alfredo write. My father listened to him. My cousin was hoping that Alfredo would not write to me.

Alfredo wrote a letter on Palm Sunday and enclosed a palm inside, hoping to make peace.

Finally, I wrote, "I am sorry. It was not meant against you, we don't even know each other."

At that time everyone was getting married by proxy. But I said, "I want to look at him first. I don't want a cat in the bag. I am not an old maid and nothing is wrong with me." I was very innocent but not stupid.

I knew people who had married by proxy. There were many problems. I knew one girl who came over already married to a man she had never met. The girl had an aunt here and he had relatives back there and they had arranged it. She had arrived all dressed up, like a bride, with a nice hat and suit. She looked like Sophia Loren, beautiful, tall, dark eyes, long hair, a perfect figure. But her husband was also like Sophia's husband, short, bald, and fat. Of course, the poor girl had a shock. She had seen pictures of him but it was impossible to tell how short or how fat he was, she only saw his face and the face looked fine. From his eyes I could see he had a good heart. As soon as she saw her husband at the train station she started to scream. She tore her hat off and she went mad, she wanted to go back.

The man also said, "She is not for me." He blamed her aunt for having arranged this. He knew he needed someone who was plainer-looking, more ordinary, not someone so beautiful. But by the time she arrived here they were already married.

How could a mother marry a beautiful daughter like that by papers? He didn't even have money. She refused to go to bed with him for the first few weeks. Right away she wrote to her mother saying she wanted to go back. The mother answered, "Don't you dare dishonour me. Don't you dare do this to me. If you do I will no longer consider you my daughter."

The poor girl started to drink. Italian women never drink, maybe they have a glass of wine with a meal. She was always drinking. She did not know where to turn, she did not have anyone here. He kept telling her, "I know it was a mistake, but what can we do? I know you are not for me and I am not for you but let's try." They finally got together and they started to have children. But I am sure she threw her life away.

I called Alfredo over as a fiancé. When I went to fill out the papers I had to say we loved each other and we had been engaged in Italy before I left. The government gave one month to all couples. If we did not get married within one month he would have to go back. Before Alfredo arrived one of my cousins said to me, "You should marry this boy. Don't let him come here for nothing and then hurt him."

We went to meet Alfredo at the train station. There were at least fifty other people from Pratola waiting for him. My father got on the train to get Alfredo and as they came down I crossed myself. I recognized him from the picture. He was nicely dressed. We didn't kiss but we embraced. The first thing he asked was if his family had written. He had been on the boat for thirteen days. He was not even twenty-four and I was going to be twenty-one in three days.

We all went back to the house. My mother had prepared supper. My father didn't want him to sleep with us in case something went wrong. Alfredo went to stay with my second cousin.

He came over to our house after work. We had supper together and talked or listened to the radio. My mother packed his lunch for the next day and he went back to sleep at my cousin's.

We all went to Welland for a big Italian dance on my twenty-first birthday. Alfredo was nervous. He was afraid to meet Vittorio. When I first danced with him I enjoyed it but he was not a dancer. He danced the slow ones well but not the fancy steps. I had always said, "I won't marry him if he is not a dancer."

I don't know if I could have done anything if I would not have liked the way Alfredo looked. Perhaps, not to hurt his feelings, I would have remained silent. Sometimes, by trying to protect other people's feelings, I only hurt myself.

My mother began to embroider my sheets when I started writing to Alfredo. Before we got married she took me out shopping. She bought me a black Persian lamb coat on sale for $200. She also bought me a pair of two-tone suede and lizard shoes with a matching envelope-style purse. I also had a white hat with a veil for after the wedding, to go to the hotel.

My mother had said nothing to me before I got married. I remembered a young girl at the cookie factory who had been married for three years. She explained her wedding night to some of us. She said, "Ten minutes, that's all it takes."

"That's all?" I said. "Not one hour?"

She said, "Do you want him to die?" But she did not really explain anything. I thought, after waiting so long it could at least last one hour.

I knew nothing about contraception. The night before we got married Alfredo said to me, "Remind me, I have to get a little box."

"What box?" I asked myself. One of the married girls I was working with explained what they were.

On the day of my wedding, as I was about to go out the door, my Aunt Lisetta kissed me and said, "Congratulations!" I started to cry. My father started shouting, "Was this the time for you to congratulate her, could you not wait?" I came down the aisle with five bridesmaids, a maid of honour, and two flower girls. All my relatives were there except Vittorio and his sister. We did not invite them. Alfredo did not want them there.

There I was in the church, with my long white dress and my head down crying. My father was beside me, very proud, but he kept saying in a low voice, "*Questa stupida.* Stop crying. Stop crying." He was nervous too. He knew why I was crying. I didn't see anybody, my head was down and the tears just kept coming. I was standing at the altar with bulgy eyes, crying.

I was surprised on our wedding night. I didn't expect it and it was not ten minutes. We went to bed at one in the morning and I did not fall asleep till 8:30. When I told Alfredo I thought it was going to be ten minutes he was proud.

I did not enjoy it the first time, maybe I did not know him that well. When you really love a person, you don't care, even if he hurts you, even if he would kill you, it would be sweet to die by his hands, I would stay there. Of course, Alfredo was not a maniac, he did the right thing, he was never rough.

153

Suddenly at twenty-one I felt like an old maid, just because I was married. My parents went out. Before I always went with them but now Alfredo did not want to go. He was afraid we would bump into Vittorio.

After I had my first baby my husband was still jealous. He said, "Where did your parents go tonight?"

I started blushing. I felt bad, embarrassed. I said, "They went to see Vittorio."

He said, "Well, I hope he doesn't start bothering us."

"How can he?" My husband would not let me near him. He kept me inside the house for a year. We did not go to parties, he was afraid to meet him. I had the worst time of my life, I was always crying. When my eyes were all swollen from crying, he said, "OK, do you want to go out now?"

"No, how can I go out with this face?" He did that all the time. There I was crying and he was so quiet and sad.

When the baby came along I started arguing. I wanted to go to weddings. Finally we went to a wedding. I had my five-month-old baby with me. And there was Vittorio with his wife who was expecting. My husband said to me, "If you dare to look at someone, it will be the end." When we sat down to eat they were across from us. Alfredo went to get food at the buffet and there I was with the baby. My cheeks were red and I saw them all smiling, looking at the baby.

The dream was always to go back, to make some money and to go back. I didn't want to think that I would grow old and die here. After we got married, Alfredo told me that his mother had lots of land and his father had promised to give land to all his children. Anytime we were ready to go back he would build a house for us on the land. I liked the idea. In every letter my father-in-law wrote, "Come, come, we can't wait till you come. We'll give you whatever you need."

Alfredo had come to marry me and to take me back. But he did not say this at the beginning because then I would not have married him. I would not have left my family. His parents had told him to stay a few years and then come back. Seven years after we got married we went back to Italy.

I went before Alfredo. I left in May because I wanted to go with the three children a few months before school started so they could get used to the language and the town. I took the boat to Naples where all of Alfredo's family was waiting for us.

We stayed in the house of my in-laws. My mother-in-law had already built villas for her other children, all close to their house. She was waiting for us to come over so we could choose the style we wanted. I did not want to make any decisions without Alfredo.

The kids got sick in Pratola. They were not used to the food and the water. They had diarrhea, were vomiting, and had developed allergies. My mother-in-law didn't know what to give them. She was cooking rice and tea every day for one month

Alfredo's father was a gentleman and an educated man. His brother, Romano, was a dentist. Every member of his family was a university graduate. But my father-in-law was a very jealous man, worse than Alfredo. The first two weeks after I arrived he was full of compliments. The third week something happened.

Alfredo had a cousin, Michele, who wanted to marry my cousin in Canada. He was very fine, he reminded me of my cousin, Vittorio. Alfredo never paid me any compliments. Vittorio always looked at the dress, the hair, everything. When I arrived, Michele came to visit me and he kissed me with such affection. To me that meant he loved my cousin.

The third week I was there Michele said to me, "I would like to buy your cousin some shoes. Would you come with me to help me choose?"

I said, "Yes."

Alfredo's youngest brother, Carlo, drove us to Sulmona. There were all my children, Michele and his two sisters and Carlo. We all went together. When we got back I sat down to talk to Michele about my family because we were going to be related. He asked me all sorts of questions. We spent a couple of hours talking. My father-in-law was in the living room and he kept calling me, trying to disturb us, to break off the conversation. Several times he would say, "Come and see this nice program on TV."

"Papa, thank you very much, not now."

He was jealous. What was I doing wrong? Before that evening he always said, eat this, take that, you did not eat enough. After that evening, he ate but he didn't look at me or talk to me. He just told me what he wanted me to cook for supper. No compliments, nothing.

From then on I could not go out. If I ever went out he put on a long face, whether it was the day or night. I went to the hairdresser the day before San Vincenzo day and I was there for seven hours. They didn't take appointments and you had to go there and wait. My niece, who was seventeen, came a couple of times and saw that I was waiting. My father-in-law came back at two o'clock from work and I was not home yet. I arrived a few minutes after him.

My niece told me that he had asked, "Where is she after all this time?"

She said, "At the hairdresser."

"I don't believe that. Who knows where she went?"

My niece said, "No, it's not true. I went there a couple of times and she was there, waiting." I was so upset when she told me this.

I had Rosa's address when I returned to Italy because we had written to each other. The last time I heard from her she had sent me an invitation to her wedding, she was getting married to a bookkeeper. But I could not look for her. My father-in-law would not let me out.

The children and I got the mumps and we had to stay in bed for a few weeks. I was crying because I felt so alone. I felt I didn't have anyone to take care of me. My mother-in-law was very old, she used to sit in a chair at the end of my bed and knit. Michele came regularly to visit me. But he never looked at me in a bad way, he was just like a brother. My father-in-law said that he came to the house to take advantage of me.

One day Michele's mother said to my mother-in-law, "Who is spreading the rumour that Michele is in love with Lina?"

I felt like two cents. In Italy the parents were responsible for a son's family. If the son did not have a job the parents had to take care of him and all his children. So it was good to have the son go away. I think my father-in-law wanted to have his own son, Carlo, marry my cousin.

When I arrived there we had a maid for two months and I said, "Oh, this is heaven. I have never had a maid." Then he kicked her out because now he had a young woman in the house. From then on he treated me like a maid. My mother-in-law came from a better family than he, she was the top of the town. She was rich and good yet he stepped on her. She was of the old generation, the man was the man and she would never answer back to him or criticize him. Now he wanted to step on me as well. I am the nervous type but I never shouted or talked back to people. The manners my parents taught me, my education, was above my nerves. I would shout at a younger person but I would never shout at an older person, I could control it.

He once said to one of his nieces, "I don't like her character." I don't know why, I did my duty. When I said, "Good night," he would not answer. I knew he liked tea and if one of my children was sick and I made them tea, I used the one tea bag to make two cups, one for him. If I would have a mean character I would just throw away the tea bag and say, "Why worry about him?" But no, I made tea for him and took it to his chair and said, "I made tea for one of the children so I made you a cup too. I know you like it." He did not say a word, not even a thank you. But when I went to get the cup, after he had gone to bed, it was empty.

I didn't want to write about this to Alfredo, I didn't want to bother him. I thought when he will come here there will be time to talk.

Alfredo arrived seven months after us. I had never seen him so happy, he looked as if he had conquered the world. A special dinner was prepared for him. They bought a baby lamb, they chose it when it was alive and it was so tender. I couldn't eat it, not after I had seen it alive. If I see the animal alive, even if it's a chicken, I cannot eat it.

His big sister knew that for a change I had to sit with my husband at the table so she said, "Lina, I told Papa to hire a maid for that day because you are the wife and you should not have to get up." She knew that I did all the work, even when they came over. I always had to prepare the coffee and everything, they would just sit.

They sent everything out to the big ovens, lasagna and the lamb. We hired a cook. Of course, I had to set the table beforehand. The maid arrived for the beginning of the meal and she was in the kitchen the whole time washing dishes for twenty-five people.

The next morning, when I woke up, Alfredo was not there. I guess he was anxious to see the house and the garden. On the weekend everything was fine. Then Monday morning he went with Carlo to Sulmona. He knew that I liked pastries and he came back home with a big tray of pastries. As they drove in toward the house I was sitting on a bench under a tree. I felt shy because I had not seen Alfredo for seven months, I felt like a new bride, I could not look at him. Instead I looked at my brother-in-law and laughed. Then I looked at Alfredo. He smiled at me and I smiled back. He gave me the pastries and quickly went into the bedroom. I followed him.

I saw him sitting on the bed with a long face, he looked so serious. I said, "What happened in Sulmona?"

"Nothing."

"Did your brother say or do anything to you?"

"No."

I begged him, "What happened? This morning you were fine."

"When we drove through the gate you didn't look at me. You looked at my brother." He was jealous.

I told him the truth, "I was shy. I felt like when we were engaged. Your brother is like a friend. I didn't care."

Then it all came out. He had arrived on Saturday and on Sunday morning I woke up at seven and he was not there. His father told him about Michele and I. He knew I would say something about it to my husband, before I had the chance he told Alfredo himself.

I was so upset, "I don't have your blood. I am like a stranger to you, yet I was concerned for you, to allow you to be completely happy for the first couple of days and he, your father, wanted to poison you right away. What kind of a father is that? He says he cares so much for his son, but as soon as the son comes he poisons his mind and heart. He does not even wait twenty-four hours. Michele is the best one in your family, the most affectionate and the kindest. How can a father spread this lie?"

Then I told him all the wrong his father had done. At the end I asked, "Well, did you believe him?"

He said, "Of course not. You will never know what I told him. I shut him up with one word, fast."

Often there is a little bit of truth to every rumour but this was a lie created and imagined by him. The father knew that his son was the jealous type, what could he want? Maybe he thought he would beat me up. What kind of satisfaction could he have wanted?

At the end Alfredo said, "I know he did wrong but he is my father." He did not want to lose respect for his father.

Alfredo was a different man in Pratola. He was not that jealous, maybe because he had all that freedom. He went to Sulmona with his brother and who knows what they did. Over there everyone had a second woman, maybe he was enjoying himself. I often saw him flirting with the women and I smiled. I went along with it. Of course, I couldn't flirt. Him, yes. We even went to a party once where I met Vittorio and his wife. They had moved back to Italy a few years earlier. I had a nice conversation with his wife but Vittorio and I did not talk.

Four months after Alfredo arrived I was pregnant again. Each time I wanted to visit my Aunt Carmina or Marcella, Alfredo took me, happily. But my father-in-law always put on a long face when we went out.

Alfredo's brother had a laboratory in Sulmona and Alfredo worked with him. We bought a car. Things seemed to be going well. I designed the villa myself with the builder and they started working on it in April. By the summer it was finished. We should have moved in right away but we continued to stay at my father-in-law's for two and a half more years. The villa stood there empty. Each time I looked out the window I could see it.

It was convenient for my father-in-law to have me there. My mother-in-law grew up with servants so she did not do the housework and she hardly did any cooking. All she did was sit, knit, and embroider. And there she was using those fancy words.

In December, when I realized that I was expecting again, I said, "I am leaving. I cannot stay here anymore." Alfredo kept hesitating. Finally, I told him that either we move to the villa or we leave. Not one day passed without some sort of a discussion or argument about it. But we had no money to buy the furniture for the villa.

His parents had sold some land in order to build the villa. But the villa had cost no more than a quarter of what they had sold the land for. There was lots of money left over. The oldest daughter always went to ask the father for a half a million lire or a million lire at a time. To some of the children he gave money, under the table, but to the others, nothing. He gave us the food and the roof over our head but I was working for it. I took care of three people plus the children. When he bought food he did not think about my children's breakfast. I had to go out and buy them milk.

Alfredo had to go to his father, "Papa, we came to a decision. We are going to move into the villa but I need one million lire to buy furniture." My father-in-law did not need any money, he was working. The house was already paid for.

Alfredo said he just wanted to borrow the money, not like the others who asked for it for good.

His father made no reply.

Then Alfredo said, "If you cannot give me the money then I have no other choice but to go back to Canada."

His father finally said, "I cannot help you."

Of course, Alfredo felt very bad about this. It took a few more months of arguing before he took any action. One day we had a particularly bad argument.

We were in the bedroom and I said, "I cannot take it anymore." I walked out and left him sitting there. I was very upset.

I joined my mother-in-law in the front room. A few minutes later Alfredo marched across the room and, without even looking at any of us, loudly said, "I am going to the travel agency."

Suddenly, I felt calm inside.

Michele

I NEVER WANTED TO LEAVE. As soon as I got on the boat at Naples I got sick. Half an hour after the boat had left the harbour I demanded that we turn back. My mother kept shaking her head and telling me we were going to see my father. But I hardly knew my father so that was not a convincing argument. I wanted to see the captain but I could not move I was so sick. All I could do was watch the land disappear, Italy was moving away from me. It was getting smaller and smaller.

Canada was supposed to be a rich land but the train which took us to Toronto was certainly no indication of any richness. It was a train powered by coal. In Italy all the trains were electric, which was a much cleaner process. As we were going through forests I saw cars abandoned in the snow, in the middle of nowhere. To me this was the first indication of the country's wealth. My god, people here are so rich they just abandon their cars, they don't need them anymore for whatever purpose. Abandoned cars were scattered along this vast countryside. In Italy I had studied the geography of Canada and I knew about the vastness of the country but studying it and seeing it were very different. To be moving through all this open space was marvellous, it was a marvellous sense of freedom.

Everyone on the boat from Italy had transferred to the train, and this herd of people descended on Union Station. At Union Station we found another mass of people. The whole place was filled with people, like the inhabitants of a small Italian town squeezed into an enormous waiting room. It seemed to take forever before we located our family.

In Italy I was used to having my own room. Naturally, I was expecting the same thing here. Instead I found myself having to sleep in the hallway. All of a sudden I had no room.

Once I stepped out of the house I did not understand what people were saying. A Canadian family lived next door to us. They had a daughter about my age and for the first two weeks all

I could say to her was, "Hi." I would actually go out of the house when I saw her leaving just to be able to say, "Hi," to her.

Our other next door neighbour was Italian and their son became a good friend of mine. He had already been here about five or six months, he was a wise kid by this time, he even knew a few words of English.

I started going to public school which was not far from our house. I found other Italian kids in the school but those who had come two years earlier, or those who had been born here, felt that the recent arrivals were taking their rightful place. It was difficult to find a niche to fit into. To top off my discomfort, I was placed two years behind. Physically I fit in because I wasn't very tall, but I felt cheated, I felt I had lost two years of my life.

The teachers wrote words on the blackboard that were meaningless to me. The only things I could decipher were the numbers. When it came to arithmetic it was easy because I had studied all that in Italy. After a few weeks a buddy was assigned to me. Every day she took me to the library and read aloud from the grade one books. She tried to get me to read the words after her. Once a day she gave me a spelling test, but just the word, there was no meaning attached. I kept saying these words, these strange sounds, without knowing their purpose. As soon as I said a word I forgot it. Sometimes there were pictures in the book and the girl would point to a lamb and repeat the word several times to me and then I had to repeat it with her. I felt like a child who was just learning to talk and I was already eleven years old. It was humiliating.

I heard the words Wop and Dago regularly. It did not take me long to realize that these words were meant to be derogatory and I was very upset. I felt that in some way I was being dismissed. I was not considered an individual, I was lumped together with a group, a group I hardly even knew. I was forced into a defensive position.

One day I went to school wearing shorts. This was what I always wore in Italy. Here none of the kids had shorts. When I got to school one of the guys kept looking me up and down and laughing. I was furious. Another Italian kid was with me and I said to him, "Watch this, the next time he looks me up and down he is going to fly." The kid once more bent down his head and I didn't even wait for him to look up again, I just gave it to him.

The first expression I learned to use was, "I'll throw a punch and break your dents." In Italian teeth translated as *dente*. Since I had taken two years of Latin in Italy, I thought the word might come from the Latin.

School was a constant fight. Fighting became our main source of physical activity. Otherwise things seemed to slow down. The games kids played here were different from what I was used to. I had never seen baseball. It was funny to watch a guy trying to hit a ball with a stick. There was very little I could get involved in. I spent ten or fifteen minutes in the school yard after school and then I went home. In Italy I was told to be home at a certain time, if not one of my brothers came to look for me. Here I just went home. There was nothing to do.

Less than a year later we moved and I changed schools. I found myself in a Catholic school where a very high percentage of students were Italian, therefore I fit in much more. We played a lot of the games I was used to back home. These were much more physical games than the Canadian kids used to play. Some of them involved running around and jumping over two or three guys at the same time. Of course, the teachers were very upset with us because they were afraid we would hurt each other. They didn't understand the Italian culture and what kids did back in Italy. They just said that these strange games should not be played because you can hurt yourself and we were stopped from playing them.

Sundays were spent going to church and visiting family and friends of my parents, or attending religious processions. Almost every Saturday or Sunday there was a religious procession in Little Italy. The statue of the saint was carried around the streets just like back home. That whole tradition was transplanted here. The older people would stop the men carrying the saint and they attached $10 or $20 to the robe of the statue and then the statue would proceed. That was fun. There were celebrations every weekend.

In Italy, I had been an altar boy and I was very involved with the church. My mother, of course, expected me to continue my church activities here. I found the priest in our local church to be a very gentle man. He took an interest in you and he was much more approachable than the one I was used to in Italy. The priest here gave me more space to think. He also moved slower which allowed me to stop and talk to him, he was not always in a hurry.

To me the priest in Italy always seemed like a giant of a man, his very stature imposed his authority and he was very strict and severe. There was no questioning. I did not have discussions about religion. I attended catechism classes which I learned by rote and I served the mass.

I was approaching my teens and I began to feel that I was becoming a man. The teachers at school were nuns and they were encouraging us to talk to the priest about personal problems or questions we might have. They also suggested talking to our parents but I never felt comfortable talking to my father about such things. The confessional was the only place I could get any advice. The priest always pointed me in the direction of being a good Catholic and a good citizen. It was certainly comforting to know he was there even though his advice was not always helpful. My body continued to change and the embarrassment of that change was not erased by advice.

I felt a certain acceptance when I switched to the Catholic school but I was constantly reminded that there was another world outside of school and church which did not totally accept me. I had a part-time job delivering for a drugstore. Sometimes I would deliver to a home and the lady who opened the door treated me with an incredible coldness. She would just grab the bag out of my hand, shove her money at me, and slam the door in my face.

I went to the Post Office one day to get a stamp to mail a letter to Italy for my parents. I said to the lady behind the counter, "A 15 cent stamp."

She insisted I say, "May I have a 15 cent stamp, please?" I was embarrassed to no end. She kept insisting I had to say, "Please." She would not give me the stamp unless I repeated her exact phrase. In our family the words please and thank you were not used. It was a matter of course that we did certain things for one another and we did not have to say please and thank you. So this lady's insistence was totally incomprehensible to me.

At the end of grade eight we moved from Little Italy to the suburbs. The high school I attended in Etobicoke was totally Anglo-Saxon, there were no Italian kids. I withdrew into myself and my relationship with my peers was practically nonexistent.

I wore a tie and suit going to grade nine. The other kids wore jeans and of course I didn't even own a pair of jeans. The kids put Brylcreme on their hair, not a hair was out of place. I was a stranger to that. There was a whole fad in the fifties that I was not a part of.

Students would get together for games and I would feel left out. I was not picked to be on teams to play football, probably because of my size but I interpreted it as not being picked because I was Italian. I spent grade nine with my school books. At the end of my first year in that school I won a scholarship which helped to pay for a new TV.

Schooling was what I had to do. From the very beginning it was expected of me to pass and do well in school. When I brought home a good report card there was no praise, I was expected to bring home a good report card. Of course, I should be doing well. Studying was supposed to be my business. If I was not doing well in school then they would be concerned. My other brothers were expected to do other things. When Roberto came here he went to work with my father. Roberto never cared for school so going to work was expected behaviour. He should be going to work with his father because he did not do well in school. But if I missed a day in school, by God, the roof would cave in.

My parents retained their links to Little Italy. They continued to go shopping there and to attend church on Dundas Street.

I joined the local church. My mother called it the English Catholic church, and I participated in the choir and the youth club. I got along very well with the priest and we had great discussions. I was going through a phase where I was beginning to question everything. I began to question some of the dogmas of the faith. Was there any need to go to church on Sundays? How could the birth of Jesus have occurred from a virgin? Miracles? Perhaps they were possible if you had faith. The priest said that without faith there were no miracles. But I never got what I considered to be satisfactory answers. I wanted to order my world and how could I believe in something that did not have a rational base?

When I was down in Little Italy finishing grade eight I had no problem with my identity, I was surrounded by Italian kids. I was very comfortable being in that community. But it was obvious that I did not fit into Etobicoke. I was the weird kid on the block.

My parents grew vegetables in the garden. None of the other parents did that. I was always asking my father, "Why are you taking away the grass to grow vegetables?" Everyone had manicured lawns, little shrubs, flowers. I was acutely aware of these differences and I suffered a great deal. I wanted to be accepted, I wanted to belong. And it was my Italian-ness that kept me apart. I had to try to erase, or at least to submerge, my true identity. I had to create a new self for this new milieu. I had to become one of them. It was a question of survival.

In my teenage years I made every attempt possible to abandon who I was and where I came from. I had to become indistinguishable. I felt I should not disclose my identity because that would mean rejection. Of course, by this time I had absolutely no accent. I started to pronounce my name with an English accent. I was lucky, with a name like Mike Pace I could easily become anonymous. Some of the other Italians were not so lucky.

I was living at home physically but mentally breaking away. My parents never came to the school for parent-teacher night. I did not want them to come. They would have only caused me a great deal of embarrassment. After all, they could not even speak English. I began to refuse to speak Italian. I rejected my culture. I wanted very little to do with Italian friends.

At first I had gone to weddings with my parents and other Italian functions. As I grew older, I broke away from that circuit. I had other interests. I no longer had time to go. Of course, when I could not go to these functions my mother would say, "Well, you know that's a sign of disrespect, we have to go and show our respect."

At that time, the image of Italians was that they did not speak English, they were uneducated, menial labourers living in a group by themselves. I adopted all the stereotype images the Anglo-Saxon world had of Italians. I had violent disagreements with my family. While they were saying we should keep our language and culture alive, I was saying rubbish, become a Canadian. I was perpetuating an act of discrimination, but when it came to my English-speaking friends I withdrew from such conversations. I did not want to expose myself.

At the same time my mother was also undergoing a change. She had to adjust to the way of life in Canada. She had one foot in the old world and did not want to put the other foot in the new world, her energies were focussed on retaining the traditions.

My parents also felt isolated in the suburbs. I had to go and do the shopping for them. I fought with them all the time, saying I did not have time for such things. They also asked me to write letters to Italy for them. My mother could write but very badly, her words ran together and it took her forever to finish one letter. If a letter came from Italy she would say, "Michele, come and read me the letter." Then, "Michele, let's sit down and answer the letter." I would hate that with a passion.

Whenever my father did not like something I was doing he would say, "Aha. *Sta diventando Canadese*" – "He is becoming a Canadian." He was suggesting I was different from them, I was no longer part of them. I heard this when I refused to go to church on Sundays. I didn't even like spaghetti. My father would often repeat this phrase when he had friends over. It was his way of apologizing to his friends for my behaviour, for my refusal to attend Italian functions.

I was becoming a Canadian. I wanted to eat white bread. I asked my mother to buy the pre-sliced white bread. Before I had to go to school with these big sandwiches made of Italian bread while everyone else had their little white sandwiches. During lunch they would look at my sandwich in a very strange way. They had never seen anything like it. My sandwiches had either a strong-smelling cheese or mortadella. The other kids had their odourless Kraft cheese slices. So, not only did my sandwich look different from everyone else's, it also smelled different.

I developed a taste for hamburgers and coke. To completely round off my assimilation, I even got a summer job in a Coca-Cola factory. After a couple of summers of working there I quickly lost my taste for coke.

When I started going out with girls I didn't ever go out with an Italian girl. In school I was going out with non-Italians. I devoted my time to socializing and, of course, my school work suffered. I was so busy fitting in that by grade twelve my marks had dropped. It was usually Frank who kept after me to do well in school. He was always the one to check my homework. But after he moved out of the house his influence was gone and I felt free to play. My parents never asked to check my work. Even if I had shown them what I had done in school, they would not have been able to read it. By grade thirteen I was so involved in all sorts of school activities that I had no time to study. I failed miserably.

The second time around there were other things which distracted me. I sat down to study for exams and instead found myself writing poetry and thinking about my Italian-ness. I was sitting in front of the books but my thoughts had nothing to do with the coming exam.

The poetry I was writing dealt with my origins. I was putting down in poetry form the struggle that was going on inside of me. I was describing myself as a monster, a cold-blooded monster as opposed to the sociable, happy-go-lucky, singing Italian. I felt that Italians were more sociable people and my life had somehow been detached from that identity. I was becoming cold, almost English cold, I was comparing myself to a cold fish. I did not like the transformation. I had succeeded in being accepted, I was part of the crowd, the Anglo-Saxon crowd. But after the acceptance had been achieved, I stopped to take stock. Yes, my Anglo-Saxon friends accepted me. But did I accept myself?

At the end of high school I was beginning to have second thoughts about what I was doing to myself as an individual. I was attempting to escape the embarrassment of discrimination. I had no accent, nonetheless I was not English-born, I was not of Anglo-Catholic background and no matter what I did, people would know about it or they would find out about it. And why was I hiding it?

For the first three years I never invited friends to my house. The school was much closer to their homes. Later on, in high school, I brought a couple of Anglo-Saxon friends home. But only after I had been over at their house many times. Of course, I did not want them to come to my house at first. Again, I was afraid of rejection. But my fears never materialized. The first time they came, they felt right at home. My father was good at making people feel comfortable. I realized there was no need to feel ashamed of my parents.

I had wanted to go to university after high school but my marks were not high enough. Instead I entered Teacher's College. Most of the papers I was writing dealt with immigrants, how schools should be adjusting to the kids. Now, not only did I accept who I was but I was saying that the process I had gone through should not be imposed on anyone. It was not a healthy process. I was openly saying that the situation had to be changed. The community and the institutions should adapt to the people and not the other way around.

When I started to teach I asked for a school where there were a large number of immigrant kids. The first day of class I was very tough and stern with them. I had learned that in Teacher's

College. Once I grabbed the flag pole, there was no flag on it, and said, "In this classroom you do three things – work, work, and work!" As I talked I was energetically swinging the pole around and the metal top of the pole just flung out and away from the stick and went straight in the blackboard. There was a hole in the blackboard for the rest of the year. Some of the other things I had learned in Teacher's College were equally useful.

I taught grade six. The majority of the students in my class were Italian and I discovered that the ethnic kids were about two years behind their grade level in reading, writing, and arithmetic. I set out to determine why that happened.

Teachers complained about the learning ability of some of the children. One would say, "They are intelligent and alert. I don't understand what is going on. Why are they not doing better?" Another teacher might say, "Well, look at their background. All they speak at home is Italian. What do you expect?"

This type of comment would really anger me. The point was that the school looked after the needs of kids who were fluent in the English language, kids who were not fluent suffered. Teachers expected children to have a certain amount of knowledge of English nursery rhymes and poems, but the immigrant kids did not have this. Naturally, the teachers thought that these students came from a deprived background. After all, what child does not know, "Mary Had a Little Lamb"? Since this basic knowledge was missing, the teachers could not expect these foreign students to do very well. I always had arguments about this with the teachers. Just because the background of a child was different, it did not mean that it was a deprived background.

I noticed the Italian parents were not coming to the school to find out about their kids and to give some kind of input to the teachers. They were not even being encouraged to come. The school only paid lip service to the community. "Yes, we would like Italian parents to come to the school, we would like to find out more about their home life and the kinds of things they consider important in the school." However, there was no real attempt to get the parents there and to listen to them.

In my first two years of teaching I became involved in actively reaching out to parents, encouraging them to come to school to meet the teachers. This was doubly difficult. First, Italian parents felt that the ultimate authority lay with the teacher. Why would the teachers be interested in their opinion? The second problem was the teachers. They resisted the participation of ethnic parents. The attitude was, what could these uneducated people possibly contribute?

The teachers looked upon me as an oddity. Here was someone who wanted them to do things they were not comfortable doing. I found an ally in the principal. He announced that in two months there was going to be parents' night. And everyone prepared for parents' night.

I organized a network of interpreters for the teachers and the parents. Language should not be a barrier to communication. If you really want to communicate, it is first of all important how the person is accepted, how a person is made to feel. The non-verbal communication can easily transmit to another person whether they are made to feel welcome or not, and if not they are going to just want to get the hell out of there. The language itself is only important to give information.

The first parents' night was a great success. There were teachers who were afraid of the experience because they never had the experience before. But some teachers became very supportive.

One of the things the parents complained about was the lack of discipline in the school and why didn't the kids get more home-work. The kids would go home after school, the parents would ask what they had done that day and the reply would be, "Well, we went out to play, we saw a film, we went on a field trip." And the parents were thinking, "What the hell is all this stuff, this is not education." The parents did not view field trips as an education. This was too much fun. The discipline back in Italy was that you sat with this book in this corner for a certain period of time. If you did not, then there were going to be physical conse-quences. Of course, those kinds of things were totally alien to the philosophy of teaching here. But they were crucial to the educational system in Italy. Parents told teachers that if their chil-dren did not behave they should just slap them. They gave the teacher permission to physically punish their children because, if they were not punished for bad behavior, then where were the consequences for that behavior? The Italian point of view was that undesirable behavior had to be hammered out of the child.

Also, there was too much choice according to the parents. What do you mean a child can choose to write a story now or to write a story later? In a classroom some children did math while others did artwork. Children did various things rather than having the whole class focused on one subject. The students were given a choice. It was hard for parents to come to grips with that. How can a child choose what to read when? You as a teacher are supposed to tell them what to do.

The Italians were considered the salt of the earth, warm and friendly but no education. As a result of that stereotype the expectations were so low, the students were not given a chance. They were two or three years behind in reading and therefore they must be dumb. It had not occurred to any of the teachers that perhaps something was wrong with the educational system instead of the learning ability of the student. Italian kids were automatically streamed into technical schools without being given a choice. I wanted to do something about that.

I did a lot of research and came up with the idea that it would be good for these kids to be taught in their mother tongue with the English language introduced gradually. During junior kindergarten almost everything would be conducted in the mother tongue and by grade eight they would have only about three-quarters of an hour in the mother tongue. By that time the kids would be bilingual anyway. Initially, all the basic skills would be taught in the mother tongue and there would be a direct transfer of those skills to the English language.

The teachers were against it. It threatened their jobs. They felt they would have to be replaced by teachers who spoke another language. They were afraid that immigrant teachers were going to be hired to do their jobs. Only the status quo would ensure the continuation of their positions. But if the teacher does not understand the cultural needs of the student, then that teacher does not understand the child.

Finally, it was agreed that in junior and senior kindergarten the teacher would conduct the program in the mother tongue of the students but by grade one students had to go into an all-English program. This was the only part of the proposal that the trustees passed. As far as I was concerned, this was the first step.

After two years of teaching I decided to go back full-time to university and I continued to teach at night. I wanted to get my BA because I thought that having a degree would give me more of an influence on the teachers in the schools. I also wanted to show that I was an educated Italian, they were not all construction workers. I was considered a rarity. In those days there were very few Italians in the teaching profession and the ones that existed had been born here. I met one of these teachers, his name was Italian but he did not speak the language at all, he was totally Anglicized.

In university I invited friends over to the house to study. After they left my mother would say, "Watch out for those Canadians, be careful, I don't like them." To her, non-Italians were Canadians. My mother believed in a strong family unit and she felt that could not happen if you mixed with people who were not from the same background.

I had non-Italian friends who tried to make me feel that there was something wrong with me because I was still living at home after the age of twenty. From my teens on I never felt that I was impeded from doing the things that I thought I should be doing. There were no restrictions on me. I did not feel I had to go away from home to get more freedom. Some people sought their independence by leaving home, but I already felt independent.

When I went back to university I started to become involved in politics at the organizational level as a volunteer. I voted for the first time in 1968 and carefully examined what each of the parties stood for. I finally voted for the New Democratic Party. I considered the other parties to stand for the status quo, they were not interested in changing anything. Politically, I came to terms with where the ethnic groups were in relationship to society as a whole. I became more and more involved in politics. There were certain things I wanted to do educationally but I was bound by an existing law which I considered outdated. Only politically could I make real changes.

I began to feel proud of being Italian. In university I took Italian literature. I also took Italian lessons because I wanted to learn the language as well as I could. When I started to get involved in the community some of my Italian friends said I was not so sure of my Italian. I had lost a good deal of it. In order to express my thoughts clearly, I would switch into English. But without speaking Italian I could not have a close contact with the community.

I went back to Italy for the first time in my last year of university. I took a tour organized by the Italian Club. Even though I was Italian-born I had never been to Florence or Venice or Milan or Sienna. My life up to the age of eleven was strictly within a ten-mile radius of my home town. I did not really know Italy.

At one point I left everyone in Rome and took the train to Pratola. The kids I had gone to school with were no longer there, they had gone up north. Everything that I had thought so grand and beautiful now seemed like little toys. The house I grew up in, as far as I was concerned was like a palace, and it turned out to be a little dinky place. Outside the house there was a place where my mother used to do her washing and I used to swim, so you would think it was quite big but it was no bigger than two by four. My memories over the fifteen years just made everything into giants, or as a kid I remembered them to be giants and I kept exactly that same view till I saw it again as an adult.

I only spent a few days in Pratola but it was important for me to fit in, to be considered part of that community. But the people knew right away I was not a local. Those people had eyes like foxes. I walked into one place and asked about a pair of shoes. This guy knew his shoes. He said, "You either come from the United States or from Canada."

I said, "How do you know?" At this point I was purposely speaking the dialect.

He said, "Because those shoes that you have on are shoes made in Italy but made for export to Canada or the u.s. Those shoes go no other place." He just had to look at my shoes and I was branded.

Florence was a place where I could have stayed for a long time. It fitted more into what I had read and studied. Seeing all the original paintings and sculptures created a great sense of awe. I did not want to leave the place. I vowed that I would return and stay there for a few years. I thought I could teach English for a living. But that was just a dream which never materialized. Once I left Italy behind that dream gradually faded.

After I got my degree I returned to teaching on a full-time basis and I continued to push for programs which reached out to the community. We formed various work groups in the school. In one of these groups there was a teacher called Phyllis. She was small, beautiful, with delicate features and I was attracted to her right away. A couple of days later I said to a friend of mine, "That's the girl I am going to marry." At that time, I had not even spoken to her.

Gradually, a group of us in school became friends. Phyllis and a good friend of hers, Connie, who was Italian, were part of the group. We often went out together. I kept asking Phyllis to go out with me alone and she always refused. Finally I asked her why. She told me that Connie had built up a whole relationship in her head about me. I was floored because I never thought that I gave her any signals in that way. I had kissed her on the cheek once when I dropped her off at home after a party. I never had any intention of getting serious. But that must have begun a whole line of thinking in her head.

I went and talked to her about our relationship and explained that it was just a professional and friendly one. I certainly did not want her to go on feeling that somehow I felt differently inside from what I was showing on the outside. Perhaps her feelings for me were because I was Italian. Perhaps she thought, here he is, Italian, and I'm Italian and therefore it's natural that we should get together. I could not allow her to continue to think that way, to hold on to a dream that would never come true.

When I started to go out with Phyllis her first concern was Connie because they were such good friends. She was afraid she might be betraying her.

We went out for five years prior to making a decision. The major stumbling block was the difference in our religion. Phyllis was Jewish.

Both my mother and father loved Phyllis. The problem occurred when I said, "Of course, you realize I am not going to get married in a church and, of course, you realize that Phyllis is not going to become a Roman Catholic." They always presumed, well, you are Roman Catholic, you will get married and she will also become a Roman Catholic. If Phyllis had converted, as far as my parents were concerned it would have been perfect.

Her parents reacted in exactly the same way. If I had converted, it would have been no problem. It was pretty difficult for her family to accept me as a non-Jew. Her mother is very religious.

At the beginning, her mother had thought that because I was not a strongly religious Catholic I would probably become Jewish. But the reason that I was not a practising Roman Catholic was exactly the reason why I would not be a practising Jew.

Personally, I do not see the value of religion per se. I think it is an imposition on human beings. Religion says to society that if you do not follow certain rules then certain things will befall you, you are going to be damned. Back in the Middle Ages and prior to that that may have been one way to control people. But as we move on, and as society becomes more sophisticated,

I think that those types of controlling techniques will just die. Human contact, respect for people's dignity, mutual understanding, such things are much more important. These are religious and spiritual values which I hold very dear but they are not necessarily confined to a particular religion. Confining such values to specific religions actually breeds discrimination, which I totally abhor.

FIRST GENERATION

Franco

AFTER I GAVE UP MY RADIO SHOW I started a live talk show on TV. One hour cost me $900 and we were allowed twelve minutes of commercials. But we were selling at least twenty minutes through the sneaky formula I learned from my radio show. Again, after a couple of years, I was only behind the scenes and I hired someone to work for me.

I gave over my hour on TV for free to try to get relief funds for the 1967 flood in Florence. I had heard about a telethon from someone but I didn't know what it was exactly. I inquired and found out. I asked the telephone company if they would provide me with seven lines in my house on College Street. They gave me the lines for free. I hired seven girls to answer the phones and the door was left open. This went on for two Sundays. The money kept coming in. One Sunday morning we collected $42,000 in cash. The girls called me at the station and I announced on TV that Mr So and So had already pledged $20, who is going to compete with him? Someone else pledged $25 and I announced their name. It was very salable, especially for the ordinary person, it was exciting to hear your own name on TV.

The flood had created a lot of damage to the works of art in Florence. The money we raised could help to repair them. There were about five or six people organizing all this and we all worked very hard canvassing for funds. Finally four of us went to Florence to present the money. We took one million dollars to Italy and nine hundred cows. The government of Canada gave us $500,000 but they could not give us the money, we had to buy something here and deliver it to the country in need. We bought nine hundred cows and we had to hire a ship to transport them to Florence. Two cows were born on the way and two died.

In Florence, when we went to present the money and the cows, we were given a special dinner. All the press were invited and my relatives in Pratola watched me on TV. The mayor of Florence presented me with the bronze wild boar. This was something very special.

By now I had already been to Italy three times and through my contacts at the Canadian Embassy I knew a lot of people in Rome. But having gone to Florence the way I did created a greater circle of connections. Part of what I had achieved was a result of the people I was associating with, I could not have done it alone. I had to adapt myself to the new class of people I was now involved with. At the beginning I was a little uncomfortable. In a certain way I was prepared to be looked down upon. I tried to put myself in their shoes and my foot was much smaller. At first their shoes were too big for me but in a short time I succeeded in coming close to filling them. It surprised even me.

In Italy, in order to move in certain circles, you have to have manners and education. You could have all the money in the world but the doors are closed to you if you don't have the right papers. A person without an education would never succeed in reaching a position of power, he would be stopped halfway. Here you have more room. You just need ability and a certain knowledge of the public.

In Italy all you have to do is open your mouth to say something and people know right away where you come from and what sort of education you have had. Italy has thousands of dialects. People could hardly understand each other when they went from one town to another. It was easy for Italians with education to judge someone with no education because good education is always in standard Italian. When you meet someone for the first time you have to talk standard Italian. If you speak in dialect you are judged to be uneducated.

The northern part of Italy was always much more exposed to what was happening in the world than the southern part. In the south, people were born in one place and died in the same place without knowing what was around them. How could such a person speak standard Italian or carry on a conversation about anything else but the little things which surround him, like the goats or the dog or the cow? Today even the south is exposed to what is happening because of television. But the old prejudices of the north against the south still remain.

Here you cannot judge people in the same way. Here it is very acceptable to speak in dialect. I would not expect a person to speak any other language than his own dialect. More than three-quarters of the people who came here had no education back home. Of course, here, they expected to be professors. I had some very bad experiences with people who had recently arrived. As soon as they had a couple of dollars in their pockets they became authorities. They thought they could do whatever they wanted without following the rules. But when I spoke to them in Italian, in two seconds I knew they had no education.

I found that it was much easier to communicate with the educated class. With the less-educated class I had to sell myself first, I had to show them what they could get from me. Educated people did not need that, they could size you up quickly and sense a potential for a good relationship or a profitable association. It was very easy to become friends with them. I met a man in the Canadian Embassy in Rome. In a few years he became my best friend, he asked me to be his daughter's godfather.

Now I have friends everywhere, I know people in all levels of society, people from the Vatican, from Parliament, and other professionals. I started to get people in Italy interested in investing in Canada. I brought quite a bit of money from Italy to Toronto. Everyone has always made money with me.

Through the Canadian Embassy in Rome I met a lot of politicians. Every time I went to Italy they met me at the airport, they took me around, they put me on TV and my relatives in Pratola watched me. Some of these politicians wanted to come to Canada to raise money. I helped to raise $7,000 for a politician who came to visit me from Rome. He needed the money to buy votes. There is a market over there, each vote is 1,000 lire, it is all commercialized, like selling potatoes. It's a shame, you almost don't feel like being Italian. I also helped to advertise their party among the Italian people here, to persuade the Italian community to vote for them.

The people I associate with are much more educated than me. Our social life has been quite high. I have tried to take my wife everywhere. We have been to dinners with ministers. We have always appeared in public arm in arm, but I was always very, very uncomfortable because I did not know what would happen in the next two seconds. I would be talking to a few people in a small group and my wife would come over and start talking without first listening to what was being said. She would just start talking nonsense and I would be shaking. She would go on and on and she would not know what the hell she was talking about. I didn't want my wife to look like an ass. If my wife looked like an ass that was a reflection on me. These people would talk about geography or history and she would not even know the meaning of such words. If she was asked something her answer would be totally inappropriate because she had not listened to the question. She didn't speak English very well either, she just got along. These people did not say anything, they just smiled. But I knew what was going on inside my stomach.

I have never insulted my wife in public. When she talked about things she had no knowledge of I would sometimes gently kick her under the table. Then when we went home she would start grunting, "Ah, ah, ah, you didn't want me to talk. You think I am stupid."

"You interfere, you throw yourself in certain discussions and you don't even know the first thing about it."

"You did not want me there."

"That's not true."

"Why did you kick me?"

"Because you are my wife. I do not know if I love you, but I think I care about you. We have children together. I don't want you to look like an ass and at the same time to make me look like an ass. You were saying things that had nothing to do with what other people were talking about. Do you think they are stupid? They are not, that is why I was trying to stop you."

We often got together with some friends who were very well educated. One of the wives had a university degree yet she hardly said anything, she sat there like a saint. I would tell my wife, "Look at her, she barely says anything and you can hardly read and write. Can't you keep quiet when others talk?" But my wife was there talking non-stop. I tried to tell her, "People will think more highly of you if you don't talk." But she could not understand.

I have had little education but I have taken a few courses at York University in commercial law and I have been reading books all my life. I also have enough experience of the world that I can deal with people on almost any level. But my wife has had a limited experience of life so it is normal she would have difficulty coping with the conversation of professional people.

I have tried to help my wife. She was never interested in dressing. If I would see a dress in a store that I thought would look good on her I would tell her to take a look. I would even go down there when she tried it on.

But my wife is arrogant. She will not accept anything, yet she is afraid of everything. I would leave at 8:30 in the morning and come back at 7:30 or 8:00 at night and sometimes she would be screaming and throwing things at me when I came in. I could have started a store with all the things she has destroyed. When a woman cannot cope at the same level as her husband she becomes hysterical. And she would do anything to bring him down, to humiliate him. That makes her feel a little more comfortable.

Then my wife started to withdraw from public life. She had complexes about being too fat or not being nice-looking. To me she was nice-looking, she lost the figure she used to have but I didn't care if she was big or small, she was my wife, she should come with me. She was the mother of my children.

The more complexes she developed about her looks the less she took care of herself. I did not like that. People need to take good care of themselves. Get dressed at night when I come home, don't let me see you sloppy. Don't spend your whole afternoon talking to your three or four friends, criticizing this and that. I didn't like her friends because I didn't think they were people on our level.

Her father had died and her mother came to live with us. That was probably where I made my mistake. When you argue with your wife, just you and her, you can go for two or three days without talking and then you have to get together because you can't live in the same house like strangers. When her mother came along she felt, "I don't need to talk to you, I don't need you, I can talk to my mother." It was very bad. When we had an argument she said, "My mother is on my side. We are right and you are wrong."

My mother-in-law is a very intelligent and beautiful lady. My wife used to say that I was in love with her mother because we respected each other very much. Of course, when she arrived it did not take her long to see what was happening. The only thing my mother-in-law told me was that I had to be patient.

I never involved my parents in this. Only my mother as a mother. My father wasn't in a position to give me the right advice. There was a confrontation between my wife and mother once. My wife complained that I was only acting for my own good, not for the good of the family, and I had other women in my life. My mother simply said, "I know my son because I made him.

He grew up in my house, I know his sentiments and I know his education. He came to Canada because he wanted to achieve something." Then my mother said, straight to her face, "And you don't deserve my son." That was it, boom. I think the mother is the first one in your life who cares about you, more than anything else. No matter how many sisters, brothers, or uncles you have, the mother is still the mother.

Of course, I thought of divorce. But in the Italian community the moment you divorce your wife you are isolated. I know people who were successful businessmen and as soon as they left their wives they were finished. My business would die if I would divorce, half of my clients are Italian.

When I told my mother I was thinking of divorce she got very upset. She said, "If you want to take ten years off my life then do it."

There is no family without a woman. The woman keeps the family together, the family belongs to a woman. The man can provide, the man can be a king or he can be an image outside. But if he comes home and there is no woman, even if there is supper on the table, there is no family with affection and unity. Children will never grow up in the same way without a mother. It is the mother who educates the children. The father comes home, eats, and then maybe reads the papers. It is the mother who says, "Don't answer back to your father."

Sometimes she loses control for nothing, she screams for nothing. All of us try to help the best we can. If she does something or if she starts screaming, we don't say anything, we let her talk, let her get it off her chest, that's it. Twenty years ago it was not like that. I was still young, I got excited because she was my wife. I hated to see her waste time on nothing, on silly worries. She had all the opportunities in the world to be a happy lady. She has a nice family, we have a good business going, she has money, she has everything but she has refused it, she has closed a little door inside herself.

She has her own room and I have my own room. If I have to go in by any chance, I knock on the door before I enter. Physically, she is very cold, I don't think she misses anything. I have had other experiences and I can tell the difference. You can feel when a person is there, you feel it. But she doesn't have it. I can't force it.

Naturally, other women came into the picture. In the Italian papers there was an article about all the married men having mistresses and they blamed the wives for this. The wives let themselves go, they have a greater difficulty in adjusting.

I live my own life the best I can with my children and work very hard. You cannot expect everything from life. We live under the same roof. We talk sometimes about our problems, not personal problems, problems in the family. When it comes to money she has her own account, she can write all the cheques she wants, she has all the credit cards, I never question what she buys. She goes bowling with the women on Tuesdays. She goes on special diets where she loses a lot of weight very fast and then she gains it all back in ten days. She has been doing that for years and years. I don't care anymore.

Perhaps it is my fault and I have not been close enough to the family but I have taken my children with me wherever I could. When they were young they never missed an Ice Capades or an Exhibition. I took them to Disneyland. My children are my great pride, particularly Patrizia who is studying to be a lawyer. She is also devoting a great deal of time to the New Democratic Party. She has recently become very political, it is all Michele's influence. She goes canvassing for him, she goes into the riding office to lick envelopes. We always get into arguments about politics. I told her that I particularly resent the New Democratic Party because they could at least have the guts to call themselves by the proper name, they are a socialist party.

Each party has to present a flag, it is normal. But I do not believe in the colour of the flag, I believe in the individual. I have friends in the Liberal Party and in the Conservative Party, not many in the NDP except Michele. I am a Conservative in Toronto and a Liberal in Ottawa. When I vote, I naturally vote for my brother. But I don't believe in politics.

At one time politicians were an asset. The financial contributions you made to their campaigns you could get back three times over in favours. But today they are a liability because, if you give them something, the next day it is all over the front page of the paper.

When Michele told me he wanted to enter politics I tried to discourage him. I do not believe there are people who truly want to help others without an ulterior motive. I have never seen such a thing. Michele doesn't agree. I tell him, "Wanting to work for the community is very admirable but in my experience, no matter what you do, you can never please the public." We are always arguing about this. I believe in politics you have to be an actor. You have to smile while you hear complaints day and night. You have to smile at everyone even if you have a stomach-ache. You always have to say yes, even if you think no. How can you cope with that sort of life?

I have never believed in politicians because I know there is always someone behind them. Politicians are put in place by the people who pay the highest price. Like in the early days, in Pratola, where people with the highest bid carried the Madonna della Libera. What a person says means nothing, it all depends on who pays the bill and he is the boss, not the one who stands up there.

With money you can buy the muscle and the brain. That is the horrible part of life but nobody has been able to change that. The three places with the best brains are the banks, the oil companies, and the church because they can afford it.

To me religion and politics are the same thing, I put them on the same level. You sell politics and you sell religion because it is necessary. Both deal in power.

If you sell, you cannot be honest, you have to be a hypocrite and you have to smile. People don't buy the truth. I reached a point while I was selling that I had to say to myself, "I am sorry but I have to lie." I didn't like it, but the customer wants to believe that he is buying God. I try to make him believe that he is buying San Vincenzo, not God. I have gone halfway, why can't he accept that? I am intelligent enough not to say you are buying gold when you are buying wood. But when people need something, they want to believe more.

There are people who say, "Mussolini is a god."

I say, "I saw him hanging head down with his mistress. How come you saw him as a god?"

How many gods do we have in this world? Which is the right one? How many religions do we have? Which is the true one? Some worship the sun, others worship the cow, and we have Christ. Why do the Jews start their calendar a few thousand years before we do? If you want to believe one thing, you have to forget all the others. But how can you forget about all the others when you are living next door to them?

These days religion has become politics. I know a priest in Sulmona who is thirty-two years old and a communist, a well-educated agitator. He appeals to the young. I like well-educated people. When I go to Pratola I often go over to Sulmona and he comes to see me. We go for a walk and talk. Last time I saw him we had an argument.

I said, "Communism is good for a certain class of people, but for people like me it's not good. I want to be free. I don't want to work for the common good because that means I have to work for people who do not want to do any work."

He said, "You know, Franco, you really disappoint me."

"Why?"

"You are talking with the mentality of a dirty American capitalist."

Then I really gave it to him. His parents were in the U.S. working who knows how many hours a day and he was able to get a good education because of the money they sent him. Since this priest arrived in Sulmona, everyone has been voting communist, he is the one who is educating them. I told him, "You are poisoning the people. That you are a communist, fine. I respect your views as a man, not as a priest. If I would go to a woman in my town and tell her to vote communist she would tell me to go to hell. If you go to tell her the same thing, she will vote for them. You have a certain influence and you are abusing that influence. Why don't you leave the church and go into politics?"

"No," he said. "I want to stay inside because I can fight the system better."

I went for a picnic on the mountain once and saw him playing tennis with a beautiful girl. The only time he dresses like a priest is on Sunday morning, otherwise he goes around like a civilian. For the communists in the area he is a hero, every time there is a strike he is there with a flag. Most of the people in my town are farmers and he helps them in the fields. Fine, but he should not get mixed up in politics.

I hate religion and politics as institutions but not the human beings who are in them. If the priest stands up on the altar and preaches to me then I hate him, but when he comes down for a coffee and we start to talk as equals, then I like him. Just because I do not like the job that someone is doing does not mean that I have to dislike him as a human being. Some of the priests I know are the sharpest people. They are also the best actors. Perhaps politicians can beat the priests in acting, but not in manners and intelligence.

I have heard some of the best jokes from priests. Here is one. A rabbi went to visit a priest one Sunday. When he arrived, the priest was in the confessional booth. The rabbi entered the booth to say hello. The priest was still busy so he sat down to wait. One person came to the screen and said, "Father, I have committed three adulteries this week."

"Oh, son, that's no good. For punishment you have to say six Ave Marias and make a $20 contribution to the church."

Two minutes later another fellow came along and said, "Father, I have committed three adulteries this week."

"You too, son? The punishment is six Ave Marias and a $20 contribution to the church."

When the next person came to the screen the priest turned to the rabbi, "Max, Max, I have to go to the washroom. Take over, they don't know who is behind here."

The rabbi sat down and the guy in the booth began, "Father, I have committed two adulteries this past week."

The rabbi said, "Oh son, it's all right don't worry. Go and have another one because it's three for $20 this week."

I use that joke a lot.

One night, a good friend of mine was giving a party. Of course, my wife did not want to go so I ended up going alone. At the party the hostess introduced me to a woman, Maria, who was a widow. She had been born here but of Italian parents. As soon as she found out that I was an investor she wanted to talk to me. She had some money her husband had left her. As soon as I heard she was interested in investing money, I stopped everything and listened. We talked for an hour or so and I drove her home.

A week later Maria came to my office with her mother and a check for $30,000. She left me the money without even asking me what I was going to do with it. A few days later she called me to invite me for dinner. I knew she had three children but when I arrived they were not there, we were alone. She told me she was forty-two years old, she looked at least ten years younger. She was a very sharp, intelligent woman and I enjoyed her company. We talked about everything, she was even interested in my business. From that night on we saw each other regularly. I started taking her to some of the social functions I had to attend. She could talk to anybody, no matter how well-educated they were. She never interrupted and always stayed close to me. If I moved from her side she would ask where I was going. But in a very nice and caring way. It was not possessive. It was beautiful being with her. There was understanding and communication.

We went everywhere together, California, Barbados, Aruba, Italy, and always first class. I bought her a car. I gave her jewellery. Even her mother loved me. Her mother would call me in the office to tell me she had made my favourite dish. She cooked very well and when I arrived everything was there, prepared. Both the mother and Maria knew all about my marriage. There was an understanding between Maria and I, in time I was going to get a divorce and we were going to get married. We got along very well, we are both the same sign, Taurus.

But we had a lot of fights. I didn't like the way she was bringing up her seventeen-year-old daughter. She allowed her to go away on ski vacations with her boyfriend but her boyfriends kept changing. I wanted her to educate her daughter in the right way.

One night, I asked Maria, "Are you going to tell your daughter that I don't like this or should I?"

"No, you are not going to tell my daughter anything."

Since both Maria and her daughter knew that I disapproved of her going out with so many boys, the two of them would lie to me to cover up what was going on.

Maria and I were in Italy when I received a phone call in the middle of the night from Michele. My father had died. I got dressed immediately and took the first plane back home. When I saw him lying on the bed, dead, I didn't know what to do. I kissed him and just stood there. I felt half dead myself, someone had to lead me to a chair. No one could talk to me for an hour. When I lost my father, I realized I had lost something forever. You can always get another wife but you cannot get another father. If I lose a child, it would almost kill me, but I could still get another one.

The father is the first one who gives you food to grow, maybe it is not the best, maybe he does not have the best. My father talked very little to me, not because he did not care about me, but he was occupied. There is an understanding between a father and a son which does not have to be talked about or explained, it is there. It is a very strong feeling of obedience, respect, and affection. These three things are the most important in life. If you have these feelings for another individual, you are truly attached to that person. If you do not have them, you are a nobody, you are a nothing.

People growing up now do not suffer the way I suffered when I came here. They do not know how to suffer, and they know nothing about discipline. When I was growing up, supper was at eight o'clock in the evening. Nothing could justify our being away from the table. We were not allowed to sit down before my grandfather came into the room, we had to stand behind our chairs to wait for him. If you say this to the younger generation, either in Canada or in Italy, they think you are talking about the Middle Ages.

When I was eighteen you did not say no to a parent. You would never dream of contradicting your parents. Today there is no such thing. If my sons want something and I don't like it, I tell them. But I also tell them, "If you want to do it, go, please yourself." I never asked my sons to come into the business with me. Of course, I was happy they wanted to, but I did not ask them to come.

Eduardo is a real estate broker. He has two diplomas and I told him he could put them in the fireplace. Reading the book is easy. I'll take you outside and you show me how you can sell. I will sell ten before you can even sell one and I don't have a degree. I tell my son, "When you entered the school you were a donkey, and you came out a monkey."

I think Eduardo made a bad choice in a wife. She used to be my receptionist and he became infatuated with her. I told him my feelings about her before he married her. He did not listen. They are living in the house and I see what is going on between the two of them. I do not like it. She is rough and uneducated and she tells him where to go. She does not know how to respect a person and neither does she know how to be a good mother.

Two days after my fiftieth birthday I was driving over to a friend's house for coffee. That morning I had concluded a very good business deal involving an important development project. It was early afternoon on Sunday and the sun was shining. I had spent Saturday night with Maria, celebrating, she had cooked my favourite things and we finished off two bottles of champagne. We agreed that within the next two months I would talk to Filomena about a divorce and then start the proceedings. The following year Maria and I would get married.

I was going along a quiet street, listening to an Italian radio program. There was a little boy sitting on the curb and as I was about to drive past him he suddenly sprung up in front of my car. I knew I was going to hit him, there was not enough room for me to stop, so I swung the car toward the curb. As I hit the curb I felt that I had hit the boy too. I jumped out of the car and ran in front thinking that I would pick him up, regardless of anything, put him in the car and take him to the hospital. But when I got to the front of the car there was no boy. I looked under the car and he was not there. Then I looked up and saw him running like a rabbit across the park. There was an immediate sense of relief.

I continued on to my friend's house. As I was telling him what had happened I felt myself getting more and more upset and I started to sweat. I thought it must be very hot but my friend still had his sweater on. I excused myself, got up and left. For some reason I felt I should be home. On the way home I started to realize that I was having a heart attack. I continued to sweat and kept feeling my hair with my hands thinking if I stopped sweating I would get over it but I didn't.

When I got in my wife was in the kitchen and she asked me if I had lunch.

I said, "No."

"Do you want me to prepare something for you?"

I said, "No."

Knowing me, no lunch and not wanting to have lunch, something was wrong. I walked into the family room and laid down on the couch. She came in, "Don't you feel well?"

"No, not really."

"Should I call the doctor?"

"I don't think you will find him. It's Sunday."

She tried to reach him at home, he was a very close friend of mine. In ten minutes he was at the house. All he had to do was look at me, he didn't even feel me, he just looked at me and called the ambulance.

In the hospital, one of the strangest things happened to me. My wife was there and the children had come. Later I was left alone and the doctor came in. He said, "You realize you had a heart attack."

"Yes."

"You know, the first twenty-four hours are the most critical ones, so if you can get over that period of time, things should be improving. Five or six hours have already passed, try to hang in there." Then the doctor left.

I was on my own in the intensive care unit. A few minutes later the nurse came in to ask if I wanted something.

I said, "Yes, a cigarette."

She said, "I have been a nurse for twenty years, I have had people asking me for a drink, for food, for a woman, but I have never had anyone ask me for a cigarette. You are the first one. Aside from the fact that everything would blow up, where are you going to put it, in your ear?"

I had an oxygen mask and needles all over the place and I was hooked up to monitors.

Finally, I was left alone and I started to think about what the doctor had said, about the twenty-four hours. I thought, probably I will get over it but on the other hand these could be the last hours that I am here. Immediately I started to think about my family. I thought about my children and wished I would have spent a little more time with them. My wife was going to cry for the next two or three weeks but she would get over it. She would have the insurance. I reviewed who I would leave behind and all of a sudden it struck me who I would meet on the other side. I thought, I am going to face my father and grandfather and the first thing they are going to ask me is what have I done with the Pace name while I was down there. What have I done with my life? I began a methodical review of my past, thinking of the things they would approve of and the things they would disapprove of. After I had settled everything in my life my father and grandfather asked me about my brothers and sister. Then I reviewed their lives, it was an account of what each one had done with the Pace name. I told them that they had done pretty well for themselves. I wanted to assure them that they had done everything to prevent the name from being tarnished. During this accounting I was not at all scared, I was ready to accept whatever happened. I felt a serenity I could not remember ever feeling in my life before. I had a long conversation with them till I fell asleep.

I was put in a regular room and, when I started thinking about this experience and realizing that I had been on the threshold of death, I started to get scared. All sorts of other considerations came up.

For the first couple of days only your family could come and visit. The nurse came in to tell me that a woman kept asking for me and wanted very much to see me. She had told the nurse that she was part of the family but the nurse did not believe her.

The nurse asked me, "Should I let her in?"

Of course I knew who it was, from the description it could be no one else but Maria. I thought for a few seconds and then shook my head, "No, she is not family."

The doctors could find no physical reasons for my heart attack except perhaps the cigarettes and a bit of overweight. The doctors said something about muscle spasms and they wrote down the cause as stress.

I was under pressure at the time but I cannot remember a period in this country when I have not been under pressure. A doctor told me that one of my problems was that I have been so busy since the age of twenty-five that I have forgotten that another twenty-five years have gone by.

After I got out of the hospital I decided to lead a more tranquil life. The doctor told me to stay at home for four weeks. But I was still in the hospital when people from the office came in to ask questions and to get me to sign this or that. After two days at home I called in and asked someone to pick me up and take me to the office. I was restless. I could not stay home and do nothing.

I have been ambitious all my life, to progress, to learn. I have educated myself, I have no certification from anybody. Nobody helped me. And I have always worked, I have always been busy. How can I stop now? I know I should slow down but it's impossible. This is the way I am. I cannot change myself.

Roberto

NOW IT IS ME WHO WANTS TO go back and live in Italy. I could do the same work over there, but my wife is right, it's not me anymore, it's the kids, they don't want to move. Even here, if I want to move to another house a half a mile away my kids are all against it. I also don't think my wife would adjust too easily to living in Italy today, she would have to give up some of her values. Maria is the actual mother and wife who is used to looking after the family, working twenty-four hours a day. In Italy things have changed. On the other hand Maria does not really have any contact with Canada because she has never worked outside of the house. She always speaks to my family in the Italian dialect, she listens to Italian radio and TV, and that is not Canada.

Four of our children were born within the first three and a half years of marriage, the fifth one came seven years later. The Italian dialect was their first language. When they started school, up to grade five, they all had to take special lessons in English as a second language. Now the kids are losing their Italian. In the house my wife and I speak in dialect. In school the kids are taking Italian classes and they are learning the standard Italian. I talk to them in English all the time and my wife talks to them in Italian and they answer her in English. Somehow they understand each other.

I prefer to talk my dialect instead of standard Italian, not because I don't know how to talk standard Italian but the dialect is more me. I used to say that if I were filthy rich I would only talk in dialect and anyone who wanted to talk to me would have to learn it or he didn't talk to me. I hear that in Italy today there is a trend toward going back to the dialect, so perhaps my dream can still come true.

Recently Maria has begun to take English classes and she talks a bit of English to the kids. I don't really know how much English she knows because when I am around and want to hear her she refuses, she is shy about talking English in front of me. Perhaps she does a better job when I am not there. The kids tell me she is advancing and she is also beginning to watch TV in English. With the kids growing up she has more time, now Maria even wants me to teach her how to dance. I tell her I don't have time and she is mad. I find the time to do other things with her and the family. We all go to the farm together and pick our own tomatoes. They charge $6 to $8 a bushel and for our family we need about twelve bushels. We bring the tomatoes home, spread them on a blanket to make sure they will all ripen evenly, and when they are ready we chop them up, put them in a huge pot and boil them for twenty minutes. Then we put them in a machine and the sauce goes one way and the peel goes the other way. My wife puts them in bottles and they are ready to use when needed. We also put away artichokes and pickles. I enjoy helping her with such things, they are relaxing but I just don't see where I am going to find the time to teach her how to dance.

In this house we never talk about divorce and I am the one who makes the decisions. They might not always be correct but that's the only way to run a family. If you have two or three different points of view you will never accomplish anything. I think this gives the kids security. Of course it could also be bad because if they marry non-Italians and they have been brought up according to our mentality they might be in for a few surprises. If my daughters would marry a non-Italian boy I think that boy would be the happiest man in the world because I know they are going to be like their mother, all the attention is for the man of the house. What more could a man want? But if my boys marry a non-Italian girl and she will say, "I am going out tonight with my girlfriends or to the bridge club instead of preparing supper," what kind of marriage is that going to be? My kids would be better off marrying someone in the same position as themselves, not an Italian, or a Canadian, but someone of Italian origin, born here. I would prefer if my kids would marry one of the neighbours because I have know these kids for fifteen years, I know the families, there would not be any surprises, you know where they are coming from.

If my daughters want to go out to dance the answer is no. A few years ago, when Teresa was twelve, I overheard a friend of hers from school say, "So that is why Teresa is good in school, she has no boyfriends." At that age they were talking about boyfriends. I was surprised. Now Teresa is sixteen and she still does not have boyfriends. She has friends but she is too young to think about boys. Now she has a part-time job as a cashier at Canada Tire. I pick her up every night and drive her home. Usually I am the taxi driver around here.

I have two boys, the first one, Luigi, is eighteen. He is an exceptional student, always on the honour roll. I bought him an old car for $200 and he took it all apart, piece by piece, and replaced everything with new parts, piece by piece. He redid the whole engine and even did the upholstery inside, everything by the book. He also has a part-time job and a girlfriend who he has been seeing for the past three years. I think it is bad to get attached to someone at this age. I am not saying she is not a good girl, even though she is not Italian, but he is too young. I told him, if you start at that age you are both going to give up many things in life. That is about the only advice I can give him. I have never tried to sit down and discuss the facts of life with him or the others because I think they already know it but also, I think, because my father never said anything to me about it. I would not know how to approach the subject.

The other son, Marco, is seventeen. He was going to school but he was not really there, he didn't bother doing his homework, he skipped school regularly. One day I said to him, "What are you doing, you are wasting your time and your teacher's time. Either you go to school or you don't."

He said, "I don't like going to school."

"All right then, quit."

He asked me to find him a job. I could have found him something but I didn't want to. I wanted him to try for himself. He got a job dishwashing. He worked for two or three months and then quit. He came to me and said, "Daddy, I want to go back to school."

But I can see that it is not working out for him there. We had a long talk the other day, I asked him what he wanted to do. He said he wanted to try sheet metal. I spoke to my boss at Massey Ferguson and told him to try out Marco but to get him to move around, not to stick him just in one position. If he is going to learn the trade, he must learn all aspects.

I see my kids really attached to their friends and I tell them that they are friends now but as they will grow older they will grow apart. Now the parents of one of Luigi's friends are away. He is all by himself in the house and a group of them go over there and play cards all day long. Sometimes the boys come home at five o'clock in the morning. I get angry at that, why do they have to come in at that hour? I don't see the point of staying out later than two in the morning. But then I think back to myself when I was young and this makes me even more angry.

I just received some sad news over the Christmas holidays. A good friend who I used to share a room with while I was in the Air Force died. We had both left the Force at the same time and we both got married. When I went to Italy to get married I borrowed $700 from the credit union and he had co-signed for me. He was from the Prairies and we were always exchanging Christmas cards. They were in town once and he came over for dinner with his wife and kids. This Christmas I received a card from his wife to say that he had died of a massive heart attack. In the card she wrote, "It is a bad time to tell you, but any time would be a bad time."

When you are young your friends are everything. But today my children and my wife are my friends. No one else counts. I think the oldest understands that. I don't know about the younger ones.

The last time we went back to Pratola was in 1973 and I tried to find some of my old friends. It was no longer the same as when we were young. We were all different, different ways, different concerns. The town had also changed, it was no longer my Pratola. A lot of strangers were living there. I wanted to talk my dialect but found that they were all talking the standard Italian, except for the older generation.

It had become an industrialized town. Cars were all over the place, over the sidewalk, double parked. The boys picked up the girls by car and took them somewhere, even the parents did not know where they went. They didn't seem to care either. In my time there were no cars, we were chasing the girls on the piazza or we went to a girl's balcony and waited till she came out. That doesn't exist anymore. Now they get in the car.

Now things come too easy to the people, they have lost their ambition. They don't have the desire to move ahead. In Pratola I went to the gas station just when the guy was closing. I met him in front of the pumps and said, "Nick, I want some gas."

He said, "I am going home, it's closing time."

I said, "But you are still here."

"Yes, but while I give you gas someone else will come along and I'll have to give him gas and then someone else will come along, and so on, and I will never close."

There was no point in arguing with him, "When are you coming back?"

"Three o'clock."

And that was that. All the stores closed from 12:30 to 3:30 and you were out of luck if you did not have what you needed.

Everybody went to work in the fields by car or motorcycle. In the old days if you went to work on a donkey you were rich. Now if you want to see a donkey you have to go to a zoo. But few people even want to work the land, a lot of land just sits there, abandoned. The people have grown lazy. Some people who went to work in other countries like Switzerland sent back money to their wives and they invested that money in land. But having land no longer means what it once did. My father-in-law told me that he was thinking of selling his land.

Every old person has a pension, sometimes even two pensions. Before you only got a pension if you had been in industry or if you had been a civil servant. Now, when I talked to friends of my father, retired seventy-year-old people, they were telling me stories about their trips to France and Assisi. In my childhood elderly people just sat around doing nothing. Beside the pensions, people receive money from relatives in the States or Canada or somewhere else. Everyone has relatives somewhere else who is sending home money. These days people living there only care about having a good life, they don't have any motivation or initiative. I have grown accustomed to the North American way of life, working hard.

This year my sister-in-law's kids were here for a couple of months from Milan. My niece is taking English and she wanted to come here to practice. This girl is seventeen and has never done a day's work but here she saw that my kids had part-time jobs and they had extra money to spend on clothes. She was surprised. In Italy, work is taboo till you have a full-time job. While you are a student, you don't lift a finger. Recently my kids got a letter from her and she writes she has a part-time job teaching English. But she had to come here to see for herself that work was not that bad.

In Italy people have too much freedom, the country needs a person like Mussolini. I regret to say this but all Italian people, myself included, want to be bosses. But we are not good at it. We all want to be leaders but most of us are followers. This is the problem they are having in Italy right now. Since the war ended Italy has had a change of government every year. They used to have fist fights in the House of Commons. Fist fights! There used to be chairs flying. We regularly heard this on the news and these were supposed to be the leaders of the country. How can you create confidence that way? Italy needs a strong man.

Take Fidel Castro. The whole world is against him but I am sure that if we talk to the Cubans they are all going to say that he is a good man, he is a good man for Cuba. Like in my family, I am the father, I might be a thief or a hoodlum but to my kids I am the best father in the world. The same thing went for Mussolini. I don't care what anybody says, he was a good man for his country. Hitler also, he saved Germany, maybe he went a little too far, but he saved Germany. He had big ideas, now they say he was crazy. Maybe he was, but maybe he wasn't.

Today no country in the world is controlled by the government, they are controlled by a small group of people, the capitalists, the ones with the money. And every head of government has to carry out their orders because, if they don't do what they say, they will not live long. Today life is cheap. Howard Hughes must have been part of this group of capitalists who control the world. He formed his own group. He advertised in a newspaper in California for a young lawyer who wanted to be the president of the United States. Richard Nixon replied to the ad. At that time he was fresh out of school. He lost so many times before he became president of the U.S., but finally he won and he was backed by Hughes' group. Because he won they managed to get all their people into government offices. I don't care what people say about Nixon, he was the best president the U.S. has ever had. This Watergate affair was just an excuse for the other group of capitalists to kick him out and to replace him with one of their men.

Every nation has a national debt which runs into billions of dollars. To whom do they owe this debt? To the capitalists. Countries have to go to the World Bank to borrow money, and these banks belong to the capitalists. When they give money to a country they say, "Fine, we will give it to you but you have to do what we want, you have to pass certain laws."

Lately, I have been reluctant to vote because if those guys are going to be the rulers anyway then why should I waste my time voting for someone who will be taking orders from someone else? It does not matter who I would vote for, they will still have to take orders from those people up there.

I sympathize with the New Democratic Party because they should be for the working class. But first of all I don't believe in any of them, as a second choice I would take the NDP. Michele and Franco always get into arguments about politics. I vote for Michele because he is my brother, he is an idealist. I wish the world could be run the way he sees it. I sympathize with Michele but I think Franco is more practical and, of course, cynical. I vote for Michele but I don't contribute anything to Franco's telethons. There were so many scandals about the earthquake in Naples, about money that never arrived. The idea for the telethons is good but the people from Naples are still there, even with all the money that was sent from all over the world. I don't know where all the money went to. It's a good excuse for people to get their hands on other people's candies.

In a way my father is also an idealist. He knows a lot of people and enjoys meeting people. If he would invite all the people he knows to a party no place would be big enough to hold them all. But considering all the people he knows he should have been able to have a different job. He has never taken advantage of his contacts. He has pictures of himself with all the big shots, for what? You might as well make them pay. He never did. He did everything for friends. If you are in trouble and you know that my father knows the right person then you go to my father and he will take you to that person for help. And my father is happy because he did you a favour. Don't try to pay him anything because he won't take it. That is the kind of person he is. Someone else in his place would say, you want that contact, it will cost you $1,000. But my father enjoys just helping. Consequently, he worked as an electrician for twenty-two years, that's it. He never wanted to start his own business because he wanted to be free.

Today I am working for Massey Ferguson as a tool-room inspector. We build agricultural machinery. I made a point of concentrating on trigonometry and with a small calculator everything is there. I became good and now I am mostly involved with the hardware. On top of that I started my own business in 1973 as a computer programmer for sheet-metal engineering. Everything I know has been self taught, my education is still only up to grade eight. When I started the travel agency I was green, I didn't know anything. When I started my own business,

I knew exactly what I was doing. At first it was only for tax reasons, not because I needed a business. Then last year it became a limited company. I am now suing Bell Canada because they didn't list me in the Yellow Pages. I want to make sure they will not forget again.

Many companies have their own programmer, but if that person is sick tomorrow the company is stuck. They can try to replace him but in the meantime they might lose a lot of money and the machine is sitting there doing nothing. Or that one programmer is really busy at certain times and he cannot handle everything. I can come in and ease the load. At this time no one is offering such a service.

I am not going to leave my full-time job until I am sure that I have enough work not only for me but for another person as well. Now with my full-time job plus the work I do with my company I hardly have time for anything else. I spend all my free time sitting at the table, calculating and figuring out the programs. I make very good money. I tell myself that in my spare time I can either try to make it on my own or I can sit down and just watch TV.

If I would have been an Anglo-Saxon working at Massey Ferguson, doing exactly what I am doing, I am sure I would have reached a much higher position. But what can you do? Open your own business. This way I can be my own boss and I will have much more freedom.

Angelina

AFTER MY FIRST CHILD I started talking to my parents as friends, to say you are wrong or right, never before. The only thing I blame my mother for is that she was never a friend to me. I was always ashamed and afraid to tell her that a boy said this or that to me. She was so severe, I could never open up to her, never.

I told my parents so many times that I gave them more than they gave me. When we were working we gave all our money to them. I always gave them everything. Now my children work part-time and I am not taking a cent of that money. I know friends who make their children pay room and board. I feel it is my duty to feed them while they are in this house. After grade twelve Carmina went to work for a publishing house, she worked for two years and I let her put all the money away. Once in a while I checked her bank account to make sure the money was there.

I recently reminded my mother that the supervisor at the cookie factory had suggested that I take a secretarial course and I asked her why she never encouraged me to do this, she knew that I always wanted to continue my studies. Just to make me feel better she said, "Well, you would have ended up at home anyway, so don't worry. Don't think about it."

After the fourth baby I started to have problems with my throat. At parties I had to force my voice in all the smoke and noise, the next day I could not speak, not even on the phone. I went to see the doctor about it and he said it was nerves. I started losing my voice because of all the screaming at the children. When they were small I remember running from one corner of the house to the other without breathing. Today it's worse, I would rather wash diapers again because now I worry much more when they are out.

I began to have a bit of time to myself when the last one was three years old and the others were in school. Thank goodness, I wasn't expecting again. One afternoon I opened the TV just to see what was on, to relax a little. Then I turned it on again the next day and I realized that it was the continuation of the story

I had seen the day before. I noticed that it was on every day. From then on I started watching the soap operas. My family teases me, sometimes when there is a very important part that I have been waiting for I take the phone off the hook. "Another World" is really like another world, they exchange husbands like peanuts. When I started to watch them twelve years ago they were cleaner, there was just a little kiss. Now you see them in bed, the man is half naked and the woman is in a nightgown or in her bra and slip. Before you did not see that. My mother also started to watch them, she does not understand every word but she knows what is going on. The other day she said to me, "They are becoming so nasty and dirty." These soap operas give you a good idea how people think nowadays.

Six years ago, just when I was beginning to enjoy some of my free time, I was beginning to relax, I realized I was expecting another baby. I was going out of my mind. I thought of so many bad things. I didn't want it. I heard stories that sometimes the husband woke up the wife in the middle of the night and told her to have a hot bath in order to lose the baby. Not Alfredo. He said, "Maybe it will be a boy."

I said, "I don't care anymore." At the time my youngest was eight and my oldest was eighteen. After two months I started to calm down and be happy, the mother instinct took over.

For two weeks I was lying on the couch, sick. I didn't do any cleaning. Then one night I had a dinner party for friends and I decided I had to clean the house, it was so dirty. To clean it properly you have to move the furniture. After dinner I put the coffee on and I started bleeding. I called the doctor and he made me go to the hospital. He said there was a 99 per cent chance I would lose the baby. The next morning I woke up in the hospital and I started to cry. The nurse came over and asked, "What is it?" I told her that I was losing the baby.

"Oh," she said. "Is it your first one?"

I could not answer her I was crying so hard. Also, I was so ashamed. Finally I said, "I have five daughters at home."

"Oh," she said. "You were hoping for a boy."

I cried for one week and then, thank God, I had to prepare a surprise party for Carmina's eighteenth birthday and that helped me.

After this happened I told Alfredo to get an operation. Why should a woman always take care of these things? "Oh, I will, I will." Then he forgot about it. When I reminded him he said,

"Are you nuts?" He thinks he is going to lose something. He never used the little box he talked about before we got married, he never liked those things. He prefers having children but he doesn't like to raise them.

Alfredo never helped me to raise the children and he admits this. If my daughters say something they should not and Alfredo is there, resting or reading, he ignores them. I always have to be the one to discipline them, that is why I have lost my voice. I would say to Alfredo, "I told Monica to come and peel the potatoes three times. Now you tell her."

He would get up and peel the potatoes himself, that's how sweet he is. Then I get mad, "Why are you doing it? Because you don't want to get upset or you don't want to bother your daughter? Why?" I don't like him to do that. I want my children to come when I call them, they have to learn.

Once I was not feeling well and I said to Alfredo, "Please, I am asking for your help because I can't anymore. I am getting sore throats and headaches. Do you want to see me in the hospital?"

He said, "Don't worry. I am going to help you."

The next day he came home from work and two of the girls were arguing. He put a stop to it. Another one did something else and he said something to her. I said to myself, "Thank goodness, I can rest. He is doing my work."

The next day Alfredo forgot about his duty. Again two of them were arguing. I said, "Alfredo, these two are arguing."

Nothing. He forgot.

I said, "Alfredo!"

Then he started swearing. That was it. The next night I didn't call him anymore. One night was enough for him. So I can really say I raised them. I did it all, the bad with the good.

I would like to be friends with my daughters, I would like them to tell me every little thing so I could advise them. They tell me I am too nosey. But no, it is because of my own experience. Even today, a twenty-year-old with all her education could not have the experience of a forty-year-old mother. I keep telling my children never to trust friends, they can betray you. Who always takes your husband or fiancé? It is the best friend because she knows everything about him, but your mother never ever wants to hurt you. I always tell my daughters, "I don't care how many more years you study, I can see things better than you." The young are so innocent, without fear, they think nothing can happen to them.

I say to my children, "If you meet a boy from school on the street, go and have a cup of coffee with him. That is the only way you are going to get to know a person. If you don't talk to him how can you know him? You won't get to know a boy in a dark room. You can only get to know people by talking to them."

In certain ways I am old fashioned. I allow my daughters to go out with boys but I keep telling them, "Please, don't let them touch you. If you do something wrong it is bad for you. Boys go after only one thing. After they get it they get tired of you and leave you. If they love you and want you so badly then they will have to marry you."

In my home town I often heard men say to women, "Give me proof of your love." And the stupid little girls did it and the parents lost their honour. What proof do we, as parents, have from them? The only proof is that they take us to the church. After they can give the boy whatever he wants. My mother always said, "Don't get tired of talking to them. From a hundred words a few will sink in." I leave my children free all day long. But at night I don't want them on the street. At night I am afraid, I get nervous. In the daytime, fine, use the time well, but don't disappoint me because if something bad happens I am capable of dying, I am that strong.

I never allowed my daughters to go to pyjama parties. They were never allowed to sleep over at a friend's house, only at my mother's. I did not trust anyone. I was always thinking something bad. Maybe because my mother was like that with me, always thinking the worst about others to protect me. The third one, Monica, is more stubborn, she lets the parents call me. Once in a while I receive a phone call, "This is Mrs So and So, can Monica come?" I say, "I am sorry, I don't have anything against you, I would like to send her, but I never allowed my two oldest to go and it is not fair now to allow Monica." "Oh, I understand." The pyjama parties might only be girls but they have fathers and brothers. Even if there are no brothers, what if the father gets drunk and bothers the young girls? Old people used to say, "You will come back safely from where you do not go." Of course, if it is meant for me to die then no matter where I am I will die, even in my own house. I believe in God.

My sixteen-year-old does not ask to go to dances but I am just preparing her. She can go to the formal this winter because I would like her to go. I have just the boy for her and the mother loves Stefania. We are close friends, she has five boys and I have five daughters. All of them are just one year apart. Her first boy was born one year before my first daughter, the age is perfect. She has one married son and I have one married daughter. We have four and four left. We often get together and talk but we wouldn't dare to say anything to the kids. This boy, the one who is perfect for Stefania, is so handsome, typically Italian with brown eyes and Stefania has blue eyes. I would love it if they got together. They are from my town. But if it does not happen I will not force it.

Anything I have ever dreamed of for myself I do for my daughters. Sometimes they don't want it, but I do it anyway. For their high school graduation I always make a party and invite my family. I prepare fancy cookies and put the green confetti everywhere and I serve green liqueur. I told them all, you won't get married, you won't leave this house unless you give me the high school diploma. After that, since you are girls, I won't push.

I am hoping Teresa will give me a university diploma. Then I will put red confetti all around. The red is for glory, the top.

When Carmina was eighteen she was signed up to go to college. I was very happy. That summer we all went to Italy. She loved Italy so much that she said, "I want to work and save enough money to come back next summer." I said, "Alone? Forget it." I was very sad that Carmina didn't want to go to college. While she was working she got engaged to a boy from Milan and ten months later they were married. I like her husband, he is a Sagittarius, like me, the nervous and happy type. He comes from a nice family in Milan.

Teresa just got engaged to a Canadian boy and he gave her a ring for her birthday. He also sent her two dozen roses, a dozen for Teresa and another dozen for me. I was very touched by that.

I wanted all my five daughters to marry Italian boys because anybody who marries a foreign person leaves their own language behind. My oldest daughter was born here but because her husband is Italian she talks to her daughter one-third of the time in Italian. But I give my daughters the freedom to choose. If they want to marry someone poor I would let them. If my daughter chooses a Chinese man or a black man and that man makes her happy, fine, but then I would suffer because society would make them suffer and society would make their children suffer.

For their eighteenth birthday I give my daughters a party, it is like a debutante party, they are ready to enter society. But they don't enjoy my parties because they say I invite all the old people. When my oldest had her eighteenth birthday she said she wanted to invite all her friends. Before the people arrived I went to check on her and I saw that she had dressed all in black, even the stockings were black. I said, "Don't, it looks like you are in mourning." She was the type to listen to me. She changed but she said, "You don't understand fashion."

The next day there was a phone call from Italy. Alfredo's aunt had died the day of the party. Then I remembered a little man who told me my fortune when I was thirteen. He had said, "Each time you will have a party a distant, distant relative will die."

I am superstitious. Every dream I have comes true in three days. One night I dreamed I was going down so many stairs. The next day Alfredo fell down and hurt his hand. When I am going up the stairs pleasant things happen to me. If I dream of sweets but just look at them then everything is fine. If I eat them then bad things happen. When my mother received a telegram from Italy saying that her brother was dead, she said to me, "I was eating so many chocolates last night in my dreams." My mother always says that when God wanted to send a message to the saints he sent the angels in their dreams.

Now, in Italy, the parents of the groom expect the parents of the bride to give an apartment. If I would have stayed in Italy I don't know how I would have managed to give an apartment to each of my five daughters. Before we left most of the people in our town were farmers. They didn't give the bride an apartment, they gave her a piece of land. Six years ago I heard that a father retired early so he could get $20,000 to marry his daughter. In Italy, if you have worked a number of years and you want to retire, you get *la buonuscita*, it is a large sum of money as a reward for having put in so many years of work. This man was willing to retire early and ruin his own life in order to be able to get his retirement money to buy his daughter an apartment for her wedding. After the wedding the couple came to Canada. Could they not have gone somewhere in Europe, a few miles from their house?

My son-in-law gets mad when I say in Italy they do this or that. He always says, "You are not talking about Italy. You are only talking about your own town."

We always have arguments because he is from Milan. I know the cities are different. City girls get married with nothing, so they say, just to prove they are not small-minded like in the small towns. But if the family gives an apartment to the boy, they are happy.

In Canada, the Italians here are doing the same thing. I just thank God my son-in-law did not have his family here for the wedding because the mother-in-law could have said something. We are not rich but people always think we are rich because of the way we dress, we go out, we travel, but we have no money. A farmer who eats beans and macaroni every day has more money. He does not travel, does not spend money on clothes, so he has more money put away and can give more to the daughter. But I gave my daughter whatever I had and nobody could criticize me. I bought her nice sheets, fancy nightgowns, bath towels, thirty-six all together. I enjoyed doing it. Why should she have to worry in the first year of her marriage? I don't want them to start with nothing. Maybe our children will not do such things.

Some friends who live here started to collect things from the time their daughters were eight years old. But I would rather give my daughters one sheet less and one more year at school. Who cares how many sheets they have? An education allows you to do anything you want. I sometimes feel bad that I could not also start collecting when my daughters were eight years old. But I have five children and Alfredo is the only one working. God provides for me. I take one step at a time.

Monica is almost twenty and I have nothing for her. Now that Teresa has become engaged I will take care of her. At Eaton's I saw beautiful sheets on sale for $400, just one set including the pillow cases and the comforter. It was all satin. I said, "Teresa, let me buy it for you, just one good one." She said, "No, no." Maybe she does not want me to spend the money. But I am happy to do it.

Sometimes it worries me that after the children will be married they will forget about going to church. Teresa has stopped going to church already and she is not even married yet. But I spoke to her fiancé privately and asked him to make sure she goes to church at least on Christmas and Easter and a few other times in between. He understood. He is a very nice boy, from a good family.

I don't go to church as regularly as I used to either. On Sunday morning I have to prepare a big meal for one o'clock. I have to cook, make the beds, get dressed, I never have time to go.

Recently I started going on Saturday night. There are two masses, one at five and one at seven. When my daughters are working they come home before five, we eat, then Alfredo takes me to church at a quarter to seven. Sometimes I go alone or with my little ones. If I am invited out for Saturday night then I go to the five o'clock mass. I feel so relaxed after mass, it is very peaceful.

Franco teases me, "I can see you are going to become like Mamma, going to church all the time." My mother goes to church every day even when there is a storm outside. We tell her, "But Mamma, it is so bad out. What if you break a leg or something?" She answers, "God will watch over me." I am afraid to go out when it is icy, but not her.

Whenever I want to go to church Alfredo does not say anything, he takes me there and picks me up. Church is the only place he lets me go without a word. When I am sloppy with my hair out of place, he is so happy. When I start getting dressed and I put makeup on he is nervous, he is that jealous. We go to parties and we come home fighting, he is even afraid to show me to people.

After I was married for fifteen years I heard that one of my nieces in Italy was going to marry her first cousin. The whole family was so happy, particularly the father, Mario, he was the happiest man in the world. When I heard this I cried. At the time that I wanted to marry Vittorio the whole family had entered into a discussion about it, not just here but in Italy as well. Each one said his piece and they were all against me, no one was for me. Mario in particular had said, "Well, I come from Sicily where they marry cousins so easily but this never occurred in my family." So when I heard that his daughter was marrying her cousin and he was such a happy man, I cried because I was mad.

I wanted to say something to his wife, my cousin, about this. We always got along and I knew she was on my side but she could not say anything at the time, she could not go against her husband. When I called her up to congratulate her, I said, "Strange, when the same thing happened to me not even a dog was my favour." I said this with tears in my eyes.

She felt bad. She said to me, "My father had said, 'It is a sin to separate two souls in love.'"

I felt even worse, "Why didn't you tell me this then?"

Later I heard from a friend of mine that Vittorio's marriage was not very good and I felt so happy that day. I kept asking myself, "Why do I feel so happy?"

209

We had not seen each other in ten years. When I went back to Italy for a visit we met once at my cousin Marcella's house. She was always inviting us over, she wanted me to meet his family but Alfredo would never go. She called me again one Sunday morning and said, "He is not going to be here, only my other brothers. Please, come to say hello at least."

We were on our way to dinner at a friend's house, I said to Alfredo, "Let's stop by for five minutes, after all, they are my cousins."

He said, "Who is going to be there?"

"Vittorio is not going to be there." He agreed to go over. We all sat in the living room. Vittorio's two daughters and his wife were there. While Alfredo was talking to someone Marcella called me in the other room. She said, "What are we going to do? I feel so bad." As we were standing there talking Vittorio came in. I grabbed Marcella's arm. I didn't know what to do. I was so afraid. Then I said to myself, "My goodness, what is he going to think?" I calmed down and we shook hands, "How are you?" He mumbled something I didn't understand and, instead of staying there to say a few words, I ran. I said, "I better get Alfredo." I was so afraid what Alfredo would do. When Alfredo saw him he was upset. He tried to talk to everybody but I knew how he felt and that made me upset.

That was also the first time I saw my father-in-law since we had left Italy back in 1963. Soon after we had returned to Toronto Alfredo's youngest brother, Carlo, got married. He took his new wife, Sonia, to live at his father's house. He had a new maid to replace me. But Sonia did not have the patience I did. She screamed at him, she argued with him. When he said something that offended her she would throw dishes or she kicked a pot. She was not Lina who cried in her room and that was it. This girl was it, no one was going to boss her around. Finally, he could not take it anymore and he yelled, "Get out of my house!"

She went crying to the oldest sister-in-law, "He kicked me out, he kicked me out." Carlo and Sonia moved into her parents' house in another town. They had to find an apartment fast.

After this happened my father-in-law began writing letters to me, "My good Lina!" All of a sudden I am good. "I am sorry for everything I did, you are welcome to come back anytime. You will always have a place in this house." He needed another maid. I still have this letter. Later Sonia wrote to me that he had told her all the garbage about me, about Michele. She said he had even gone to her parents' house, before the marriage, and told them all these things. I was furious. I told Alfredo, "You should have talked to him. You should have told him to stop it." But he never said anything. Alfredo kept telling me, "He is an old man."

I decided to write a letter to my oldest sister-in-law. Alfredo did not even read the letter, he did not have to. I wrote, "What sort of person is your father? I am asking from the point of view of a parent. If I had a daughter-in-law, such as he thinks I am, I would try to cover up for her for the sake of my son. I would defend her from such rumours. Instead, he is the one spreading these lies. I do not understand how he can do this."

She answered me with an old saying, "The devil is not as black as you paint him."

I answered back, "What has this devil ever done to deserve a lighter shade from my palette?"

I did not write to him after that for five months. Each time I saw a picture of him I started to shiver. I could not look at his face. I hated him.

When we went back to Italy I was nervous about seeing him. But he treated me very nicely. Maybe he said things behind my back but I would have heard. Of course, he was older, he had mellowed. I know older people like attention and affection so each time I went away or came back I gave him a kiss on the forehead. I could see from his face that he enjoyed it.

Once I overheard him say to my mother-in-law, "That Sonia didn't even bring money into the family. She had no dowry, nothing. She could not even obey orders and do her duty."

My mother-in-law said, "Well, Lina didn't have land or a house either."

Then I heard him say, "At least she brought her beauty." I could not believe my ears. During those six weeks we spent with them the relationship was very good and I thought, "Thank God, now I cannot hate him."

Since we had left Italy Alfredo's oldest brother, Romano, had become a millionaire. Now all he cares about are cars and women. His wife, Luciana, stays quietly at home, like Roberto's wife. I like to stay at home but I also like to go out. They don't go anywhere together. He is tall and well dressed. She is chubby and homely. Now that Romano was doing really well he wanted Alfredo to go back and join him in business. Alfredo wanted to go back.

He always wanted to go back, but I could not. Romano tried to persuade me as well. He even gave me one of his small busts of Mussolini. He has so many little pictures and statues of Mussolini and he had three small busts. I particularly liked one of them, the one made of marble. When we were there he gave it to me and said, "Watch out, don't give it to anyone and don't break it." He likes me because I think like him.

They taught us to love Mussolini and I still do. My younger brother, Michele, was only two or three when Mussolini died, he picked up what the books wrote. I loved fascism because there was discipline. Too much freedom is not good. If I am afraid to go for a walk at midnight, what good is freedom to me? There are so many riots, terrorism has become a plague. Is this freedom? I want to be protected, for me that is freedom.

Even now Alfredo dreams of going back. He dreams that when the girls are all married we will go back and live in our villa. I can come back here for the white Christmas and my children could come over for visits.

My son-in-law likes that idea. He enjoys visiting Pratola. I think he finds it different, quaint. But the last time they went there he was so disappointed. He said to me, "I wanted to hear the local dialect and everyone spoke the standard Italian." But now the new generation wants to bring back the dialect. They don't want it to die. I always speak in proper Italian to the children. Most people here speak only in dialect and when they go back to their home town people laugh at the way they talk. Alfredo knows how to talk standard Italian but he prefers the dialect. He loves talking in dialect. I hate that.

When I go back to Italy I am careful about how I speak. I never mix in English words. People cannot tell that I am from Canada. They say I talk as if I was from Italy.

The last time we were in Italy my Aunt Carmina, Vittorio's mother, died. God meant for me to be there, to be with her in her last hours. The two of us had some time alone. I sat beside her bed and we talked. She mentioned the boy she had loved in her youth, the policeman. I mentioned Vittorio and she looked up at me, "You too?" Then she said, "Still, my husband is a good man but not my type. The other one loved to read, like me." My Uncle Eduardo had taught her how to read and had brought books home for her. In those days few people could read and when she found this policeman she was so happy. He also liked to travel but not her husband. Just like Alfredo. He does not want to go anywhere. Later my aunt Carmina travelled alone with her children. Even on her deathbed she thought of this boy. She mourned his memory.

As I listened to her talk about her past, about her desires, I thought of Vittorio who once said to me, "If ever I have you one day, I will keep you on a pedestal." And I was so naive. I could have said, "I'll wait till I am forty and then I'll marry him." But I was so young and inexperienced. At twenty I knew less than my twelve-year-old does today.

Vittorio loved to dance and to go to the theatre. Alfredo grew up hunting. Now he goes fishing. He goes to hockey games alone or with one of my daughters. He watches the sports on TV and I go to the opera by myself. But we have arguments over that, he does not want to send me alone. He suffers when I go alone. But now that I am older I am going to put my foot down. If I like to do something why shouldn't I? I am not doing anything bad when I go to the opera. When I go I feel so good inside and I dream that someone who would also appreciate it would be sitting by my side.

Vittorio used to say to me, "We are going to choose our friends." Alfredo does not care. All his friends are older than him. They are not handsome, they are not those fine types. They are nice but sometimes I say to him, "You should have more sophisticated friends."

"Those are the friends you pick for me."

"No, dear, most of them knew you, not me." Those people had come to meet him at the station when he arrived. They had known him back in Pratola, but only to exchange a greeting, nothing more. But here he was like a brother to them. They are nice people and now all of them have made money and they travel and we don't.

If we would have stayed in Italy we would never have been friends with these people. They would have been a different class. But maybe if I would have stayed in Italy I would never have been able to marry Alfredo because my family did not have very much money. To marry into his family I would have had to have a house or an apartment of my own. My parents could not have given that to me.

And maybe if we would have stayed in Italy my father would not have been so fussy. He would have allowed me to marry Vittorio. Maybe.

Michele

I DIDN'T GET MARRIED TILL I was thirty-two years old. At that stage in my life I was mentally ready for marriage, I felt reasonably certain that I would not be unemployed, that no matter what would happen I would always be able to find some sort of a position. One of the things I picked up from my parents was that you get married when you have a secure job, therefore the thought of getting married prior to that wasn't there.

The location of our wedding was a compromise position. We were not going to get married in a church and neither was it going to be in a synagogue. We went to City Hall. Both my mother and Phyllis's mother were very upset.

Afterwards we had a small reception for about fifty people at my mother-in-law's house. Originally my mother had drawn up a list of more than 250 people she wanted to invite. In the end it was narrowed down to immediate family. Naturally, what occurred was that Phyllis's family sat together on one side of the room and my family sat together on the other side of the room. This division was due to language. Few people in my family could communicate with members of Phyllis's family. A cousin of mine had come up for the wedding from Argentina and Phyllis had an uncle whose family had come from Argentina so they could talk to each other in Spanish.

My mother still does not speak very much English, therefore the relationship between the two mothers is virtually nonexistent. They are also each steeped in their own culture which is an added difficulty. My mother likes to go to church almost every day and twice a day she sits down to pray. She is an orthodox Roman Catholic. Phyllis's mother is a conservative Jew. On Friday night and Saturday she does not turn the light switch on, she does not want to answer the phone, and she walks to the synagogue. These two religious backgrounds have their prejudices built in. According to the Catholic religion the Jews killed Jesus Christ. And my mother-in-law at one particular time could not stand to see me wear a cross.

I used to wear a cross around my neck, under my shirt. If I came out of the bathroom after a shower with no shirt and my mother-in-law happened to be in the house she would see the cross hanging from my neck. Her reaction was unmistakable. I did not know if it was a reaction of disgust or just a reminder to her that her son-in-law was not Jewish. It does not take very long to know how my mother-in-law feels about things and certainly her feeling was that she would rather I did not wear it. She never actually said this to me but the non-verbal language speaks loudly. However, Phyllis did ask me not to wear the cross when her mother was there. At first when she asked me I said, "Well, if it is really going to upset your mother then I will not wear it." To me that cross is a symbol, I do not wear it because of religious beliefs. I also wear the star of David and the mezuzah because I happen to like the way they look. Once I tried to fit the cross into the mezuzah but it would not fit, they are too different in shape.

At the beginning I was careful to take the cross off when I came out of the bathroom and I knew my mother-in-law was there. But then I thought, sure, I can go on protecting Phyllis from her mother's responses and I can make sure that I do not forget my actions to protect her and be on my guard all the time. Or I can act as I have always done and allow my mother-in-law to see who I am and what I am and, if she does not like it, she can say something to me. So I stopped taking if off and if my mother-in-law was there then she saw it and that was fine. She can either learn to accept it or she can talk to me about it. Of course, I don't know if she will ever get used to me not being Jewish.

I don't think that Phyllis is that deeply religious. I think she wants to carry on a cultural tradition, she wants to have a kosher home and she lights candles on Friday night. The kids and I partake in the lighting of the candles during the eight days before Hanukkah. But I do not know to what extent they have a religious impact. I think it is a cultural impact. Of course, I am trying to separate them and there may be no separation. It is a very difficult question. I can be culturally Italian without being a practising Roman Catholic but with the Jews the identity is the religion – there is no separation between nationality and religion, they are all tied together.

There are various dimensions to us. We always talk about an emotional dimension, or a psychological dimension, I think we also have a cultural dimension but we don't talk about that at all. Very few people acknowledge the cultural aspect of their character, yet this is very integral to our sense of identity and without a total sense of identity people cannot realize their potential and therefore they cannot really make a contribution to the society they live in.

When immigration started in the late forties and early fifties, to be proud of one's background was a no-no, and some people probably went through exactly what I went through, a total identification with the culture of the new country, almost to the point of discarding their own background.

While I was growing up I was moving away from my family mentally, socially, and emotionally because I was also ashamed of them. I went through that experience and was capable of coming out of it. However, there are a lot of people who are not so fortunate, they close off a side of themselves and they never get the chance to re-evaluate what is behind that enclosure. This is very much an immigrant experience and I see no need for people to go through that. I don't want to prove that I am a strong Canadian by having to assimilate totally. One is not a Canadian by being English or by being Italian but by being both.

I do not believe that people want to deny a part of their identity. People need and want to go back to roots and I don't think that the government in Ontario understands that. The government needs the immigrant vote, therefore at election time they say, "We'll support your culture, we'll give you the few thousand dollars for your queer dances and your puppet shows." This is their multicultural philosophy.

I never agreed with this attitude. As I began to devote more and more time to the community I began to form my own ideas and thoughts on the subject. Due to some of my beliefs and convictions that certain things had to be done, certain attitudes had to be changed, I decided to run for office. After nine years of teaching I was elected to the provincial Parliament.

The goodies the Conservative government offers immigrants are shallow. They are paying lip service to a facade, just like the teachers were paying lip service to the community without really examining the needs of that comunity. It is not the dances that are important, though that is an expression of culture, it's the spirit that created those dances that is important. You recognize that spirit by saying that many founding nations developed this country, not just two founding nations. The Ukrainians had a lot to do with developing the west and if it were not for the Ukrainians the west would not be developed to this day. The Italians had a lot to do with building Toronto, physically building Toronto. In not recognizing the contributions that we, as ethnics make, that contribution is of no value. "Isn't it nice," is not enough.

My father and brothers worked on some of the buildings I see around Toronto today, that was their physical contribution. But beside that physical contribution we have also made a contribution to this country in terms of its spiritual and emotional content. And that is a very real, though more subtle, contribution. It goes much deeper than getting up on stage and performing a few national dances.

The political bend here is that we want you to maintain your background. But their attitude really encourages a separateness rather than an acceptance. The government's image of the ethnics borders on caricature and by saying that they want them to maintain that image what they are really saying is that these people will always remain hyphenated Canadians, such as the Italo-Canadians. In Canada the pressure to assimilate has always been more subtle than in the States. The States has a very definite culture. Canada does not and therefore you don't have an identification. The conclusion that I and others around my age have come to is that the Canadian culture is not yet here, it is in the process of becoming, and one has to allow for that evolutionary process. When someone of Italian background can feel that this is their country, their land, then they will be truly Canadian.

I hope to be able to transmit to my children the things that are important to me, and my wife will transmit those things that are important to her. To me that is what a multicultural individual is about.

I think it is tremendous that Phyllis expects the kids to learn Hebrew. I would like them to learn Italian so that they will be able to move in as many cultures as possible. Most of the immigrant parents today, like myself, speak the language of the country, but if the child is not encouraged to continue to speak the mother tongue there will be a cultural break.

The need to have people's language recognized in the educational system is a fundamental need. Without the language the culture would disappear within two or three generations.

The language is a pivotal point. The kids going to school will learn the English language but they will forget their mother tongue. Concurrently, if the parents do not learn the English language and do not adapt as fast as the children, the family unit will break up, and it is the family unit which carries the cultural values. Breaking up the family unit is equivalent to erasing that particular identity. The forces of assimilation will wipe out values which I consider important.

There are a lot of people who are totally assimilated, and those people say in their adult life, "Ah, those Italians, they can't learn English, they can't do this and they can't do that." My feeling is that the person doing that rejecting is not a complete person, and that person has personal problems of a cultural nature.

When two people from two different cultures get together, a lot of things which are understood all of a sudden are no longer understood. Phyllis and I had a lot of problems to iron out and they are still not all ironed out. You really cannot iron them out before you encounter them. You can indulge in an intellectual exercise but that is about it.

My household is kosher. I am not kosher outside of the house. When I go to my mother's I eat Italian sauages. The kosher tradition was totally new to me. I had to be careful with the dishes, you don't just wash them and put them away. One set is for dairy and the other for meat. The first year or two of our marriage I made a lot of mistakes and mixed everything up.

One thing that took a lot of discussion was how the kids would be brought up. I don't think that is resolved even today. We have two boys, and we decided not to confirm them, or baptize them, or have them circumcised according to the Jewish law, or bar mitzvah them. Should they go to parochial school or not? We had to consider the question when our son was ready to go to school. We decided that he would go to public school. It was a compromise position.

We keep Christmas in the sense that we spend it with the family. Having a Christmas tree was one of the things that had to be discussed and debated for two or three years. This year we bought a Christmas tree and decorated it. We feel that the kids should not be deprived of this.

I think Phyllis worried about how her mother would feel upon seeing a Christmas tree in her daughter's house. Her mother never voiced her reaction to me. She might have said something to Phyllis. But what happens in our house is determined by Phyllis and me.

I think I can deal with cultural differences, I embrace cultural differences. But there are different kinds of thinking processes that go on in different cultures and that part of the cultural difference we have not settled yet. I don't know if it will ever be settled.

I think Phyllis feels that her mother will never forgive her for marrying me. The two of us probably have the best of relationships. But in her mother's eyes the fact remains that I am not a Jew.

Phyllis's family is very close but at the same time distant. They have a love/hate relationship which was a new phenomenon for me. If I have something to say to my brother and I am angry with him I just get it off my chest and it is dealt with and forgotten and we continue on. But it seems to me that in Phyllis's family things are talked about but not dealt with. My mother-in-law is an expert user of the pause and the silence. Naturally they affect Phyllis. Since her mother is not in the best of health, particularly mentally, Phyllis feels she cannot be straight with her and get things off her chest because how would it affect her mother? It is the guilt working away – if something happens to my mother it will be my fault. It is a vicious circle.

Phyllis often says, "I am tired of this, I feel that I am her mother and not she my mother." But then the feeling dies down till the next crisis.

The little problems and the big problems that exist between Phyllis and her mother always come to the surface but there is never a resolution. The same sort of relationship exists between the mother and the other sisters and these problems are forever and forever discussed. Sometimes I say to Phyllis that if her mother and sisters do not have problems they are not happy, they feel they are not living. Then she gets very upset and she transfers her anger onto me. Then a by-now familiar process begins, she pushes me into a corner, in the psychological sense. She pushes me away saying I do not understand. My reaction to that is to keep quiet. This sometimes upsets her even more because she sees my silence as detachment.

Often when the family gets together around the dinner table and the discussions begin I feel like an outsider trying to find out what is happening. I try to approach the problem from a rational angle, not an emotional angle, and then I am told I do not care or I do not understand. They are caught up in the process of constant analysis and rehashings. I sometimes refuse to get caught up.

When we have dinner at my mother-in-law's house sometimes I find myself wanting to get up after an hour and a half of sitting at the dinner table with the whole family. I want to do something, I want to be active, they still want to talk. I go to the den and smoke a cigarette, I just take a break. Phyllis says, "You are not interested in what we are talking about." Sometimes I say, "You are right, I have heard all these things before, not once but several times." I consider myself to be a listener but I need to have new things to listen to. I cannot listen to old stuff all the time. It might seem that the problems they are discussing have a different face but the underlying principles are the same. It is an incredible web.

When members of my family get together we talk about other things, we don't go into great depth about problems that we have, we just deal with them ourselves. We sit down and have a nice game of cards. We find that very enjoyable, very relaxing. Phyllis of course says, "What is this card playing? The women go off and do one thing and you guys go off and do another." This is foreign to her because when her family sits down all they do is talk, talk, talk. In Phyllis's family, if they stop talking there is a void and somehow all the gaps have to be filled with words. With my family there is no compelling need to talk, you have something to say, you talk, but you don't force yourself to talk even though you feel you might want to be quiet. Roberto's wife by nature is a very quiet individual and Phyllis finds it excruciating to spend any time with her.

Both my parents love Phyllis but they are not able to express that love with words. Phyllis is a very verbal person, therefore when she is with my parents who are not verbal she feels very much at odds. I have no doubt that my mother-in-law loves me, I feel it. And whatever my mother-in-law has in terms of barriers, my parents also have in terms of barriers, religious barriers. But I make a distinction between religious and human barriers.

Some of the cultural problems I encounter in my personal life I try to apply to my political philosophy, I try to see them on a larger scale, in society. It is very difficult to understand the cultural attitudes of people but it is not impossible. The most important element to any problem solving is a common desire for a solution. If the common desire to find an answer is there, an answer which will often be a compromise, then a lot of problems can be surmounted.

I like to take a bit of credit in being partially responsible for bringing the arguments for the necessity of an ethnic program to the legislature for the first time and putting them before the government.

I went into politics wanting to raise the level of consciousness in a group or a community. I am motivated by principles, and if I cannot hold onto my ideals then what is the point of being in politics? To a certain extent it is similar to the old Biblical concept of being your brother's keeper. I believe it is possible to translate that politically in terms of the poor versus the rich. Once I forget about this principle, I should get out of politics. The power comes from achieving what you think ought to be achieved. If the power I would be seeking was a personal power, for myself, for my family and for the people around me, then I could have gone into any other line of endeavour and not necessarily the political one. I could have gone into business and achieved material wealth. I could have worked with my brother. Franco translates power into material wealth and material wealth into power but that is not my interest.

Certainly money is one concept of power. One can contribute to a given party in power and say, "If this particular thing is discussed in Cabinet, make sure a positive decision is reached." That is buying a politician. If someone would come to me with that kind of approach I would say to him, "Keep your money, I have no need for your money." And if I do not get elected next time, then I do not get elected next time. It will not be the end of my world.

To me it is power when you have the ability to affect the lives of people at the bottom and say that they cannot be treated in the way they have been treated in the past.

I think it is to the advantage of certain elements in the community to maintain a community that does not understand its rights, because understanding how to go through the system lessens the power of those elements.

The mentality and social awareness of the immigrants are shaped by their cultural background. Mussolini represented a kind of law and order to the generation of my parents. Obviously he was a dictator, but he was a socialist until he realized that socialism was not the route to power and he abandoned those principles.

One of the stories that my parents told me was how impressed they were by the amount of sugar that flowed to the south during Mussolini's time. There was a shortage of sugar and Mussolini managed to make sure that a trickle of sugar got down there. From time to time a truck load of sugar would arrive and it would be deposited on the main square in front of the church. That's all it took to impress them, that was the peasant mentality.

When my mother goes back to Pratola she stays there a couple of months with people she used to know, with relatives, and they talk about the things they used to do. When they look at some of the kids walking together in the piazza they say, "Look at those kids, they are no good, when we were growing up those were the kids, not these here." She sees them but doesn't approve of them. She knows there have been changes but she has not been a part of those changes and does not understand their application.

My mother's reaction to present-day Italy might be negative and she might not be totally conscious of Canada either but I, as her son, am capable of understanding the past that she holds on to and with that understanding I can shed light on the present. The past experiences of our parents have obviously shaped them but they have also shaped us. These experiences have been handed down to us, they are part of our cultural heritage. The combination of my past and Phyllis's past is the future. Just because I have embraced another culture does not mean that I have given up my own. In fact that other culture helps me to better understand my own, to see it more clearly.

A multicultural person is one who can feel at home anywhere because he or she is already familiar with the process of adaptation. That person will be more versatile, will be able to adjust to the system of the new country faster. Integration within the new society will not take fifteen years. The people today are constantly on the move for whatever reason. People moving to a new country should be made to feel at home because by their arrival they have changed the country. Why should people have geographical confines? My sense of Canada is not static, it is changing all the time. To me the Canadian identity is not Anglo-Saxon anymore. Today I am as much a part of this country as a person whose family has been here for over two hundred years.

I could be of Italian background, or of German background, or of Spanish background, and with that background and with my ideas I will make my contribution to the country and in the process I will change as a person and I will also change the country. I am not a passive subject to be acted upon. But without a sense of identity people cannot make a contribution.

I understand that as people grow they become hardened in their ways and attitudes and they naturally think that their way is the best way, because that is what works for them. If everyone around them shares those particular values then everything is fine. But if 65 per cent of the population does not, then either the rest of the population changes or the minority imposes a change on the majority. This is where power comes in. I want to have the power to say that there has to be an adaptation on both sides, to meet halfway. One segment cannot stand on one corner and the other segment on another corner and never meet, talk, or try to understand one another because if the distance continues to be maintained you are asking for trouble. Either the power is shared or it is going to be taken away and then it will be taken away violently.

EPILOGUE

Teresa

FOR OUR GOLDEN ANNIVERSARY the children gave us a big party. Lina made up the invitations, there was a photograph of us when we got married and right underneath there was another photograph of us today. They were both framed in gold. It was beautiful. All the people from my home town were there. They had rented a big hall. My husband gave me a gold ring with diamonds to replace the one I had given to Mussolini during the war.

A few months later my husband got sick and he went into St Michael's Hospital. He had cancer. I went to visit him every day. He suffered for one year before he died in June 1977. He liked everything, sports, dancing, singing. Every Christmas he dressed up as Santa Claus. In Italy, when he was young, he would always put on a mask and go the the Carnival in February. Once he went dressed up as a nun and he won the prize for the best costume, no one recognized him. Everybody liked him, he never stopped talking, he enjoyed life. But he didn't like money very much. He didn't want to hold on to the money and put it in the bank. He liked to live.

I didn't have very much money to live on after my husband died. I thought of renting out a few rooms in my house but Roberto did not like that. He said, "I cannot leave you alone, something might happen."

I said, "I live in a six-room house, I can stay on the first floor and rent out the other rooms."

But he said, "Mamma, I don't know what type of people you will find. I can't sleep at home knowing you have people you don't know in your home."

So I sold the house. I cried all night when I sold this house. I had to have an eye operation because I had also cried too much when my husband died and I broke something inside. Now my eyes get tired easily.

I moved into my son's house and now help my daughter-in-law with the children. I try to carry on a conversation with my grandchildren in English and they laugh at me. But I say, "You can laugh all you want, at least I try."

My grandchildren speak some Italian but their freedom is Canadian. The Italians don't like freedom very much. One granddaughter goes to college and works on weekends. But how do you know where she is?

Lina tells me, "I never went anywhere. Now my daughters want to go everywhere."

Everything is changing. My husband always said, "You have to go with the times." But what kind of morality is there today?

One day I was coming home on the bus and I saw a boy of about ten smoking. I went to sit beside him. "How old are you?"

"It's none of your business."

I said, "No, it's none of my business."

He looked me up and down. I guess he was wondering why I was dressed all in black. "Where are you from?"

"From Italy."

"So?"

"You are a very nice boy. Why do you smoke like that?"

"Lots of people smoke."

"Who gave you the money to buy cigarettes?"

He said, "Huh! You think somebody gave me the money? I stole them. Once from my mother and once from my father."

I said, "Don't they see that their cigarettes are missing?"

"I am not stupid. I take one at a time." He got up and went to the door. Just as he was about to get off he said to me, "Next time you watch yourself. This is none of your business. OK?"

One day it was raining and I saw a boy and girl of about twelve scratching up a car. I went over there and yelled at them, "I am going to phone your mother right now. What are you doing to that car?"

Sometimes if you make something your business you can stop it. If I see something, I go over there, I can't just pass by. When I tell this to my son he says, "Mamma, please, why do you do this?" Most people do not think like that today, they do not think about other people.

I see people talking to themselves while they walk on the street, maybe about the mortgage, or something. It hasn't happened to me, thank God, but I never saw people like that back home. Peopled talked to each other, not to themselves. The hell with the mortgage. The first few years when we were here I asked myself why we had to come to Canada. How many times I asked myself that? Canada has nothing, just the dollar.

The TV gives bad ideas to young people. I sometimes watch the soap operas and they change wives like they change ties. Even in Italy this year there are 25 per cent more divorces than last year. People don't have time to raise their children properly and they do not have time for the family. What do they have time for? Other people's families?

Children are not brought up to appreciate religion. There are little religious pictures hanging inside Roberto's house. Whenever I can, I take my grandchildren and make them kneel down to pray in front of these pictures. If they have friends with them that's all the better. I make them all kneel down and pray. All it takes is a few minutes. They hardly ever go to church, especially the boys. A little prayer here and there is better than no prayer at all. Of course, it would be best if they would go to church regularly but what can I do?

I used to go every year with my husband to the festival for the Madonna della Libera, but since he died I don't go. My son is too busy to take me. In Toronto the Pratolani Club holds a mass for the Madonna in the first week of May and each year it is held in a different church. I go to that with Lina and we take as many of the children as possible. They do not all want to come, they are not interested.

The last time I went back to Pratola with my husband was in 1975. I didn't like it. You could no longer keep chickens near your house. Before I left you could have horses and cows near the home, no more. All the homes are beautiful, there are washing machines and washrooms, everything. But people don't have much respect anymore. When I was a little girl and saw an old person carrying something I would say, give that to me, let me help you. Or sometimes when you were sitting on the bus or train and saw an old person standing you would give them your place. All this has changed, the new generation does not care about the old one. The young people don't get up for the old ones. I went to visit my sister-in-law who was eighty-four years old. She has very bad arthritis. She had to go and buy some wood for the stove. There was a boy nearby and I said, "Come here, I will give you $2 to help this old lady buy wood."

He said, "Are you crazy? Give me $10,000."

You see old men sitting outside, sometimes they cannot walk and they ask one of the boys to go and buy them a packet of cigarettes. The boy says, "Go yourself."

Before it was, "Good morning. How are you? Do you need something?"

You find girls who go to dances alone or to the movies with the boys. My nephew's daughter is fourteen, right after supper she goes out and walks up and down between the two piazzas, up and down, up and down, just showing off for the boys. Before the war the girls could not go out of the house alone. I blame the parents. If you give them too much today, tomorrow they will want a little more.

Everything has changed. Before you saw people in the morning going out of town to work, now you don't see that. Before towns had a shoemaker, a tailor, a barber, that's all finished in some towns. People don't have haircuts, the boys have shoulder-length hair. People buy dresses in the store, nobody makes suits to measure. Some towns have mobile stores, a big bus goes around, it has two doors, one on one side and another on the other side. It goes from town to town, like a moving department store. We had two big ovens in town and they worked day and night, we had to sign up for a time. But people don't make bread anymore, they go and buy it. People don't even make their own pasta. Everything can be bought in a store. People have grown lazy, they do not even bother with the ringing of the church bells. The bells are still there but now they have a tape recorder and big speakers in the tower. At noon they turn on the tape.

People don't work, most of Pratola is on a pension. There is a pension for everything. My sister who is a few years older than me applied for a pension because she was overweight. There is a chart which says that at a certain age you should weigh so much according to your height and if you weigh more you are entitled to a pension. My sister has just been notified that she is eligible.

Today the parents kill themselves to help their children become somebody, like an architect or a surveyor, but then the children go to Rome to find a job but there are no jobs. I have one friend whose daughter is a teacher and she has been supply teaching for twelve years now. She goes to one place for two weeks and then to another place for another two weeks.

Before, to go from my home town to Rome took four hours, you had to go around the mountains. Now, with the new highway,

it takes an hour and a half. But I do not see the advantage
of this, all it means is that ideas from the big cities arrive
much faster to the small towns to pollute the minds of the young.
The young now go to Communist rallies, that is their entertain-
ment on Saturday nights. I think politics tries to take people
away from the church, particularly communism. My town has
lots of troubles because the Communists want to have their
podestà, the Socialists want their *podestà*, the Catholics also
want one. It's not like before, when you had one man. Now
they change him all the time. It's not good, it takes at least six
months to learn the job and then after a year you are kicked out.
In 1978 the *podestà* was a woman. One time there was a *podestà*
who stole a lot of things.

When I heard that the Pope had said that some saints are no
longer saints I was very confused. There are 365 days and there
are 365 saints. But probably there are over a million saints. How
can you say that now I am crossing off this name from the
calendar because he is no longer a saint? The Neapolitans have
San Gennaro as their protector, he is still San Gennaro. They still
have a festival for him. According to the Pope, San Gennaro is no
longer a saint. But they say that his statue still bleeds every year
and he still performs miracles. The people in Naples don't care
what the Pope says. For them San Gennaro is still a saint. The
same thing for the other saints. The Pope can't just cross off a
saint and say he is no longer a saint. A saint is a saint for three or
five hundred years and all of a sudden is not a saint? How can
you do that?

A few years ago my sister was on the committee to organize
the *fèsta* for the Madonna della Libera and she worked on it for
one year. Everyone wrote to relatives asking for contributions.
I collected $250 and sent it to my sister.

Today, in Pratola, nobody wants to carry the Madonna. People
do not have faith in her. After the war the young people didn't
care anymore. If you want them to carry the statue you have to
pay them. People say, "Why should I walk for two or three hours
with this? It's heavy and it's hot." Before the war people made
sacrifices to be able to carry the Madonna. The last time I was
in Italy lots of people were there from Canada and the States
and they wanted to carry her. My cousin is seventy years old
and for him it is still an honour to take the Madonna. He carries
her every year.

But now the procession is not what it used to be and the church is almost empty. I don't understand the young. What do they believe in? They stand there in their blue jeans and they don't look happy to me.

Today nothing happens anymore anywhere, no miracles, because the people are bad, they do not have faith, not like my grandfather who helped to build the Church of the Madonna della Libera. A lot of miracles happened in those days. But today there is nothing. The people do not have faith, they do not have time for such things. Since the war people have become polluted.

But something happened the other day that made me think that perhaps there is hope, people might have abandoned the faith but the faith has not abandoned us. Michele had a terrible accident on the highway. The accident was even on TV, on the news. Two cars collided, his small car and a truck. Michele walked out of his car unharmed, he just had a few minor scratches. As he stepped out after this big accident on the highway he found a medal on the ground. He picked it up and it was a medal of St Christopher. Every driver in Italy has at least a small St Christopher medal hanging somewhere in the car because St Christopher protects the drivers. Michele, of course, has never had it except he heard about it and he knew about it but he did not believe in such things. How did this medal get there, on a highway? I wrote about this to all my relatives. To me this was a miracle. St Christopher saved Michele's life. After this happened I felt very comforted.

I was too old when I came to Canada. I had a *testa dura* – a hard head. A lot of times I said to my husband, "As soon as the children are all married I will go back to Italy." Then I wanted to see my grandchildren. We kept postponing and postponing the time. There were always reasons. My husband finally said, "OK, as soon as I have the pension we will go back to Italy." Now I don't want to go back because my husband is buried here, I want to stay with him.

I have lived my life. I have done what I could for my family, perhaps not always the best according to some but still, the best that I was capable of at any given time. Now I am calm and I am ready. I am ready for when God will call me.